34.95

D1212296

Paul Brent

LAGER HEADS

**Labatt and Molson Face Off
for Canada's Beer Money**

HarperCollins*PublishersLtd*

Lager Heads

© 2004 by Paul Brent. All rights reserved.

Published by HarperCollins Publishers Ltd

Text of "The Rant" ("I Am Canadian" commercial) reproduced by permission of Molson Canada, © 2000.

First Edition

HarperCollins books may be purchased for educational, business, or sales promotional use through our Special Markets Department.

HarperCollins Publishers Ltd
2 Bloor Street East, 20th Floor
Toronto, Ontario, Canada
M4W 1A8

www.harpercollins.ca

National Library of Canada Cataloguing in Publication

Brent, Paul, 1964–
Lager heads : Labatt and Molson face off for Canada's beer money / Paul Brent. – 1st ed.

Includes index.
ISBN 0-00-200649-9

1. Brewing industry – Canada – History.
2. John Labatt Limited – History.
3. Molson Companies – History. I. Title.

HD9397.C22B72 2004   338.4'76633'0971
C2003-903768-1

FRI 9 8 7 6 5 4 3 2 1

Printed and bound in Canada
Set in Monotype Joanna

Contents

Acknowledgements

This book began, appropriately enough, over backyard beers with HarperCollins editor Don Loney and author and friend Lee Lamothe, who both suggested a book about the companies behind Canada's obsession with beer. The result is a story about how business empires were built – and squandered – based on Canadians' steady thirst for their brew.

The enterprise would not have been possible without the willingness of the "beer guys" from all the brewers – Carling O'Keefe, Labatt, and Molson – to share their stories.

From the Carling side there was Bill Bourne, who provided a wealth of knowledge and a directory of past beer management colleagues.

From Labatt, the task was made easier by access to those on the marketing, sales, and public relations sides, including: David Kincaid, Terry Zuk, James Villeneuve, Cal Bricker, Paul Smith, Troy Taylor, John Diakiw, Mike Rapino, Glen Cavanagh, Dick Walker, Tom Errath, Mike Hurst, Dick Bradbeer, and sales legends Howie Larke and Paul Bourque. Labatt senior management also made themselves available, including past presidents Don McDougall, Peter Widdrington, Sid Oland, George Taylor, and Hugo Powell. Thanks also go to Bob Vaux, Sam Pollock, Bruce Peer, and Lorne Stephenson. Special thanks to Nellie Swart, Labatt's historian.

At Molson, I would like especially to thank Barry Joslin and Marilyn McCrae, who gave valuable insights about what it was like to work over the years at North America's oldest brewer. Marketers Michael Downey, Rob Guenette, Brett Marchand, Blair Shier, Brent Scrimshaw, Jim Grundy, John Hay, and Jeff Carefoote were insightful and knowledgeable. Former executives Sheldon Bell, Norman Seagram, and John Barnett were also gracious and helpful.

Because this book is as much about beer marketing as it is about the business, a great deal of time is spent detailing life within the advertising industry. The ad business, which I began writing about in 1989, is full of characters and right-brain creative thinkers. Due to the massive dollars the breweries had to throw around at the height of the beer wars, they have had a disproportionate influence upon the Canadian advertising industry. Beer accounts have always been among the most coveted, both for their lucrative nature and for the creative opportunities they provide an agency. No advertising agency is complete, it seems, without a beer brand on its client roster. The competition for beer accounts has always been fierce and, with the exception of Molson's lengthy relationship with MacLaren McCann, often brief and tumultuous. Labatt, for example, played a decisive role in the creation, and ultimate demise, of ad agency Ammirati Puris. One of the most vocal critics of agencies, Labatt was also instrumental in creating Toronto advertising agency Grip Ltd., which began with just one client.

Many "ad guys," led by the inimitable Gary Prouk, detailed the behind-the-scenes drama of the beer wars. That list includes Bill Durnan, Glen Hunt, Andy Krupski, and Rick Davis.

The book would also not have been possible without the insights, analysis, and opinions of Michael Palmer, beer industry analyst extraordinaire, and independent brewers such as Jim Brickman of Brick Brewing, John Sleeman of Sleeman Brewing, and Bill Sharpe of Lakeport Brewing.

At HarperCollins, thanks for the diligence and patience of editors

Chris Bucci and Kathryn Dean, and legal expert and cross-examiner Alison Woodbury.

Thank you for the encouragement, proofreading, and critical commentary from friends Brenda Bouw, Jodi MacDonald, and Karen Howe.

Finally, this book would never have been written without the unflagging support of my incredible wife, Mary Donohue, who put up with scattered piles of paper, author moodiness, and a long period of slim paycheques.

Cast of Characters

The Presidents

LABATT

Peter Widdrington, president and CEO, John Labatt Ltd.

Don McDougall, president, Labatt Breweries of Canada

Sid Oland, president, Labatt Breweries of Canada; later, president and CEO, John Labatt Ltd.

George Taylor, president and CEO, John Labatt Ltd.

Hugo Powell, president, Labatt Breweries of Canada

MOLSON

Marshall (Mickey) Cohen, president and CEO, Molson Cos. Ltd.

Ted Kunkel, president, Molson Breweries

Bruce Pope, president, Molson Breweries

John Barnett, president, Molson USA; later, president, Molson Breweries

James Arnett, president and CEO, Molson Cos. Ltd.

Dan O'Neill, president, Molson Breweries; later, president and CEO, Molson Inc.

Eric Molson, chairman, Molson Inc.

Ian Molson, vice-chairman (and heir apparent), Molson Inc.

The Marketers

Tom Errath, vice-president of marketing, Labatt
Dave Barbour, vice-president of marketing, Molson
Blair Shier, marketing, Carling O'Keefe; later, president,
  Molson USA
Glen Cavanagh, director of business development, Labatt
Michael Downey, vice-president of marketing, Molson
David Kincaid, vice-president of marketing, Labatt

The Ad Men

Gary Prouk, chairman and CEO, Scali McCabe Sloves
Bill Durnan, creative, MacLaren McCann; later, president, Ammirati
  Puris
Glen Hunt, copywriter, Ammirati Puris; later, with Bensimon Byrne
Andy Krupski, president, J. Walter Thompson

Part One
Catching Lightning in a Bottle

I

The Rant

In that big, mostly empty country north of the 49th parallel, more than the usual Oscar buffs were anticipating the upcoming Academy Awards. The animated movie *South Park: Bigger, Longer & Uncut*, nearly as famous for its depiction of a Canada-US war as for its gratuitous use of the F-word, was up for an Oscar. Even better, comedian Robin Williams was slated to sing the movie's big song, "Blame Canada."

In Canada, at least, the speculation about how Hollywood would deal with the profanity was overshadowed by the lyrics' harsh treatment of the country's national treasures. Songbird Anne Murray, for example, was called a "bitch."

When the time came for Williams' performance in the middle of a predictable Oscar night (Phil Collins beat out the *South Park*-ers with a sweet trademark number for Disney's animated *Tarzan*), Oscar viewers were ready for something a little gritty.

They were not disappointed. Williams' send-up of Canada, complete with a kicking chorus line of buxom female "Mounties" in hot pants, was the highlight of an Oscar show otherwise devoid of much surprise.

Canadian viewers, famously tolerant and secretly proud of their fleeting *South Park* fame, took the ribbing with typical good humour. Of the 5.32 million who took in the telecast, just seven called to complain about the *South Park* bit, said the Global Television Network.

Nearly lost in the Oscar hubbub was a coming-out party of sorts for Molson Canadian, a beer at times alternatively cursed and blessed by its brand name. Tucked in among the tearful acceptance speeches and musical numbers – airing, in fact, just after Williams' act – was a 60-second beer commercial featuring a flannel-shirted Canuck everyman spouting those universal truisms Canadians have hoarded for so long in resentful little piles to use against their ignorant American neighbours.

> Hey. I'm not a lumberjack, or a fur trader.
> And I don't live in an igloo, or eat blubber, or own a dogsled.
> And I don't know Jimmy, Sally, or Suzy from Canada, although I'm certain they're really, really nice.
> I have a Prime Minister, not a President.
> I speak English and French, not American.
> And I pronounce it "about," not "aboot."
> I can proudly sew my country's flag on my backpack.
> I believe in peacekeeping, not policing,
> Diversity, not assimilation,
> And that the beaver is a truly proud and noble animal.
> A toque is a hat, a chesterfield is a couch,
> And it is pronounced "zed," not "zee," "zed."
> Canada is the second-largest landmass,
> The first nation of hockey,
> And the best part of North America.
> My name is Joe! And I am Canadian!
> Thank you.

Epitomizing the plain old good luck that played a role in Molson's new ad campaign for Canadian, the brewer didn't even have any air time reserved for the sold-out, March 2000 Oscars telecast. Its media planning agency managed to squeeze the ad onto the broadcast and "Joe" – dressed as a lumberjack but professing not to be one – got his chance to rant.

The rest is advertising history.

Tapping a rich vein of dormant national pride, the commercial developed into a topic of conversation at water-coolers country-wide. It quickly became the subject of ethnic parodies, everything from "I Am Jamaican" to "I Am Not Canadian" ("I Am Québécois"). Federal politicians were spouting the lines outside the country, and with the backdrop of the Parliament Buildings looming behind him, Joe even appeared as a half-page picture on the front cover of the *National Post*. All this for a beer commercial. Joe actor Jeff Douglas became a national celebrity. Even his departure for the lure and lucre of a Hollywood acting career didn't dim the appeal of the "Rant."

To this day, Molson does not completely understand how the "Rant" struck such a chord with the general public. At the time, Americans were treating their northern cousins with the same benign indifference that had generally characterized relations along the world's longest undefended border. Most of their attention was focused inward, in fact, on a technology-led stock market boom and a president who seemed in danger of total political destruction. When pressed, the only indignity one Molson exec could come up with was the defeat of Canada's hockey team by the US squad of all-stars in the 1998 Canada Cup, which had been renamed the World Cup that year.

What *was* clear before Joe took the stage and ranted for his country was that Molson needed a win for its flagship beer.

In the last two decades, once Molson Canadian had emerged as a national presence to battle it out with Labatt Blue, who was win-ning and who was losing the battle to be the best-selling brand had become an ongoing struggle. The state of morale at the big brew-eries could be tracked by the rising or failing fortunes of their respective flagship beers.

Labatt management is obsessed with the health of Blue. Undisput-edly the top-selling beer in the seventies and eighties, its position has eroded steadily since then, while Canadian has gained ground. There's a lot more to the Molson-Labatt beer wars than Canadian and Blue, but no single struggle better illustrates the lengths the two companies will go to and the money each will spend to lay claim to the status of market leader.

In the beer business, like the advertising business, there is a telling axiom. *You're either going up or you're going down.* Prior to the "Rant," the Canadian brand was doing poorly, as was Molson as a company. The state of Canadian, losing share to a resurgent Blue, was one more symptom of the problems plaguing the company. Molson Breweries had just lost another president (this one quit rather than being fired), and the new guy was in place, busily hacking at costs to close the famous "profit gap" the analysts were always harping about when talking with the management of parent Molson Inc. With the gap in mind, Molson announced the closure of the Barrie plant in Ontario and the loss of jobs for the workers there, along with the termination of hundreds of white-collar employees across the country. Morale was in the toilet. No longer did a job with Molson mean a job for life.

Advertising can't fix everything – even desperate beer executives know that – but Molson needed a win. The company's ad agency for nearly four decades, MacLaren McCann, a Toronto shop that had built both the Molson Export and Canadian brands, was unceremoniously dumped in the spring of 1999. In advertising circles, it was a bombshell. Molson had always treated its advertising hirelings well and MacLaren's record of success was second to none. Its perceived transgression, the creation of the too-clever-by-half "Monkeys" campaign of 1998, seemed pretty forgivable. Featuring a teaser commercial with a roomful of typing monkeys, it promised, "An infinite number of monkeys on an infinite number of typewriters will eventually define all that is Canada." The ad conjured up images of banking or telecommunications firms – anything but a beer – and provoked joking speculation that the campaign was for the upcoming launch of Conrad Black's national newspaper. The effort was a flop: nobody got beyond the chimps clattering away to the beer commercial vignettes that followed, and the agency and its monkeys were shown the door.

Still, even after the summer of the monkeys, the agency likely figured it could keep the business. After all, hadn't it made the magical connection between rock music and beer? As the only agency to work on Canadian, it had helped build the brand from scratch into the country's best-selling beer. It had invented "I Am Canadian," the brand's most successful tag line of all time, and made Canadian synonymous with rock 'n' roll, the only prop besides women in bikinis that seemed to sell beer.

But MacLaren, one of the only constants during a string of Molson presidents and marketing heads, was not going to survive this time. The comfortable agency-client relationship, which had worked brilliantly for so long, was nearing an end. Months before the agency was axed, MacLaren president Dom Caruso knew it was over when the obligatory congratulations-and-let's-do-lunch telephone call to newly hired Molson Breweries president Dan O'Neill went unanswered.

The search for a replacement agency touched off a feeding frenzy in the advertising community. One of the beer industry's biggest brands up for grabs? Automotive and banking accounts may pay the bills at advertising agencies, but beer assignments are what agency presidents lie awake obsessing about. Breweries are always among the top spenders, throwing Hollywood production dollars at commercials that are then launched in heavy rotation on the top shows. For beer, that means sports programming and TV shows geared to that coveted 19 – 24 age group. No pandering to the Murder, She Wrote set.

Apart from the obvious attractions of January commercial shoots in California, producing great advertising for mainstream beers is also probably the most difficult work agency creative types can tackle. With Molson and Labatt both producing world-class beer, or "liquid" (the jargon-obsessed beer marketers' term for brew), it's all about lifestyle for the people in the ad factories. Figuring out the likes and dislikes of the notoriously fickle 19-to-24-year-olds, in other words. The reasons for the concentration on the youth market are pretty straightforward. They drink the most of any age group. They also enter their heaviest drinking years with little or no brand loyalty. In the fifties and sixties, Dad's beer was something to be embraced. Today, Dad's beer has as much status with young drinkers as a wood-panelled station wagon, complete with a silver roof rack.

That's why both Molson and Labatt spend millions each year on research alone. Middle-aged guys on one side of a mirror, the sought-after youth demographic on the other, deciding the fate of marketing campaigns that cost in the tens of millions. Getting it right means the difference between having a hot-selling brand and being consigned to "Dad's beer" status. With no price difference in heavily regulated Canada (the beer companies like it that way) and no effort to create large differences in the taste of the suds, creatives quickly thrive or die on beer. When Bill Durnan, one of the few real legends in the beer advertising game in Canada, began working on his first beer account, he was told, "Welcome to the male cosmetics business."

In the spring of 1999, when Molson fired its distress flare into the skies above Toronto, the ad world came as close to a wartime footing as it could. Vacations were cancelled and dozens of agencies clambered onto Molson's long list of possibilities. As July was nearing an end, the brewer was down to five agencies: three big multinationals, a small Toronto agency with a good creative reputation, and a hot British ad agency, which eventually landed the Export business as a consolation prize.

Molson's review was run by British-born Richard Kelly, a veteran ad man notable for his work as a consultant for Labatt, who then a few years later shifted nearly all Labatt's business to a tiny Canadian branch plant office of a US agency. The balding, publicity-averse Kelly was an unlikely arbiter of what was "in" among the country's youth.

While Molson was mulling over its future direction, Labatt took ownership of the key spring season with the miniature Stanley Cup promotion and advertising that made it plain Labatt finally held sway over hockey – at least during the playoffs. Hockey may seem a strange pastime to link to a spring advertising campaign, however spring has also been the season to launch new campaigns for beer brands as that is the time a young man's fancy turns to suds. Establish their preferences by the Victoria Day, May "two-four" long weekend, the thinking goes, and you have them all summer.

Having split with MacLaren McCann, Molson was muddling through. Its promotion agency, Encore Encore Strategic Marketing Ltd., produced two summer spots with the new tag line "Here's where we get Canadian."

Up against two smaller shops, Taxi Advertising & Design and HHCL, the other short-listed agencies did what big multinationals do best: they called on the strength of their US offices. As surprised as anyone that it was still in the running for Molson's business, Toronto-based Bensimon Byrne D'Arcy (which soon after simply became Bensimon Byrne) called its St. Louis sister shop for help. St. Louis just happens to be headquarters for Anheuser-Busch and was home base for the creative team responsible for Budweiser's successful talking frogs campaign.

Also getting a call from Bensimon Byrne was New York–based writer Glen Hunt. A Canadian, Hunt was a relative unknown in the small, self-perpetuating Toronto ad crowd because he'd moved to the US market a few years earlier, determined to swim in a bigger pond. Still, Hunt should have been a household name in ad circles. On loan from Ammirati Puris Lintas of New York, he'd written the famous "Street Hockey" commercial for Labatt two years earlier that kicked off the brewer's successful "Out of the Blue" campaign. Hunt, by working on the ad for Labatt, was, as much as anyone, responsible for the current mess Molson Canadian found itself in, though few knew it at the time.

Hunt was described by one ad agency president as the Chevy Chase character in the movie *Caddyshack*, a six foot one laconic golfer who, like most on the creative side of the business, got into advertising by accident. A leather-goods salesman after graduating from university, Hunt started as a copywriter with J. Walter Thompson. He later worked for Geoffrey Roche at Roche Macaulay in Toronto before the agency was partially acquired by a UK ad firm in 1996. With a hefty merger payout, Hunt bummed around for six months before joining Ammirati in New York.

Fortunately for Bensimon Byrne, Hunt was wrapping up his stint at

Ammirati and deciding whether to sign on with another US shop or come back to the cozy confines of Canada. While still on the first long list, agency president Jack Bensimon invited Hunt to join the Molson pitch team if the agency got to the short strokes. As Hunt said later, "Jack kept calling and saying, 'Jesus, it's down to 15 and we're still in it. It's got down to 8 and we're still in it. Oh my God, it's down to 5 and we're still in it. Fuck, you're going to have to come back.'"

Hunt accepted, and with its creative dream team established, Bensimon Byrne got to work. Apart from noting the friendship of agency creative director Peter Byrne and Molson ad man Richard Kelly, few in the ad business thought the agency had a chance of actually winning the business. The shop had little beer experience (beyond its hired guns) and its output to date was rarely putting it on the awards podium. Maybe they would get Molson Export or some other brand for their efforts, but friendship would get you only so far, the thinking went.

Research, that time-consuming and expensive process deemed so necessary in the beer business – another reason agency presidents are kept awake thinking about beer accounts – opened the door for Bensimon Byrne. A lowly intern armed with a video camera was instructed to go native and seek out the mysterious youthful beer drinker. The intern came back with some startling results for the 30- and 40-something agency executives.

The youth target group, who might as well have been space aliens for long-time agency people (especially if they harboured 19- or 20-year-olds at home), were revealed in research to be a far more patriotic bunch than their parents. Apparently, they weren't the cynical, anarchistic bunch of slackers they were dismissed as being, and that recently abandoned "I Am Canadian" tag line actually meant something to them.

Bensimon Byrne realized that it had to convince Molson it had committed an unforgivable advertising sin, the one they teach you about in Marketing 101. Molson had thrown away its bedrock positioning, its unique selling proposition, the main thing that set it apart in the same-same sea of mainstream beer.

Telling your prospective employer that it has screwed up the marketing of its most important brand, its cash cow, is not the sort of potentially suicidal act that ad agencies are known for. Most of the other short-listed agencies suggested returning to the "I Am" positioning along with other ideas, but only Bensimon Byrne said it was the only solution, take it or leave it.

Glen Hunt credits Dan O'Neill, the results-in-a-hurry CEO, for overcoming the bias of Molson's marketing department. "He came in, we started talking about 'I Am Canadian' and he looked us square in the eye and he said, 'Are you guys brave enough to come back to me and recommend "I Am Canadian"?' It's one of those points where you say, 'Well, does he mean are we stupid enough? Or does he mean are we smart enough?'

"We looked him back square in the eye and said, 'There is no other answer for you except that, and if we win or lose the business on that, that's our recommendation.'" Bensimon Byrne won the business.

At the meeting where the agency was awarded the contract, Hunt stood up, unbuttoned his shirt, and showed the Molson executives the little piece of Canada he'd kept tucked away during his time in the States, a bright red maple leaf tattooed on his left breast.

As August was winding down, Molson instructed its new agency to start dreaming up some hockey-themed advertising, a few weeks prior to officially naming Bensimon Byrne the winner and giving the other shops the bad news. It was hardly an easy test. Molson had the mid-week local broadcast rights to the six domestic teams, but a couple of years earlier had given up sponsorship rights to *Hockey Night in Canada* to Labatt. Molson had handed over its unchallenged link to the one sport Canadians felt truly passionate about. Thanks to Hunt and others at Ammirati, Labatt could now lay claim to being the beer of professional shinny. At least on CBC telecasts on Saturday nights and during the playoffs, when it became the exclusive broadcast sponsor.

Molson, which owned the Montreal Canadiens, and had its name plastered on the boards in NHL rinks across the country, had to re-establish the dominance of hockey it had held for decades but had so recently surrendered to Labatt.

"Within three days we had written 23 different executions for hockey and we decided not to unveil the positioning of 'I Am Canadian,'" remembers Hunt. The hockey-themed ads depicted ordinary target-group-aged males' obsession for the game and all ended with the tag line "It's a Canadian Game," voiced by long-time Toronto Maple Leafs announcer Paul Morris.

Shot hurriedly in September for the start of the hockey season, the ads delivered their message with humour. The best of the bunch featured a happy young man walking to the rink with a bag slung over his shoulder, hockey stick in the other hand, as people and dogs collapsed in his wake. He stops finally, alerted by the birds falling dead from the trees, notices his bag is open, and tentatively sniffs the interior. After suppressing a gag, the "hero" zips his bag closed and grimly continues on.

While the "It's a Canadian Game" spots allowed Molson to at least share hockey with Labatt, Bensimon Byrne was secretly working on the launch of the "I Am Canadian" campaign. Rather than tactically tying the beer to Canada's frozen sport, the new effort had to steal back the momentum from Blue and rebuild Canadian's image. The brand was still the market leader, regardless of the fact that it wasn't sold in Quebec, but it sure didn't act like it.

For once, the paranoia that permeated the beer business paid off. Despite lengthy waves of testing imposed upon the new agency by Molson's research-obsessed O'Neill (up to two months of testing was done on prospective ads), word never leaked out that "I Am Canadian" was being resurrected. Pretty much in plain sight, Bensimon Bryne held a cross-country audition for Joe. Actor Jeff Douglas – "good looking but not too good looking" – was identified immediately by the agency as "the guy" out of a group of 20 or so in Toronto, but a series of cross-Canada casting calls was held before Douglas was retained.

Puzzled by Bensimon Bryne's initial effort on the brand, Ammirati kept a watchful eye on the long-running Cold War between Blue and

Canadian. "I would play golf with [Ammirati president] Doug Robinson and he would say, 'Geez, are you going back to "I Am Canadian"?' I don't know why he thought I would tell him what we were doing, but I would say, 'No, that "It's a Canadian Game" stuff, that's what we're doing.'"

Then, right under everyone's noses in a Toronto soundstage in the city's east end, Jeff Douglas belted out his rant 30 or 40 times so the cameras could shoot him from every conceivable angle in preparation for a marathon editing session. Backing up Hunt's copywriting, an unheard-of four art directors worked on the project. The process included three weeks of editing and sorting through Canadiana imagery that was lengthened further still by personal objections to certain images from Molson's Dan O'Neill and others.

"Dan understood that this was going to be his opening salvo, and it was important that it felt right to him," Hunt said later. "At heart he was a brand manager and "I Am Canadian" was his brand. He deals with the [Molson] family. He wanted to ensure that they felt good about what they were going to put out there. He took it to the board, shared it with them, told them how well it tested, what was going to happen next, and how strongly he felt about it, and they supported him."

Like all great advertising, "Rant" was infused with insights that viewers immediately identified with. Written in an hour before the computer screen at Bensimon Bryne, Hunt's "Rant" was autobiographical. With a federal government so eager to promote people's pasts through ethnic programs – the opposite of the United States' flag-waving, Pledge of Allegiance melting pot – Canadians have a pretty hazy idea of who they are. At the end of the day, all you can get a roomful of Canadians to agree upon is that they aren't Americans (and Canadians who have travelled overseas can get pretty indignant about it).

That defensive anti-Americanism was something Hunt and the top Molson brass understood. Like Hunt, Dan O'Neill and Molson Canadian marketing vice-president Brett Marchand had worked in the States and endured the jibes and ignorance of their American co-workers.

Writing the "Rant" came easily to Hunt, so much so that it took longer to trim the speech to fit the original 60-second format than it took to write it. Stridently anti-American in the first draft, "Rant" was also softened, and nasty comparisons between the bald eagle and the beaver were dropped. Surprisingly, given how many good ads are killed in anonymous little research rooms every year, "Rant" survived the opinions of the youth market largely unaltered. The one change brought about by focus groups was the deletion of the lines, "And I like ketchup on my macaroni and cheese, and lots of it, because I like it like that." About half the people in the groups didn't understand the apparent culture chasm between US and Canadian macaroni-and-cheese-eating habits (something that is also played up in *South Park*). Ultimately, and rightly, the line "And the beaver is a proud and noble animal" was substituted.

Even the ending, in which a suddenly self-conscious Joe returns to the microphone to utter a humble "thank you," had to survive some high-level criticism. At least as American as he was Canadian from all his years in the States working with the likes of the Campbell Soup Company and Heinz, the Ottawa-raised Dan O'Neill thought the ending was a cop-out. "I remember O'Neill said, 'Oh no, he wimps out in the end!'" related Michael Downey, Molson's vice-president of marketing. "I said, 'Dan, that is the American in you, the American in you says he wimps out. The Canadian in you says he becomes a Canadian again.'"

Striking the right balance between that latent anti-Americanism and nationalistic pride ruffled by the urban legends about Americans driving across the border in July with snow skis on the roof rack proved to be a hit. To O'Neill, partway through a painful restructuring of the company and looking for any sort of win, "Rant" was flotsam for a shipwrecked man. Months after "Rant" aired, Jeff Douglas' boy-next-door mug was featured in Molson's annual report.

Those cold-eyed stock analysts might have looked at O'Neill's chainsaw initiatives as long overdue, but employees and shareholders wanted to see something other than cost-cutting. The 2000 annual report, a scorecard on the first year of the O'Neill era at Molson, prominently displays the "Rant," devoting more than a page to what is arguably the most famous ad in the country's history. The report even burbled about how marketing would become more scientific. "In our advertising, for example, we are rigorously testing ads both qualitatively and quantitatively with consumers while the ads are still in development." No more monkeys, Molson appeared to be promising to shareholders. With the gods of research willing, there would instead be a few more rants.

Bensimon Byrne's follow-on commercial, "No Doot Aboot It," was another autobiographical piece of work for Hunt. It depicts a clean-cut Canadian who, roused to action by an annoying American's mocking of Canada, resorts to the ultimate weapon of the hockey thug. The Canuck "jerseys" the oaf, pulling his suit jacket up over his head as countless on-ice pugilists have done on Hockey Night in Canada. Hunt did that very thing to a co-worker while at Ammirati in New York.

"I would say 'How's it going, eh?' and he would say, 'Oh pretty good, no doot aboot it.' He'd fucking make fun of me all the time. It burned me, so I jerseyed him, and then I took him from office to office to show him this is how you take care of troublemakers Canadian-style."

Fanatical as O'Neill was about testing – Molson claimed the follow-on "No Doot Aboot It" ad scored better than the "Rant" in research – the brewing chief recognized what few in the industry seem to appreciate: the beer business is much more about marketing than it is about brewing. O'Neill, whose constant influence upon the launch of Canadian was so apparent, had a career that was eerily in sync with that of Labatt's Hugo Powell, another outsider who understood that cost-cutting and marketing were the ways to succeed in the business.

With the "Rant," Molson had got the public's – and investors' – attention. Only time would tell whether the company had put its most important beer brand back on track or if the brewery had just got lucky and released the country's most famous advertisement.

2
Blue Dancing

Before 1984, if a Molson executive awoke shaking and sweating, chances were good that he'd been dreaming of balloons – blue ones. Labatt's decades-long ad campaign for its flagship brand had firmly fixed Blue in the consciousness of the Canadian beer drinker. Literally launched in 1968, the first Blue balloon was, in fact, red. In all, more than 200 television commercials featured a balloon serenely floating across the sky during the "When You're Smiling" campaign's 18-year run.

Created by J. Walter Thompson, one of the largest and most successful ad agencies in Canada, the campaign when viewed today seems almost too ethereal to describe. "Smile," as it was called at Labatt, came about just as Blue became a national beer brand, and the campaign was perfected in the 1970s. The typical Blue commercial featured some faddish sport such as grass skiing, water walking, or paraskiing across a frozen lake. The ads ended with a helicopter's view of the Blue balloon, followed by a quick shot of a foamy beer glass all accompanied by the line of music, "When you're smiling, keep on smiling. Blue smiles along with you." (Singer Peggy Lee belted out the tune for one ad.)

Even inside Labatt, the "Smile" campaign was hard to pin down.

But the marketing people knew they'd hit upon a winning formula, even if they couldn't describe what "Smile" was all about. The commercials were described as aspirational. After all, who could afford all the James Bond–style toys shown in the ads? The hedonistic, get-away-from-all-your-cares slant of the ads also had little to do with beer, beyond the promise that at some time after the screen went blank, the playboys and their fresh-faced girlfriends might get around to drinking a couple of Blues, among other things.

J. Walter Thompson had managed to keep the campaign going by spending a lot of time in California, North America's hothouse for weird and wacky trends. By the end of the campaign, inventors were approaching the agency and Labatt with gadgets, hoping they'd be featured in the next Blue commercial. (To this day, California continues to be an ad mecca for beer companies because the summer's sweaty TV commercials tend to be shot in January and February, hardly beach weather in Canada.)

Tom Errath, the top marketing executive at Labatt from 1979 to the mid-1980s, described the ad this way: "The 'Smile' campaign did not say 'get rich and buy a whole bunch of toys' as much as it said, 'There is a certain amount of freedom, a certain amount of fantasy, and obviously a certain amount of aspiration associated with smiling along with Blue.' It takes you through something that would almost be described as fantasy."

A US import, Mr. Errath had been headhunted from Schlitz Brewing Co. and his first job was to determine what to do with Blue. At the time, Labatt knew that the smiling and balloon act had likely run its course but the brewer just didn't know where to take the campaign. Famously cautious, Errath ordered research to see whether "Smile" was doing the job. The answer came back fairly quickly: the campaign wasn't connecting with the legal-drinking-age-to-24 cohort that made up the biggest portion of beer drinkers, remembers Errath. Labatt Blue was in danger of becoming "Dad's beer."

Those words, which sent shudders through brand managers everywhere, were precisely the ones being applied to Blue's major rival, Molson Canadian. Introduced in 1959, a little later than Blue,

Canadian was provoking that dreaded description in Molson's own internal research, according to those who worked on the brand at the time.

The slow, unhurried evolution of Blue to the status of Canada's top-selling beer illustrates how much the industry has changed. Today, when marketers launch a new beer brand, they get one chance to nail the positioning or, missing the mark, their product is consigned to discount beer status.

According to Labatt's official history, Blue was conceived after brewmaster Hugh Labatt, John Labatt's grandson, travelled to a brewery in Pilsen, in what is now the Czech Republic. He returned to Canada with a recipe for a lager-style beer, introduced by the brewery in 1951 as Labatt Pilsener. Although Labatt hired Eva Gabor and Harpo Marx to appear in Pilsener TV ads in the early sixties, the name was awkward to say when ordering the brand in a tavern or store, according to former Labatt president and CEO Peter Widdrington.

Similarly, Molson was finding that its long-running panorama campaign for Canadian wasn't exactly capturing the imagination of the country's youthful and thirsty beer drinkers. The ads featured majestic shots of mountains, seashore, and prairies, a Canadian tourism-type ad with a foamy glass of beer tacked on to the end.

Canadian wasn't in danger of becoming Dad's beer. Research of the youth market conducted in the early 1980s found it *was* Dad's beer. Canadian's market share was sliding and Molson's ad agency, MacLaren Advertising (later MacLaren McCann), was charged with turning it around or looking for other work.

At the time, ads for Canadian were not much different from Blue's "Smile" campaign, both featuring buff, beautiful people, and wholesome, outdoorsy sports. Canadian even had a balloon, though it didn't appear in every ad, like Labatt's gasbag. To conform to legislated ad restrictions, beer commercials followed a formula: beautiful people, physical activity, balloon, social scene (such as a bar), product shot, and the onscreen "super" which displayed the brand tag line. (The beer couldn't be shown before the wholesome fun play because the provincial and federal regulators – which have included the CRTC and Advertising Standards Canada – didn't want alcohol linked with physical activity.) The two competitors' ads were so much the same that MacLaren McCann once switched the product shots and supers on the brands' ads in an agency presentation to show just how similar the commercials had become. The low point came in the early eighties when Molson dispatched its ad team to film a commercial in Australia, taking advantage of the weather and a healthy exchange rate. The team ended up on a peninsula near Sydney shooting windsurfing and beach scenes, and to their horror they found a group from Labatt filming the exact same thing. Later on, the incident provoked laughter at Molson, but it was a signal that Canadian, with just one-third the sales of Blue at that time, could not keep doing the same safe, predictable advertising.

Dave Barbour, a long-time Molson marketer, pushed the panic button in 1983. Well known in the tight-knit beer community as a street fighter, Barbour was a curious choice to head up marketing at the staid, family-controlled brewery. Unlike the Molsons, who were brewmasters above all, Barbour didn't believe you simply had to brew great beer to find a following. *A great beer finds its own friends!* was the famous, oft-quoted phrase that originated with long-dead founder John Molson. Barbour, on the other hand, sought out those friends, living the beer drinkers' life. He hung out in the bars, saw what people were drinking, and learned first-hand how ineffective Molson was at reaching them.

With Canadian's share sinking, Barbour's directions to MacLaren were simple: blow the dust off Canadian. "Junk the entire positioning for the brand, throw out all the rules, and give me advertising I have never seen before" was the marching order, a directive that was exhilarating for creative types, but also frightening since all the safety devices, all the excuses for failure, had been removed.

. . .

As a desperate stop-gap, the agency heaped together some youthful imagery, did up some versions of contemporary pop songs, and literally threw the concoction on the air. That seemed to hold for the summer of 1983, but the youth-oriented campaign highlighted the dilemma encountered by most big beer brands. How do you retain the older, loyal drinkers, who aren't quaffing them quite as frequently as they used to, while still attracting the young "entry" drinkers who consume the stuff in vast quantities? That was Molson's only caveat in its throw-out-the-rules instructions to its agency: the new ads have to solve that young drinker–core drinker riddle.

MacLaren's response was typical of agencies in crisis: throw as many bodies as possible at the creative wall and hope something they come up with sticks. The desperate call to action included the junior creative team of copywriter Bill Durnan and art director Richard Clewes. The duo was scheduled to travel to St. Lucia for an Export Light commercial that featured footage of tall ships, so it was suggested they go down to the island a week earlier so that they could also work on ideas for Canadian. (The fact that the two were sent to a resort island to dream up ideas for an account they weren't even assigned at the agency shows how much the ad world has changed since then.)

There on the beach came the idea for the campaign tag line "Taste That Will Stop You Cold," which Durnan thought nicely "dusted off" Canadian and negated the Dad's beer image.

Famous in the advertising industry today for his ability to distill complex advertising problems into one or two simple core ideas, Durnan soon found another part of the solution: music. The simplest and most powerful way to reach the legal-drinking-age-to-24 target group was to put their music on a pedestal. As Durnan recalls, "The analysis – it sounds incredibly simple now but it wasn't to us – was that we determined the voice of music, using simple music as your voice was probably the most powerful way to speak [to] or connect to this target audience."

Rock videos were just emerging as an adjunct to recorded music sales, and Durnan came up with the idea of beer commercials with the music and feel of rock videos. That marriage of well-known popular music – either purchased from the artist or re-recorded by anonymous studio musicians – would soon become the new standard for mainstream beer advertising. Durnan and Clewes spent a week on the beaches of St. Lucia listening to stacks of cassette tapes, plotting out rock videos, and trying to find the right song to accompany Canadian's new commercials.

Personal experience solved the youth–older drinker dilemma. Durnan recalled going to a Christmas party at a Latvian centre with his wife, and during the festivities he heard a young group play a cover version of Barry McGuire's 1965 hit song "Eve of Destruction." "The place erupted," said Durnan. "I found it a very interesting dynamic that these young people were getting up. They were kind of aware of the song and found it pretty cool. Yet as an older person I went, 'Jesus, does that take me back.'"

Back in Toronto, a simple test of the idea was carried out. "For research purposes we just took still pictures, almost like a slide show with a theme, and put music to it, and a picture of the bottle stuck at the end. We took it into research and sure enough, it did well. It did very well," Durnan remembers.

For the initial 1984 spring and summer launch, Durnan and Clewes settled on two songs that conformed to the Old Rock Song/ Young Rock Video formula. "Dancing in the Street," the sixties Motown classic by Martha and the Vandellas, and Frankie Ford's "Sea Cruise" would take Canadian out of the gate. The two songs were thought to be old enough to appeal to the loyal "Dad" drinkers, while still grabbing the attention of high school and college kids. Different and expensive, the ads were dangerous for a life-long marketing type like Molson's Dave Barbour. "It took balls because a typical beer commercial in the early eighties was expensive and they were costing about $150,000 [each]," said Bill MacDonald, a group account director with MacLaren at the time. "[Barbour] rolled the dice on a brand called Canadian with a 6[%] market share and agreed to spend almost double that per spot."

"Dancing in the Street" was an instant hit and became the prototypical Canadian ad. "Sea Cruise," which had an artificial, shot-in-a-studio feel, was quickly judged to be the inferior commercial to

"Dancing," according to Durnan. Shooting the spot, which featured three black female singers in leopard-skin outfits, MacLaren had the trio singing and grinding away atop the marquee of Filmore's strip club in Toronto. "My wife, I'll never forget, she said, 'Bill, are you sure this thing is going to be okay?'" Not so sure himself, Durnan thought, "I'm going to have either the shortest career or the biggest."

The new Canadian spots didn't even feature beer. Because of the complicated rules that dictated all activity, all "fun" having to cease once beer appeared on the screen, MacLaren decided to junk the standard convivial bar/patio scene and keep the fun scenes rolling, opting for a short product identifier at the end of the ad. The spots were truly mini rock videos, except with better production values than the primitive rock videos of the time.

Not surprisingly, Labatt knew Molson was coming up with a new campaign for Canadian, and it began analyzing the latest creative salvo the Monday after the ads first aired. Labatt's marketers came to the quick and hardly startling conclusion that the other guy had changed the rules. Forget the metaphor wrapped in a fantasy of getting away from it all. Molson promised gritty good times with ads that married the universal language (for the target group, anyway), of rock music with images of beautiful people having a great time.

Molson had pulled a roadster out of the garage while Labatt was riding along in a Model T. Or, more appropriately, Molson's marketing team had created the first jet plane while Labatt was putt-putting along in its balloon. "The balloon didn't last long after that," admitted Labatt's Tom Errath.

Labatt would have a difficult time gauging just how revolutionary the new Canadian advertising was, since in the same summer of 1984 Blue roiled the waters with a revolution of its own, the surprise launch of tall bottles with twist-off caps. A true product innovation, the twist-off cap rang the death knell for the stubby, and the new packaging by Labatt masked any market share momentum that Canadian may have been building. Consumers who drank beer out of stubby, brown bottles with pry-off caps embraced the novelty of tall bottles topped with twist-off caps. In the industry at the time, it was generally believed that product innovation was pretty much finished. The three main product categories – light beer, ales such as Export and Labatt 50, and lagers like Canadian and Blue – are where the real battles have taken place. And with such a small range of products, advertising and packaging innovations were the most effective weapons.

Constantly looking for new ways to push brand share, Labatt rolled out a slew of packaging innovations to flank the tall bottles with twist-off caps. There was the short-lived 500-mL bottle (a he-man bottle about 50% larger than the standard bottle), mixed cases of Blue and Blue Light, and aluminum cans to replace the old-fashioned steel cans. The bigger bottles were a flop. Europeans may buy their beer in half-litre bottles, but conservative Canuck drinkers preferred theirs standard sized. The failure of the 500-mL size also had to do with consumer differences. Europeans tend to drink out of a glass not (gasp) from the bottle, and most nip into a local store to buy their tipple, rather than being forced to lug a case of the stuff home from a distant outlet, as Canadians are obliged to do. Fortunately for Labatt, it had better luck with mixed cases and aluminum cans.

Despite these successes on the packaging front, Labatt called an advertising review in September of 1984. After a six-month, full-blown agency review that cost the participating ad shops hundreds of thousands of dollars each in staff time and production costs – who didn't want a beer company for a client, after all – Labatt settled on a dark-horse candidate, Scali, McCabe, Sloves, which most observers thought had been thrown into the mix of big multinational agencies as an afterthought.

Gary Prouk, the former chairman and creative director of Scali, recalls the 1984 pitch with the clarity of a person who has told the story a thousand times. Scali then had the reputation for being a creative hot shop, if a tad small to handle the biggest beer account in the land. "The amount of money that was spent [by the ad agencies] . . . vast amounts," said Prouk. "The pitch went on for a year and a half. It was the biggest pitch in the history of Canadian advertising. For this one fucking brand of beer."

In fact, the pitch involved five agencies, including Scali. It lasted for a lengthy six months and cost the agencies an estimated $1 million combined. Even in the unlimited-expense-accounts-and-limos era of the mid-1980s, it was serious bucks. Dangling the prize of the $20-million Blue account, reported to be the single biggest brand account in Canada at the time, Labatt demanded and received a Manhattan Project–like effort from the agencies, and the agency presidents worried about paying for the pitch later.

J. Walter Thompson, desperate to keep the business, called in its international shooters, as did the others. Nearly 100 JWT staff, some parachuted in from Germany and the United Kingdom, worked on the Blue pitch at one time or another, augmenting a core team of 30. Young & Rubicam split the pitch between its New York and Toronto offices, and airlifted creatives from Brazil and Belgium at one point. Scali relied on six or seven people in its Toronto office, as Prouk refused all offers of assistance from the US headquarters.

Scali didn't work as desperately as the other shops to win Blue. Prouk, if not the rest of the Scali people working on the pitch, knew that Labatt could be a challenging client, simply because of its structure, and said he entered the process reluctantly and was ambivalent about winning the business. Adhering to the brewery-in-every-province structure imposed upon it by government wanting to keep jobs spread across the country, Labatt operated as a series of regional fiefdoms. Not only would Scali have to satisfy the suits at Labatt in Toronto, advertising would also have to please the marketing and sales types in the regional offices from Montreal to Vancouver.

Prouk also had his doubts as to whether anyone could turn the Blue supertanker around. Once a brand peaks and starts losing market share, it's all but impossible to do anything but slow the fall. "There used to be a cliché – an old chestnut in the business," said Prouk, "something like 'God makes the share, we fight for the volume.'" Finally, and most presciently, Prouk worried that the huge Labatt account would come to dominate Scali, at the time a mid-size firm with billings of $30 million to $35 million annually.

All the same, the five senior Scali people on the pitch met at the agency, as Prouk remembers it, on a Sunday morning in November 1984, the day of the Santa Claus parade. Three of the five were watching the clock, since they had to take their kids out to see Santa, which created a built-in deadline. After a few hours of furiously scribbling links between "Canada's beer" and "Blue," the five came up with the line, "There's a Heart in This Land," and the agency's top writer, Bill Martin, wrote down what would be the lyrics to a theme song on an envelope.

The other agencies, who felt they had more to lose than Scali, were unwilling to put all their eggs in one creative basket. JWT proposed three different campaign ideas, Labatt's maximum. The others presented two. Only Scali came forward with just one creative idea.

As *Canadian Business* observed in a 1985 article chronicling the review, the big winners were the suppliers to the ad industry: the photographers, film editors, recording studios, and jingle houses. When JWT swarmed into a recording studio to tape its soundtrack, the agency's two backup singers confessed that they were also working for Young & Rubicam, which was locked away in another studio down the hall, recording their top-secret jingles. The singers spent the night jumping from one studio to the other.

Scali also called in the jingle men to put Bill Martin's words to song, and fashion bare-bones ripomatic versions of the ads – rough drafts of TV ads put together with existing footage that was shot for other uses – for the presentation to Labatt. Rather than restrict itself to the same talent pool of Toronto singers, though, Scali unearthed unheralded tavern singer Paul Langiell, a bearded bear of a man from Labatt's hometown of London, Ontario. Langiell, probably the only non-union singer in the entire pitch, sang a few versions of "There's a Heart in This Land," then went on his way.

Presenting in Scali's boardroom, Prouk and his team were soon outnumbered as 10 Labatt people marched in, prepared to be inscrutable. Scali had a tape prepared of three ripomatic versions of the "There's a Heart in This Land" commercial with Langiell's vocals in the background. After a short preamble, the Scali team played the tape. Prouk recalls, "It was like G-Forces, they were being shoved back in their chairs. I think it dawned on them at that moment how wrong what they were doing was. Whether or not they believed what we'd done was really right was not the point. I think they realized, 'Oh my God, is what we are doing really wrong?'"

Tom Errath's response to the Scali presentation was a muttered "That's it!" But the cautious American, with the thick glasses and combed-over hair, was still determined to put every agency's work through the research wringer. Finally, after nearly two months of testing, Scali was summoned to Labatt's head office.

"Might we, might we take this opportunity to offer you our business?" intoned Sid Oland, the president of Labatt Breweries. "Might we accept?" retorted Bill Martin.

From there, Scali's relationship with Labatt quickly went beyond producing advertising for the country's biggest brand of beer. And the relationship with J. Walter Thompson, already on the rocks, turned into a full-blown divorce. Labatt began walking boxes of business into Scali's offices; the agency had never handled such a huge volume of business from one client. Besides Blue, the creative hot shop was now responsible for the Toronto Blue Jays' advertising, along with all the other company brands previously handled by JWT. As well, the lucrative agency-of-record assignment went to Scali, which meant the agency received a fee for keeping track of all the national and international ads run for Labatt by any ad agency.

In the wake of their one-shot presentation, Scali was being vaulted into the advertising big leagues while JWT was dealt a blow from which it took years to recover. Through the advertising agency turmoil, Blue was enjoying a revival: it was up four or five national share points, a surge worth about $60 million in gross profit at the time. Advertising, however, had little to do with Blue's surge. Rather, people were lugging home cases of the stuff because of the novel twist-off cap and the tall, lanky bottle.

The Labatt windfall created its own set of headaches for Scali, although few in the business would feel sorry for Prouk. "We had to hire 40 people. We had to take another floor in our building, computerize, and everything else to handle it. But we took it. We then, of course, used the clout of that. All of a sudden we had the third-largest [agency-of-record assignment] in the country," Prouk said. That clout, and the beige army of computers in the agency's new media department, was put to work for existing clients like Ralston Purina and Apple Canada. But working for the country's third-largest advertiser behind the federal government and Procter & Gamble brought with it other problems.

Scali had been handed the Western Canada regional brands (such as Kokanee) in the JWT dismemberment, but to cope with the new business, the Toronto creatives had to buy a Vancouver ad agency, Bryant, Fulton & Shee. Along with that agency came a small Calgary office. Whether Prouk liked it or not, Scali was reshaping itself to fit the Labatt mould.

In the early honeymoon period, everything seemed great. Those soaring, peaceful days of the balloon were like a distant memory, and Labatt was prepared to spend gargantuan sums of money to keep Blue's momentum. For the initial "There's a Heart in This Land" campaign, Scali scattered teams of crews to some of Canada's most inaccessible places to capture the good honest sweat of the country's everymen. The people at Labatt may not have realized it, as focused as they were on measuring Blue's every market share blip, but Scali was taking an approach much like the one that had worked so well with Anheuser-Busch's Budweiser brand in the United States. The St. Louis brewer had built its Budweiser brand into the country's biggest beer brand by using real people, not actors, in a series of commercials under the long-running "For all you do, this Bud's for you" tag line.

All the same, Scali would quickly learn that Labatt was no Anheuser-Busch. Decentralized into five geographic regions that sported their own presidents and marketing chiefs, Labatt was like a mini version of the Canadian government. Before the agency could hope to shill Blue to the masses, it had to convince Tom Errath at head office and the marketing guys from Vancouver to St. John's of the worth of a particular campaign or ad. Because of decentralization, ads also had to feature scenery from each region. "There was this fucking circus that went across the country," Prouk said, remembering. "We would have creative teams on the road, away from home, for a month. I'd get phone calls from the interior of British Columbia in logging camps. It was crazy, and it got crazier and crazier as it went on."

Prouk, who had refused all offers of assistance from Scali's US headquarters, was finding Labatt to be a difficult master. Besides the pricey commercial shoots, the brewery wanted the attention that a big spender deserves. Constant attention meant more client-services people – guys and gals in suits paid to attend meetings with the brewery and run interference whenever possible for the agency's creative department. Labatt wanted to see its mirror image at "its agency" and Scali conformed.

Most of the agency's meetings with the serried ranks of product and marketing folks concerned what to do about Canadian, which had punched all those holes in the Blue balloon, and was now inexorably taking share away from the market leader. The Blue brand now found itself in the tough spot Canadian had been in just a few years earlier. Because Blue was the number one beer, virtually every group drank it. So if Labatt went too young with its advertising, it would risk alienating the people who made it the Budweiser of the north. But if it ignored those thirsty under-24 drinkers, Blue would become Dad's beer.

Labatt executives who worried about the fate of the flagship needed to look no further than the company's BC bastion, where Blue in its heyday accounted for more than 40% of the province's beer sales. Mike Hurst, who quit Labatt's national marketing department in Ontario to move to British Columbia, was hired on a contract basis to fill in as marketing vice-president in 1980. In his opinion, Blue had risen too high, so its plunge was bound to be equally spectacular.

Back in Ontario, Molson Canadian, still directed by Bill Durnan, the ad writer at MacLaren Advertising, and Dave Barbour, the brewer's street-smart marketing tactician, continued to hold the high ground in the youth market. Canadian was positioned as the gritty urban beer for the legal-drinking-age-to-24 group. Beer marketers would often stretch the group to 29 or 35 years of age, but it was college-aged people who were drinking a disproportionate share of suds and viewed to be more easily swayed with advertising. Barbour, a 20-year veteran of the beer wars at the time, was applying a marketing credo the Labatt Blue folks seemed to have forgotten: stake out your territory and don't stray from it. First, Scali flailed away at the Blue puzzle with enough footage of trees, prairie vastness, and mountain scenery to make Tourism Canada proud. Within Labatt, the brewer searched for a formula to stall Canadian, which was sticking with its good-times-and-beautiful-people rock-music video ads.

Labatt decided to tackle Blue's youth problem on its own. In 1988, Labatt tapped Dave Kincaid, a professional marketer who was about as far from the Barbour mould as he could be. Instead of gut instinct and years of experience, Kincaid brought the formal marketing experience Labatt so treasured. In his early 30s, blond, slim, and runner-fit, Kincaid could have been an extra for a beer commercial himself. Earnest and fond of using product management slang, Kincaid, national brand manager for Labatt Blue, was asked to direct an internal task force of the brewery's younger sales and promotions staff. It had a straightforward mission: make Blue appealing to the legal-drinking-age-to-24 crowd, the impressionable college guzzlers Molson Canadian now seemed to own. Unwilling to change its mainstream advertising and risk losing Blue's older drinkers, Labatt management gave its task force carte blanche – share of entry-age drinkers couldn't get worse – as long as there was no chance what it produced might annoy the core Blue audience. Labatt couldn't be faulted for its caution; Blue was still the country's biggest brand with an 18% national share, although the foundation was eroding away as youthful drinkers avoided it.

Scouring the reams of posters, bar banners, and beer coasters used for Blue across the country, Kincaid came across a triangular "tent card," intended to be plunked on a bar or table, which had the line "Enter the Blue Zone" emblazoned upon it. The Labatt task force fixated upon "Blue Zone" and Scali assigned two junior staffers to the "Blue Zone" business, account executive David Martin and Vaughn Whelan from Scali's creative department.

The sales and promotions guys, so frustrated with pitting "Dad's beer" Blue against Canadian on campuses, decided "Blue Zone" could in no way be confused with the Blue of older drinkers. They'd launch an anti-campaign: it would be raucous and depict situations that Blue's national ads never would. With an initial development budget of $50,000, a paltry amount for a brewery that spends $5-million a year on consumer research, the group tested its approach. The first effort was a ripomatic version of a rock video set to Sweet's "Ballroom Blitz." After testing that across the country two different times for audience feedback, Labatt decided to have the commercial become the launch ad for "Blue Zone." "Literally about three weeks before we were to go into production on that television ad, Molson launches a Taste That Will Stop You Cold spot using 'Ballroom Blitz,'" said Kincaid. "I'm still positive to this day that there was a leak somewhere and they found out about our intent to use this song. It was the first time Blue would have used a known rock song."

Frustrated, the "Blue Zone" group went with original music for the two initial TV ads for the campaign's launch in the fall of 1988. It hired Hamilton, Ontario, band The Kings, which had the 1980 hit song "This Beat Goes On," to write and perform original music for the ads. The campaign also featured 15-second ads, a pioneering length at the time, which depicted a dancing carrot and other strange subjects, and appeared during youth-oriented TV programs such as *Saturday Night Live*.

Based on the reactions of college drinkers collected by Labatt's campus reps, the "Blue Zone" budget ballooned. "It went very quickly from $50,000 of development stuff, to a $5- to $6-million program," Kincaid recalled. "Then we added all the media components to it and it quickly became a $35- to $45-million program."

The advertising got noticed and made an impact. Much of the campaign's success can be attributed to the fact that it was very different from mainstream beer ads and that it was created outside the normal channels. With no real budget, at least to start, the internal group didn't spend time on the rounds of research, focus groups, and concept testing then choking the beer business. Young for beer guys, the "Blue Zoners" understood what the mainstream campaign *wasn't* doing for the college crowd – especially the promotions types whose job it was to push Labatt suds at college pubs.

Besides the deliberately non-mainstream advertising, Labatt relied on one of its favourite under-the-radar marketing weapons: free stuff. Name virtually any consumer product, from refrigerators to golf bags to leather bomber jackets, and chances are one of the breweries has emblazoned its name on it for promotional giveaways. "Blue Zone" hats, T-shirts, party kits of coolers stuffed with everything but the beer reminded the beer-guzzling college crowd what brand to drink, just in case they forgot.

Free "Blue Zone" stuff played a starring role in Labatt's "discovery" of Pamela Anderson, the buxom BC girl who became a star in the nineties thanks to a role in *Baywatch*. According to Labatt legend, Pamela Anderson's Hollywood career came about accidentally. She appeared on the jumbo screen at a BC Lions football game in a "Blue Zone" sweatshirt cut off at the midriff, and commanded rapt attention from the crowd and some on the field, according to her roommate. In actual fact, her discovery was not that accidental.

Still in her teens, Pamela was living in Vancouver with someone who just happened to be a campus rep for Labatt. In his mid-20s and fresh out of college, Jamie Moberg's job, as he recalls, was to try to resuscitate Blue. Pamela, whose ambitions belied her age and wholesome good looks, and Moberg, the results-oriented beer salesman, were a good match.

Not long after the first shipments of "Blue Zone" wear arrived from Toronto, Moberg had Pamela modelling the gear. Decking her out in the most alluring of Labatt's beer fashions – the "crop top" – the two headed off to the Lions game. "My objective was to get her up on the Diamond Vision screen, not to promote her but to promote the 'Blue Zone,' of course," remembers Moberg, who along with Anderson went around the stadium until they found one of the camera operators whose job was to take shots of the crowd. "We moved all over the stadium trying to get this cameraman to notice us. Finally, she ended up on the screen." Playing to the crowd, Anderson tugged at the short top and motioned as if she was going to flip it up as the control room was getting the feed on her. "The game practically stopped. The crowd just went stupid."

Hoping to capitalize on her football fame, the duo had Anderson's fiancé at the time, a local photographer, shoot her for a "Blue Zone" poster. According to Moberg, Labatt initially passed up the opportunity to have Anderson appear as a poster girl. There were lots of pretty girls vying to be "Blue Zone" poster girls. Undeterred, Anderson ended up on the cover of *Playboy* magazine as the October '89 Playmate of the Month – and a few issues later, as the Playmate of the Year. For those unfamiliar with the publication, her fact sheet, which lists hobbies and aspirations, featured the standard three photos: one from childhood, another from high school, and a present-day picture that just happened to be the "Blue Zone" poster that never was. "Of course, as soon as that appeared in there, she became known nationally as the 'Blue Zone' girl, and I think [Labatt] purchased 10,000 copies of that poster," said Moberg.

Free posters of attractive girls like Anderson, and bar games like "Get Wet in the Blue Zone" in campus-area bars, were dusting Blue off, but the campaign's very success was revealing "Blue Zone" to those who were concerned about alcohol being marketed to impressionable college kids in a sophisticated way.

Labatt unwittingly gave ammunition to its critics by boasting of the campaign's success in the advertising trade press. Kincaid candidly talked about how the brewery was targeting the 19-to-24 market, but referred to it constantly as the "youth campaign" using Labatt's internal description. The promotion's success quickly became a *cause célèbre* for a suddenly health-conscious Mulroney government, which had just slapped tough advertising restrictions on the tobacco industry. Federal Health Minister Jake Epp fired off a letter to Labatt and ad industry journal *Marketing* criticizing the brewer for its "deliberate and insistent attempt" to court college kids with the "Blue Zone." "You can understand my concern at the thought of Labatt's sales representatives creating a Blue Zone on campus to attract those students who are 'inclined to party hard,'" the letter said.

Publicly, Labatt said the "Blue Zone" would continue unaltered, just as gritty as ever. The reality was quite different. The program may have been reaching the college crowd, but the fast-cut, rock 'n' roll–style ads designed to make Canadian look tame were annoying the core Blue drinker. "Blue Zone" commercials had started creeping into mainstream advertising slots such as Blue Jays baseball telecasts. A year after the "youth" furor, "Blue Zone" lost its champion when Kincaid was shifted to manage the Budweiser brand, and the ad effort was soon dropped.

From a market-share perspective, Blue was hanging in there. The brand was still the undisputed king of beer land, with about 17% of sales nationally and an even higher share in the all-important Ontario market, due in part to the success of the Labatt-owned Blue Jays. Labatt did its best to link the brewery, and Blue in particular, to the team, advertising heavily during game telecasts. The ball club became popular as a perennial contender every year following its surprise playoff appearance in 1985.

Still, poring over long-term sales trends and market research, Labatt was not satisfied with managing what was viewed as Blue's inevitable long-term slide. The brewer wanted to regain share at Molson Canadian's expense. The solution presented itself in the form of Dave Barbour, suddenly looking for work after having been squeezed out in the merger of Molson and Carling O'Keefe. Barbour was named executive vice-president of marketing (Tom Errath became president of Labatt's entertainment group). Labatt had finally captured its long-time nemesis, who Scali's Gary Prouk had suggested a few years before would help solve Blue's seemingly intractable problems with the youth market. Joining Labatt at the start of 1990, his immediate task was to breathe some life into Labatt's advertising.

Barbour could now lay claim to being the only senior executive to work at all three major breweries. He'd left Molson a few years earlier to join Carling O'Keefe, where he directed the "Legend Is Black" campaign for the flagging Black Label brand. A creative success, the campaign also made the brand popular with Toronto's hip downtown crowd for the summer of 1988.

At Labatt, Barbour wasted little time surveying the scene. Less than a year into the top marketing job, Barbour decided to put the Blue account up for review for the third time in five years. Scali managed to hold onto the account in an ad review just two years into its mandate, but it now looked to be on shaky ground with the demise of "Blue Zone," even though the effort was Labatt's idea. Scali was also never able to find the next Blue balloon – the breakthrough campaign that could run year after year. In retrospect, when Labatt researchers raked over the Scali years, they discovered that "Blue Zone" was the best-recalled creative work for the country's biggest brand, evidence that Labatt's other campaigns were not striking a chord with the public.

When Barbour joined the brewer, the health of Blue was the main preoccupation at Labatt HQ. The company had become a diversified conglomerate in the go-go eighties, but Labatt management knew beer paid the bills. In the mid-1980s, when Blue commanded a 17%–18% share of the market and a stunning 27% of the rich Ontario market, the brand was the brewery's cash cow, accounting for 40% of the profits.

In 1990, Barbour called in two other Labatt shops from the bullpen to compete with Scali – Chiat\Day\Mojo, a hotshot California agency responsible for the ubiquitous "La Dry" campaign for Labatt Dry, and Carder Gray DDB Needham, which worked on Budweiser, the Anheuser-Busch brand made and marketed by Labatt in Canada.

At Scali, Gary Prouk had other things on his mind. The news of the Blue review was leaked to the business press on a Friday, appearing in newspapers on the lovely Saturday morning when Prouk was getting married for the second time, and Labatt executive vice-president Graham Freeman was acting as his best man. John Labatt president

Sid Oland and entertainment group president Tom Errath, also in attendance, but not wanting to ruin the day, didn't raise the subject of the review. Prouk, who'd skipped his morning newspaper routine on his wedding day, was not informed of the change in Scali's situation until just before he and his bride stepped on an airplane bound for Florence.

Soon unhappy with the ideas from the shops within the Labatt stable, Barbour called in two more agencies, including J. Walter Thompson, the creator of the long-crashed balloon. Hardly an unknown quantity to Labatt, JWT was also well familiar to Barbour, having worked for him while he was at Carling O'Keefe. As JWT president Andy Krupski recalled, he'd run into Barbour in the cathedral-like lobby of BCE Place before the creative search was expanded. Suddenly inspired by a passage in a book on UK agency Saatchi & Saatchi, Krupski said his shop had been working on beer creative since Barbour joined Labatt and had full-fledged campaign ideas to run. "Of course I had nothing," Krupski said, retelling the story. Krupski then had a couple of weeks to throw a presentation together while Barbour did a cross-country tour of Labatt. Krupski set his creative teams loose, and when Barbour returned, JWT did an informal presentation in an anonymous downtown hotel suite. The show failed to sway Barbour, but the agency was once again on the radar screen and got the call when Barbour decided to look outside the current Labatt agency lineup.

The Labatt that J. Walter Thompson had left was a different entity than the one it was attempting to return to. Senior management was turning over at a rate that seemed improbable for the undisputed leader in the beer business. During Scali's five-year hitch on Blue, the agency had worked for three different presidents. The musical chairs could be blamed at least in part on parent company John Labatt's incredible non-beer growth. Like rival Molson, the steady stream of beer profits was being funnelled into businesses that had little or no connection with brewing. Executives were being plucked from the familiar suds game to run companies they knew little or nothing about.

Given the radical changes at Labatt during the eighties, it should have been no surprise when in 1990 it handed the prized Blue account to J. Walter Thompson. JWT had been hurt in 1985 when the brewer stripped it of all Labatt-related business and now it was Scali's turn, although with the well-connected and persuasive Prouk in charge, it clung onto non-Blue portions of the business for a number of years.

Labatt's Barbour era hardly got off to a roaring start. For the first three months of 1990, the brewer was banned by the Liquor Licence Board of Ontario from advertising Blue and Blue Light because of illegal inducements the brewery paid to bar owners and unauthorized advertising. Labatt was also fined $400,000 by the LLBO for the overexuberant actions of some of its sales staff, but it was the ad ban that the marketers at the brewer thought would hurt the most. Inducements to bar owners, whether cash discounts per keg, free equipment, or free trips to exotic locales, were common practice. Getting caught at it was embarrassing, and a sign of just how the push was on among the Labatt troops to move market share at the time.

The internal joke at Labatt following the lifting of the ad ban was how little impact the hiatus from the airwaves had had on Blue's share. January to March is hardly prime beer-swilling time, but Blue's share hardly fell.

Under Dave Barbour's direction, JWT responded with a series of commercials using the tag line "Now You're Laughing," which first aired in the spring of 1991 and harkened back to the "Now You're Smiling" theme of yesteryear. Surprisingly, given Barbour's initiatives on the hip-grinding, sex-drenched Molson Canadian rock 'n' roll ads (which were still pummelling Blue), the new Labatt creative junked the "easy times, easy women" approach. "We're appealing more to the intellect of the individual, as opposed to the libido," Barbour told The Globe and Mail, whose headline writer wrote, "Labatt's Ads Lose Their La-Bido."

The male-dominated marketing department at Labatt may suddenly have developed a more moderated view. But according to former Labatt employees, the shift in strategy was brought about by the heat

"Blue Zone" had generated. It was one thing to try to boost the fortunes of Labatt Blue; it was quite another to attract the unwelcome attention of the government, as Health Minister Epp's letter had shown.

With JWT's more high-minded beer ads, Labatt was also hoping to steer clear of a suddenly feminist Ontario government. Following the surprise 1990 election of Bob Rae's New Democratic Party in the beer industry's bellwether province, Molson and Labatt found themselves under sporadic attack by the government and a feminist group called Media Watch. First it was Peter Kormos, the Ontario minister of consumer and corporate relations, who later was tossed from Cabinet after appearing in the *Toronto Sun* as a "Sunshine Boy." Kormos was about to launch a campaign to get beer companies to clean up their advertising, having felt that beer companies used too many bikini-clad women in exploitive ways. The minister was replaced by Marilyn Churley, and she similarly pledged to make the war on sexist advertising a top priority.

Labatt's decision to run politically correct ads was also influenced by the rough going-over Molson was enduring. One Molson Canadian advertisement in particular, the "Rare Long-Haired Fox," was generating a lot of political heat. The Fox, a comely lass in a halter top who also appeared in a Molson Canadian TV commercial, was featured in a newspaper ad along with the copy: "She is usually courted by a large number of males," is selective when choosing a mate, and has "superior agility and intelligence to enable her to outrun and outwit other animals, such as wolves."

Males characters such as the Bellowing Moose and Howling Wolf also made the transition from TV to print. Depicting young males as beer-guzzling fun-seekers raised no government objections, but the Fox was deemed to be over the line. "The Fox is the only woman portrayed in that series and the impression is given that she exists solely for the pleasure of men and to fulfill male fantasies," reported one newspaper, quoting Mary Ambrose, Ontario director of Media Watch.

Ms. Ambrose seemed to understand beer advertising and no doubt the marketers of Molson and Labatt wished they had her on their team. The beer companies were getting themselves into trouble because theirs was such a male-dominated profession; a male creative team at what was now called MacLaren McCann had dreamt up the wildlife ad series and it was approved by a male-dominated marketing and sales team at Molson. The only time Molson or Labatt would know they had crossed the line would be if they received feedback from a focus group, or if a feminist group lodged a complaint.

For the public, the beer companies' clashes with the feminist activists and the provincial NDP government provided some welcome comic relief from the tough economic times of most of the Bob Rae regime. The Globe and Mail's editorial cartoonist was moved to depict a group of pilgrims in severe black garb and old-fashioned hats playing beach volleyball in front of a group of curious onlookers. "What's going on?" the caption read, and the response was, "They are shooting a beer commercial for some place called Ontario."

The team at MacLaren showed they had a sense of humour about the Fox affair. The next year they ran a print spot featuring the same long-limbed, single-mother model, this time bundled in a parka, and the ad was entitled "Arctic Fox."

Meanwhile, Labatt was now unhappy with its "Now You're Laughing" advertising, conceived by J. Walter Thompson. "Laughing" was junked after just one summer in favour of a new blues music campaign with the theme "You Bet it's Blue." Showing yet again that the only consistent thing about Blue was its frequently changing ads, the brewer said the logical link of the brand with blues music would be a hit. David Kincaid – the architect of "Blue Zone" and now elevated to the position of director of marketing – defended the new tack. "What blues is to music, Labatt Blue is to Canada's beer," he told one newspaper.

JWT's Andy Krupski supported the new campaign, providing some competition on the music front for Canadian and its continued rock 'n' roll theme. The blues music approach was a hit. (That meant it lasted two seasons rather than the traditional one for Blue.) However, JWT found itself on shaky ground with Labatt once more.

Labatt was the scene of management turmoil and the company was promising to trim the agency stable from seven to two or three. In the summer of 1992, Labatt Breweries president John Morgan was abruptly fired (his subsequent suit for wrongful dismissal was settled out of court) and the Ontario division president, Hugo Powell, took over. The beer industry didn't it know it just yet, but the simmering beer wars were going to heat up another notch.

3
The Blue Shuffle

Whether or not the industry recognized it at the time, Hugo Powell, the ambitious Indian-born and British-raised executive, was going to revolutionize the beer business. Unlike his predecessors, Powell was not a "beer guy." He wasn't born into it like Sid Oland, scion of the East Coast Oland beer clan; he wasn't a professional athlete turned beer executive like former Labatt Breweries president Pierre Desjardins; or a long-time sales guy climbing through the ranks like John Morgan. First and foremost, Powell was a marketer who had been a troubleshooter in Labatt's underperforming food empire. He'd run the company's bread business in the mid-1980s in British Columbia and then headed its US juice business prior to becoming president of Labatt's linchpin Ontario division.

Before joining Labatt, Powell had made his reputation at Nabob Foods, where he'd championed a series of ads featuring actor/spokesman Mike Reynolds bashing open industry leader Maxwell House's soft coffee bag with a hammer to demonstrate the superiority of Nabob's brick-like, vacuum-sealed foil-and-paper bag. Nabob, with a minuscule share of the coffee market, had this particular packaging innovation, and the ad agency seized upon it. Scali's Gary Prouk, who'd first met Powell when his agency proposed the advertising to Nabob, remembers the queasy reaction of the company's marketers as they viewed the commercials that showed their genial spokesman bashing the competition quite literally.

Following the well-worn path of marketers everywhere, Nabob ordered up rounds of consumer research. According to Prouk, it came back showing that 61% of consumers loved the ads and the other 39% hated them with a venom that startled the researchers. "So under normal circumstances in advertising – certainly in this country," Prouk recalls, "after everyone had cleaned their seats because their sphincters went, they would say, 'We had better get rid of that stuff.'" Not so for Labatt's new president, as Prouk relates. "Hugo said something that was so great. He said, 'Well, I guess we'll have to settle for a 61 share.' It was exactly what you have to say in front of everyone who is in this room, which is a little company taking on a big guy. Behind this kind of polished, patrician British veneer, he's a slugger."

George Taylor, the president of Labatt's food businesses and the man who would soon replace Sid Oland as the chief executive officer of the John Labatt empire, pushed mightily for Powell to be named president of Labatt Breweries' Ontario division in 1990. According to Taylor, Powell's appointment was resisted by Labatt management, who knew running the biggest and most profitable region was traditionally a stepping stone to the top job, but eventually they relented. When Morgan was ousted in 1992, Powell was the logical replacement.

Powell, or simply Hugo, as he was called by friends and enemies alike, was hardly what central casting would have ordered up as a brewery president. Slim, old-world polite, and so soft-spoken one often had to strain to hear him, he was the antithesis of the popular perception of the booming, brash beer executive.

In fact, Hugo had much in common with his opposite number over at Molson, Bruce Pope. Both brewery presidents were packaged-goods marketers from Warner-Lambert Canada Inc., and both were prone to rely on research rather than gut instinct. The difference was that Hugo, the beer outsider, quickly developed fanatical loyalty at Labatt unlike Pope. Hugo certainly didn't smother his underlings with love, but like a natural leader in a time of crisis, he convinced them he would do the right thing, no matter how painful it would be.

One of the first requests he made of his staff, Hugo remembers, was for them to prepare a 10-year financial chart on market share, marketing spending, costs, revenue, and other key indicators. The one caveat he stipulated was that all of the data had to be contained on one page, free of the usual corporate bafflegab and double-talk. Hugo's simple guide to Labatt, when assembled, told the true tale: efforts to reduce costs had stalled and profit growth was sluggish. The financial analysis was called for in the wake of the surprise 1989 merger of the country's two other big brewers: Molson and Carling O'Keefe, owned by Australia's Elders IXL. The combination of the two created a beer company that was bigger and more profitable than Labatt.

"It looked to me like a business that had stood still for 10 years and the competitive set was reflecting that as well," recollects Hugo. "There was lots of action, lots of things the media would like to write about and lots of things the management would like to promote. But if you got beneath the skirmishing, the industry was sort of frozen in time and not going anywhere. We had spent large amounts of capital to buy productivity and there was zero productivity [improvement] in the business."

In the midst of much angst within Labatt's ranks, Hugo quickly took charge. Just weeks into the top job, he called Labatt Breweries' national office staff to a meeting at a Toronto airport hotel and famously said, "Look to your left; look to your right. In six months one of those people won't be working here." True to the new boss's word, Labatt fired about one-half the staff not long afterwards.

Hugo's elevation was clearly no bolt from the blue. Besides cutting head office staff, Hugo planned to beat Molson-Carling, and chop $300 million in costs. That included a $50-million savings created by eliminating the dizzying profusion of glass packaging, and moving to a standard long-necked bottle in tandem with Molson, which was suffering from an even greater burden of odd bottles.

Hugo also pledged to trim the $250-million marketing budget by $100 million annually over three years, a brave pledge considering the industry-wide obsession with market share.

Ex-president John Morgan, however, claimed that he too had a plan, and argued that Labatt should have given him the time to carry it out. As part of his $2.5-million wrongful-dismissal suit (which the parties settled out of court), Morgan claimed he had developed a five-year plan to grow share to 47%, slash costs by $100 million annually, and slow Blue's decline. Labatt's share at the time of his firing was 43.5%, and profit had risen 29% to $218 million for the most recent fiscal year. Morgan had decided to close the company's Waterloo, Ontario, brewery, an obvious candidate for closure given Labatt had two larger breweries operating in the province.

Although clearly not a beer man, and with next to nothing in common with the 19-to-24 party-hard crowd, Hugo considered himself responsible for marketing. Whether people recognized it or not, he was a believer in the tenet that the CEO, not some marketing guru, had to have firm control of the brand. That meant Barbour, so long admired and feared at Labatt, was working for his last brewery. Labatt executives toiling with Hugo and Barbour at the time say they never clashed, but it was immediately clear one would have to go, and that it wasn't going to be Hugo. Barbour was out the Labatt House glass doors at Toronto's BCE Place just weeks into the Powell era.

Hugo would soon look at streamlining beyond Labatt's hallways. Besides quickening the pace of product and packaging innovations, a traditional Labatt strength, Hugo scrutinized the ad industry in the fall of 1992. With Dave Barbour's chair still warm, Hugo called in Prouk's former colleague Richard Kelly, who in the old Scali days had worked on Nabob. Kelly had left the agency a few years prior to Scali's Labatt win. Fresh from California, where he'd gone to run the West Coast outpost of Wells Rich Greene, Kelly began advising Hugo on how to deal with Labatt's complex agency relationships.

Kelly helped write Hugo's famous "fire the handlers" speech in which he called on agencies to eliminate their ranks of "handlers," the account executives – the go-betweens who linked up the advertisers and the people who made the ads. "I don't want to pay for handlers and I certainly don't want to be handled," Hugo said in a speech to the Canadian Congress of Advertising at the beginning of 1993. He called on bright agency types to show some guts and strike out on their own. "Please, somebody start a revolution. Not with bullets, but with ideas." "Fire the handlers" may have been the wake-up call for the ad industry, but Labatt wasn't going to wait around for the ad industry to roll out of bed. Behind the scenes, the brewer was soon exploring a way out of its profusion of agency entanglements.

Hugo's early corporate statements showed he was an executive in a hurry. Although Labatt had a record of innovation in the beer industry, he wanted to pick up the pace, keeping Molson off balance and obliged to play by Labatt's rules. Despite Labatt's innovation successes, the beer business as a whole had been content to lag behind consumer trends where new product introduction was concerned. The only place competing beer companies seemed to keep pace was in advertising. Part of the sluggishness was regulatory, as many of the weapons available to other consumer-products companies were forbidden to suds makers, but there was also a tendency to be satisfied with the status quo. It made sense in a way. If you were making so much money and your rivals were not overly aggressive, why rock the boat?

Hugo wanted to rock the boat. During his first three years as president of Labatt's brewing arm (1992–1994) he set a blistering pace, shutting down breweries, introducing new products, spearheading the largest foreign acquisition in the company's history, and reducing the company's ballooning marketing and advertising costs.

Andy Krupski, president of J. Walter Thompson, was confident his shop would be one of the survivors of the agency-roster trimming, and would be working on more, not less, Labatt business. JWT was given repeated reassurances to that effect, Krupski contends. "I think the numbers that the blues campaign ["You Bet it's Blue"] was driving – it was record scores at the time for whatever they were measuring: awareness and purchase intent and share, that stuff," the ad man said. Then in the fall of 1993, US advertising heavyweight Ammirati Puris said it was opening a Canadian office – in Toronto's BCE Place near Labatt's corporate digs – and that it had accepted an undisclosed "strategic project" from the brewer. Confident in the assurances that it would be part of Labatt's future, JWT staffers ignored the rumours about their imminent demise.

In January, one year after Hugo's infamous "handlers" speech, Krupski got a call alerting him to a visit from the Labatt brass. A stretch limo pulled up to the agency's Bloor Street office and out spilled Hugo, marketing vice-president Dave Kincaid, and other senior executives of the brewery. "I was convinced that we were actually going to get the business, so I had two boardrooms, one where they were going to come in and talk to us, and one where we were going to celebrate with our employees," Krupski said. At the last minute, he decided to hold off on the party idea and simply met the Labatt gang with his creative director.

"They all came in, which was the most amazing thing I have ever seen." The meeting was short and blunt. J. Walter Thompson was out and most of its work was going to Ammirati. Krupski was floored. "By virtue of the fact that they came by limousine, one was led to believe . . . why would you think anything but the positives?" Krupski recalls in a wondering tone. "Because generally you get called down to be told the negatives."

The Labatt executive road trip would make a number of similar stops at Toronto ad shops that day before ending up back at BCE Place, the new home of Ammirati. In the end, Ammirati, untried and unproven in Canada, was handed responsibility for every beer brand that bore the Labatt name, and three agencies were terminated outright (Young & Rubicam and D'Arcy Masius Benton & Bowles, as well as JWT), while Bozell Palmer Bonner gave up the Labatt Genuine Draft youth brand for Labatt's licensed beers, Budweiser and Carlsberg. Scali's Toronto office, not so long ago the darling of the industry, lost the assignment for Labatt Ice and was given the consolation prize of new product development.

In one day, Labatt had made it official: Ammirati would be a force on the Canadian ad scene, and not just a Toronto outpost established mere months before. While Ammirati's billings would soar 150%, JWT and Scali continued their long-term declines – first set in motion by the brewer years earlier, and given an extra shove with Labatt's final agency cull. "They injured us very, very badly, not as badly as Thompson, but they [the Labatt decision] really fucking hurt Scali," says Gary Prouk, who, today, is head of a four-person consultancy. "You know how they hurt us? It wasn't even money. What they did was they seduced us with all of the trappings of money and power that made us forget what got us there was not money and power."

Two years later, the agency once known as Scali disappeared when it merged with another Toronto ad shop and Prouk departed. JWT, in its Blue-balloon heyday the biggest agency in the land, managed to survive as a shrunken shadow of itself after losing Labatt, Ford Canada, and Pepsi in the late eighties and early nineties.

Predictably, the tight little Toronto ad community, where everyone knew your name and what you were doing, was in an uproar over the Ammirati hiring. Here was a little shop of Americans who were seen as not having paid their dues north of the border, taking one of the sexiest, most lucrative ad assignments in the industry. And just who was this Tom Nelson guy anyway?

Few would ever really get to know Nelson, a soft-spoken fellow blinking shyly behind oversized glasses, and often sporting a too-big pullover sweater. Nelson, an associate creative director at Ammirati's New York office, had hired two Canadians to help replicate the agency's unquestioned southern success in the United States. He was chairman, creative director, and writer – ambitious roles for an agency of three. His creative partner was Doug Robinson, an art director, and Dennis Stief, a "suit," or account person, was hired on as president. For clients such as United Postal Service, RCA, and MasterCard, the agency had built a reputation in the United States for breathing new life into well-known, venerable brands. They had set up shop in Canada to service UPS and Compaq, which meant adapting US ads for a Canadian market.

Ammirati had been elevated to Labatt's attention by Richard Kelly, the same man who'd advised Hugo on the beer company's web of ad agencies.

To succeed in the advertising game, you need to have patrons. Scali had John Labatt's executive vice-president Graham Freeman; J. Walter Thompson had marketing vice-president Dave Barbour; and Ammirati had Richard Kelly. Kelly provided Hugo with information outside brewery channels, and gave him the background he needed to challenge accepted thinking in the business. Gary Prouk performed a similar function when Scali still worked for Labatt. He was often asked to come in and brief Hugo before Labatt sales and marketing meetings, ducking out side entrances so as not to be seen leaving. It was a tactic Prouk believes the Labatt president used to keep a step ahead of his employees. Although Hugo cultivated a fierce loyalty among his executives, he sought outside opinions rather than simply relying on what had worked before.

Hugo's commissioning of Ammirati was a good example of his willingness to change the way the brewer operated. The first strategic project Ammirati was given by Labatt, months prior to winning most of Labatt's work, involved charting out a new strategy with Kelly and Toronto researcher Henry Fiorillo, another outsider who had Hugo's ear.

Besides trimming staff and expenditures at Labatt Breweries, the next logical fix, discussed even prior to Hugo's ascension to president, was pruning the ad agency roster. Kelly sold Hugo on Ammirati, convincing him an agency free of the Toronto mindset could help Labatt regain its momentum. "[Hugo] wanted his own agency, he wanted to structure it with very senior people, and he believed, he had been convinced by Ammirati, that there should be corporate advertising," explained Michael Downey, the marketer in charge of Blue at the time. "It was that whole, 'Labatt, Good Things Brewing,' and the whole corporate name was going to become more important than the brand names."

Downey, who after his Labatt days worked at both Toronto's SkyDome and the Toronto Maple Leafs hockey and Raptors basketball organizations before ending up as senior vice-president of marketing for Molson, remembers that the first thing Ammirati did was junk the blues-oriented campaign for Labatt Blue, even though it had managed to break the campaign-a-year cycle. Ammirati's first work out of the gate for Blue featured a self-satisfied beer drinker sitting in his backyard, dreaming he was parked on the Canada-US border drinking his Blue while "taunting and teasing them . . . with the finest example of a true Canadian lager." If that didn't do the trick, the ad went on to say, he might finish the job by throwing a tape of the last year's World Series in the VCR, or the one before that. (The commercial aired in the spring of 1994 following the Labatt-owned Blue Jays' second baseball championship win, and ran during the season that ended prematurely with the 1994 World Series inconceivably cancelled by a labour dispute between the players and team owners. The Labatt Blue–Blue Jays link – and major-league baseball – had peaked in 1993 and all three were headed for a long-term slide.)

After Ammirati ran its first ads for four Labatt brands, Barry Base, a Toronto ad man and industry columnist, wrote in ad journal *Strategy* that the agency "must have crossed at Niagara Falls and spent a night in Grimsby, Ontario, to soak in Canadian cultural and architectural nuances." There were similar comments from the notoriously hostile and judgmental Canadian ad industry, but in the main, Ammirati's effort was ignored, which is likely worse, considering the profile and budget Labatt had given it. Even Labatt insiders at the time, such as David Kincaid, concur. "The individual brand executions were highly mixed," he said, noting that the best effort was produced for Labatt Genuine Draft, Blue's advertising was "acceptable," and the work for Blue Light was less disappointing.

Ammirati created the first real campaign for Blue two years later with an interesting spot featuring two voyageurs, one of whom envisioned a great country with a great lager, ending with the joke that it was a perfect place except for something called the GST. The ad sparked a series of follow-on commercials featuring Jacques and William. After the voyageur series had run its course, Labatt executives asked for a new direction. Meanwhile, Tom Nelson returned to New

York in 1996 to take on his reward for putting his Big Apple life on hold while putting Ammirati on the map in Canada – the job of vice-chairman and co-creative director for the New York agency office.

While Blue was chewing through campaigns, marketing executives, and agencies with seasonal regularity, Canadian continued its assault on Blue's Ontario bastion, and, year by year, came closer to unseating it as Canada's best-selling beer. A great deal of Molson's success with Canadian can be traced back to the original rock video music formula, sparked by former marketing vice-president Dave Barbour's willingness to take chances and MacLaren McCann's determination to stick with the format. In the period when Scali, J. Walter Thompson, and then Ammirati worked on Blue's positioning, Canadian ads promised great music, a good time with your buddies, and more than the hint of sex. MacLaren writer Bill Durnan, creator of the Canadian formula with "Dancing in the Street," directed the brand long enough to see it muscled up a little more. The pop-rock tunes were weeded out in favour of what the agency termed "classic rock."

Durnan, an undisputed rising star in the advertising world, took on the creative director's role at MacLaren McCann, a job that meant his time had to be spent winning business, stroking existing clients, and keeping various egos in the agency's creative teams in check. While Durnan was creative director, Canadian used the long-running (1988–1992) "Taste That Will Stop You Cold" campaign, which ended with the tag line "What Beer's All About."

The MacLaren-Molson marketing team settled into a successful formula on Canadian, although Durnan himself believed the "Taste That Will Stop You Cold" effort had gone on too long. Canadian's sales gains had halted and market share in fact was slipping. Much of the credit for the halt in Canadian's momentum goes to Labatt, which, in an effort to take the heat off Blue, was busily launching Labatt Genuine Draft, Labatt Ice, and the discount brand Wildcat, tempting Molson to take its eye off Canadian. In a submission to the Cassies ad competition in 1997, Durnan conceded that the brand had lost 1.5 points of market share "and also share of mind."

So again, MacLaren McCann was in trouble with Molson. Unlike in 1983, Canadian had not achieved "Dad's beer" status, however, it was in need of a creative rejuvenation. With the account in jeopardy, Durnan worked with one of the agency's teams on what eventually became known as the "I Am Canadian" campaign. Music took centre stage in the brand's advertising, which in the first year featured hip imagery and disjointed "beat poetry" to appeal to a young, culturally diverse demographic. In 1995, following the launch of "I Am Canadian," which has run continuously but for one significant interruption, Durnan left MacLaren McCann and set up his own advertising consultancy, although he rented space from his former employer, acting as a consultant on Canadian in the early days of his venture.

His decision to strike out on his own meant Durnan was far away when the stench created by the 1998 "Typing Monkeys" commercials found their way to air. Those ads, and a rival that seemed to be figuring out what to do with Blue, spelled the end for MacLaren McCann on Molson.

Durnan, who'd caught lightning in a bottle for Molson on a couple of occasions, in the fall of 1997 had grown weary of the hassles associated with running his own shop, and in short order, he sold his consultancy to Ammirati, becoming president in the process. The hiring was not accidental. "I wanted Bill Durnan on our business," said David Kincaid. "I had talked with Martin Puris [the founder and chairman of Ammirati Puris] about buying Durnan's agency, which they did." After more than three years on his own, Durnan was ready for something new: running an agency a lot smaller than MacLaren McCann, but a shop that gave him the chance to work on a beer he knew so well, stalking it as he had from Molson's camp all those years. Months later, Kincaid arrived at Ammirati's offices for a scheduled lunch with Durnan and agency chairman and creative director Doug Robinson. Instead of going out to eat as previously planned, a brusque Kincaid demanded that the agency people sit down in a meeting room for an impromptu working lunch, and trays of sandwiches were brought in. Kincaid had been told by the brewery's top brass that Blue's advertising needed a fix. "The inconsistency is unacceptable and the results are unacceptable," is how the Labatt marketing vice-president summed up the conversation. "They didn't say fix it or you're fired, but the fact that somebody is saying 'It ain't good enough,' that kind of scared the bejesus out of me and motivated me."

Kincaid's message was simple and not dissimilar to Dave Barbour's direction 15 years earlier to his agency when Molson Canadian was in trouble: the account is on the line, come up with something spectacular, or else. Labatt had reason to be concerned. After straying from Blue and devoting energy and marketing spending to Labatt Ice and Genuine Draft, the brewer was again determined to turn Blue around. In only a few months, the 1998 Winter Olympics would be held in Japan, and Labatt was a sponsor. The company had also spent tens of millions on the National Hockey League to wrestle away *Hockey Night in Canada* from Molson. Saturday evening telecasts of *Hockey Night in Canada*, like Monday Night Football in the United States, came to represent the most important games for the sport. Now with rights to the NHL's flagship broadcast in Canada, Labatt had nothing to air.

After not so subtly putting an end to Jacques and William – they jumped over a cliff à la Butch and Sundance in an ad that was never followed up – Ammirati came out the following summer with two ads using the "I Will" tag line and voiceovers such as, "I will jump on the bandwagon and stay on it." It was a good thing the ads featured shots of the Blue bottle considering Molson was spouting "I Am" in its campaign for Canadian. "This is simply creative that reflects what our consumers were saying they wanted to see," said Labatt spokesman Bob Chant, explaining the similar-sounding tag line to *Marketing* magazine.

After Kincaid's challenge, Ammirati came back a week later with storyboards for four or five different campaigns. The winner, which Kincaid remembers Durnan presenting last, involved wacky, "spontaneous fun" – the party that sprang from nowhere – that would end in every commercial with the tag line "Out of the Blue." Kincaid seized on the idea, just as research subjects did when presented with the prospective Blue campaigns. From being on the firing line in

November, Ammirati went into high gear writing, shooting, and editing for a February debut.

"Out of the Blue" was deemed to be the perfect campaign idea because it forced the writer to use the brand in the tag line every time, just like "I Am Canadian," and unlike the blues music campaign, the voyageurs waiting for the invention of the beer store, or even Molson's rock 'n' roll videos for that matter, the "Out of the Blue" concept seemed to promise virtually limitless variations. To stay consistent, the ads only had to deliver spontaneity and the promise of a good time.

By now, Ammirati had parachuted in creative talent from the New York office to help in crafting a winning campaign for Blue. One team included Glen Hunt, the Canadian copywriter who'd left the cozy confines of the Canadian ad scene for the larger US stage. Expecting to be in Toronto for a couple of weeks in the run-up to the Labatt presentation, he and his art director instead set up shop in the Royal York Hotel for three months, pounding out "5 or 10" potential ideas for commercials.

One of Hunt's proposed scripts involved a man with his buddies at an outdoor concert waiting in line for a porta-potty. As a joke, his friends manage to lock him in the toilet, which then gets passed human-wave-style through the stadium before ending up on stage with the band. Set free on stage, he gyrates with the group, and the last shots show him hoisting a beer – Blue, of course – with the band as the tour bus pulls away, the portable toilet strapped to the back of the bus.

One of the commercials, which fit neatly with Labatt's newfound interest in hockey, involved an impromptu game of street hockey that grows out of nowhere in Toronto's financial core. "Street Hockey," the only spot proposed by Hunt that made it to production and airing, proved to be the quintessential "Out of the Blue" commercial. It started modestly, with a young guy carrying a hockey bag and stick shooting a stomped aluminum can down the street. The "puck" is soon stopped by a briefcase-and-umbrella-carrying businessman, who ends up playing goal in a spontaneous game of road hockey, which attracts a growing number of players, and an ever larger crowd of spectators. The "game" ends when one of the participants looks over his shoulder and yells a variant of the kids' side-street road-hockey warning – "Streetcar!"

In the typically catty and backstabbing Canadian advertising community, "Street Hockey" was criticized as much as it was celebrated. One ad executive was even moved to write a column in one of the trade journals, suggesting that the commercial was a rip-off of an earlier Nike ad featuring Pete Sampras and Andre Agassi playing a game of tennis in midtown Manhattan. But agency staffers dismissed the criticism, saying they were well aware of the Nike ad but figured their execution was different enough to escape criticism. "Street Hockey" did not feature celebrities and involved a spontaneous game, which was hardly what Nike depicted when Agassi and Sampras unrolled a net across a busy city street.

Created for the 1998 Winter Olympics, "Street Hockey" gave beer drinkers their first real inkling that Labatt might be involved in some way with the one sport Canadians were really passionate about. Molson had been intricately linked not only with rock music but also with hockey through its ownership of the Montreal Canadiens, its decades-long role as lead sponsor on Molson's *Hockey Night in Canada* broadcasts on CBC, and local sponsorships of the country's NHL clubs. The advertising link between Blue and hockey didn't reverse Blue's long decline, but it arrested it, Kincaid said.

To a large extent, Labatt had now also broken Molson's grip on hockey. It had the 1998 Olympics, which featured a team led by Wayne Gretzky and Eric Lindros (that finished a disappointing fourth), but, for the first time ever, it would also have *Hockey Night in Canada*, for the 1998–1999 season. Besides putting Blue on Saturday night, Labatt's HNIC contract gave the brewer exclusive rights to the NHL playoff marathon, while Molson was shut out for the first time that anyone could remember.

Molson had given up the rights to HNIC in Canada because it said falling ratings couldn't justify the escalating costs demanded by the league under new commissioner Gary Bettman. Molson was correct in its assessment; the Saturday night audience, particularly the 19-to-24 target demographic, thought they had better things to do than sit at home and watch the game. The economics of hockey had also changed in such a way as to reduce Canadian interest in the league during the playoffs. The falling dollar hit Canadian clubs financially, paying for top stars became harder and harder, so much so that Canadian-based teams were lucky to make the playoffs, and when they did, they were usually eliminated in the first round, leaving just hard-core fans watching the final playoff rounds. The storied Habs were the last team north of the border to win the Stanley Cup, in 1993, and it was a safe bet the Cup would be monopolized by rich American teams for years to come.

Labatt Breweries, headed at the time by president Don Kitchen, didn't care about that. A protege of Hugo Powell, he wanted to make a Hugo-like impact on the business. So despite objections from the brewer's regional management, he dispatched Dave Kincaid and Blue marketing man Mike Rapino to New York to land the HNIC rights regardless of the cost. If Labatt was to resuscitate Blue, it had to have hockey

The NHL's commissioner, Bettman, had been recruited to run the league from the National Basketball Association, an organization that was the model for how to market a sport. He had made it clear that he was unhappy with the state of affairs of the NHL in Canada.

Jeff Carefoote, in charge of Molson's sports properties, recalls the first time he met Bettman and the league's new management team in New York. Molson and the CBC had just agreed to air "double-header" broadcasts regularly on Saturday nights, a move that would end the scheduling of early-evening games in places like Vancouver, Calgary, and Edmonton – a phenomenon that had long annoyed Western fans.

The NHL had courted Labatt for quite some time, hoping to lessen Molson's dominance of the league in Canada. At the annual All Star game, the league's mid-season showcase, advertisers were grouped strategically around the commissioner and his staff. Nearest were primary sponsor Anheuser-Busch and other big US advertisers.

Molson executives were a few rows back, and Labatt's people, who as yet had no connection with the league, were four or five rows behind, a not-so-subtle reminder that all things change in sports sponsorship.

Bettman got his wish when Labatt's Kincaid and Rapino outbid Molson for the national sponsorship rights, and Molson was forced to scramble to secure the local rights to the six Canadian clubs. The way it worked out, Labatt paid a premium to land the rights and similarly Molson, faced with the prospect of being benched, was forced to hand the Canadian clubs a substantial raise. Molson wanted to remain linked to hockey, it just didn't believe the national broadcast rights were worth the league's price.

"[Bettman] doubled his price," said Rapino. "We knew we were overpaying, we knew we weren't being coy or strategic in terms of how we were negotiating. It was simple, Molson was going to pay this and we knew we needed a takeout bid or Molson would come back in. So we went in for our takeout punch and got the deal. We just knew at that time that Labatt Blue needed a massive change, and we needed the biggest thing we could do."

In the first year of its hockey sponsorship, 1998, Labatt played up the association for all it was worth and, unlike Molson, made the Stanley Cup a star in its ads. Kincaid and Durnan, two Canadians who understood the bitter irony, trooped down to New York to humbly ask the league's permission to use the celebrated trophy in Blue advertising. Bettman, who recognized free advertising for the game when he saw it, gave immediate approval for the scheme.

The effort could have gone the wrong way, the most recognizable sports trophy in the world getting star treatment in a beer commercial. But rather than recoiling in horror, the public loved it. The first TV ad starring the Cup depicted a trio of guys attempting to get into a hot Detroit nightclub, only to be blocked at the door by surly bouncers. Then the wall of muscle is magically parted for a bunch of professional hockey players from the Cup-winning Red Wings. Rebuffed, the guys clamber into the cab that brought the players, only to find the Stanley Cup inside. The ad ends with the line, "Can you take us to Canada?" sparking a series of ads featuring the same guys and the silverware.

Labatt also used its new advertising link to the Stanley Cup in a more direct pitch to consumers. Starting with the 1999 NHL play-offs, the brewer began inserting miniature versions of the Cup inside two-fours of Blue, starting up a collectibles frenzy in the country. Retailers began complaining of ripped open cases, and the mini Cups were selling on eBay as crazed collectors were attempting to finish their sets. Camera operators were even using the little Cups in shots during the playoffs. It was madness and Labatt loved it. During the first year of the Cup promotion (it ran again in 2000), Blue's share increased two points nationally, Kincaid remembers.

Blue proved it was back with "Street Hockey" and the Cup pro-motion, but Ammirati quickly followed with a run of non-hockey creative that proved to the skeptics its creative drought with Blue was over. Whether it was Durnan's influence or not, Ammirati seemed to realize what Molson and MacLaren had as their operating assumption all along: music made the ads. In the first years it had the Labatt business, Ammirati preferred to commission original tunes from jingle houses rather than buy music from established artists. It may have been more creatively satisfying for the agency, but it was frustrating Labatt's marketers who saw Molson using well-known rock songs to good effect.

Labatt signalled its change of mind when it spent "a couple hun-dred thousand" for the right to use the "Song 2" better known as "Woo-Hoo," the hit by British group Blur in commercials, recalls Rapino. The brewery certainly got its money's worth. The high-energy song was first used as four characters raced down busy streets on shopping carts in what became the second "Out of the Blue" ad after "Street Hockey." It carried on the theme of sponta-neous – if dangerous – fun. The 60-second "Cart Chase" spot depicts a group of friends madly racing down hills on the carts, screaming around corners and narrowly missing cars and pedestri-ans. Shot in Los Angeles, it includes a brief pan of a pretty woman in a business suit looking upon the impromptu race in an amused way. The up-and-coming actress Jolene Blalock, who later became the Vulcan babe on the Star Trek spinoff series Enterprise, also became Rapino's live-in girlfriend.

Labatt and Ammirati knew "Cart Chase" was an expensive risk. The brewer had sunk hundreds of thousands into the shooting of the ad in addition to the money spent on the music, and here they were, an alcohol marketer, showing young twentysomethings careening down city streets on rickety shopping carts. Labatt put a 30-second version of the ad in heavy rotation, determined to get as much consumer attention as possible. Predictably, "Cart Chase" was ordered back to the supermarket and off the air after Advertising Standards Canada ruled the commercial violated a code that states ads "must not display a disregard for public safety or depict situations which might encourage unsafe or dangerous practices." Advertisers and marketers tend to bristle at the ASC, a volunteer group of industry and public appointees who respond to complaints from members of the public. But Labatt had little to whine about in this case. In its regular six-month report, the ASC said "Cart Chase" caused the most complaints of any commercial in that time. Still, Labatt aired the spot for nearly eight weeks before it was forced by the standards watchdog to yank it off the air.

"We were trying hard to push Blue into a very uncomfortable place," explained Mike Rapino of the ad. "It was a good statement internally that Labatt Blue was going to quit being a fake brand and we were going to start pushing it. We knew as we were going forward it was going to be pulled and that it was going to be talked about, but we knew it was going to be a good statement for Labatt Blue."

Blue was definitely in that uncomfortable but happy place where Kincaid, Rapino, and the rest of the Labatt marketers wanted the brand to be. It was now the beer of the NHL, the Stanley Cup, and Hockey Night in Canada. Labatt even got its money's worth with the catchy Blur song, using it in a number of different commercials through that summer. Ammirati and Labatt were in their second honeymoon, but for how long was anybody's guess.

Part Two

Facing Off for Market Share

4

Miller and the King

There are a number of reasons to pick 1980 as the start of the "modern" era in the Canadian beer business. For one, Labatt Blue, thanks to the decline of ales like Export, O'Keefe, and even Labatt 50, was near its peak in terms of market share (with Molson Canadian barely cracking the top five at the time). Having gobbled share from the megabrands that preceded it, Blue claimed more than 20% of the market. But such a huge number would not likely be repeated in Canada, given the market fragmentation that followed. The start of the eighties also pretty much ended the demographic bulge of thirsty baby boomers in their prime drinking years. As nervous Labatt executives had predicted in the early seventies, the days of easy annual sales gains based on the population finishing high school and entering their peak drinking years would now be nothing but a fond memory. Nineteen-eighty is also a nice round number, the start of an era in the beer industry, a time after which it all changed into the industry we know today. The fact that Blue is still near the top of the beer heap – along with Canadian – is testimony to the efforts of savvy marketers and their agencies to keep the brands going. However, the foreign brand names that keep them company would surprise most beer executives of the time who might have tried to predict the future.

Most significantly, 1980 was the year of Budweiser. Always the innovator, Labatt decided near the end of the seventies to break the stalemate that had developed between itself and Molson. Having watched a full 2.2 points of market share evaporate in 1978, the market-share-obsessed executives in London unhappily witnessed Molson pull even, and then slightly ahead. Molson had about 37% of the market (or 37 share points), with Labatt about half a share point behind, while Carling O'Keefe, which held undisputed market leadership in the sixties and seventies with brands like Red Cap and Black Label, accounting for only about one of every four beers sold in the country.

Then Labatt announced in the spring of 1980 that it was introducing Budweiser – the "King of Beers" – to Canada (in Alberta first, the most "American" of provinces, and in Ontario and Quebec the following year). The new contender was greeted with predictable Canadian snobbishness. The 1972 Summit Series may have shown Canadians that the Russians were every bit as good at hockey as we were, but beer remained the last bastion of self-perceived Canuck superiority. American beer, the story went, was weak and watery, and Budweiser would never get beyond fad status.

Demonstrating that view, marketing wizard Dave Barbour, from his perch at Molson, told the *Financial Post* that his brewery's research showed Canadian drinkers have a "marked preference [for Canadian products] over blander American beers." Michael Palmer, the dean of beverage analysts and the most quoted of Bay Street pundits because of his love of the quip, was also cool to bringing the King north. "The history of new brand introductions has been quite iffy and there haven't been too many successes lately," he pronounced to the *Financial Post*. Were they ever wrong. An open secret at Labatt, the imminent Budweiser invasion may have even filtered into the halls of Molson and Carling O'Keefe, but they, like the Canadian beer drinkers, were secure in their chauvinism. "Of course we were so superior because all our research had shown that Canadians would flatly reject goddamn American horse piss," said a long-time senior executive with Molson. "So what did we know?"

Labatt may have been desperate for a lever to shift the balance of market power back in its favour, but the rollout of Budweiser, so destined for failure in the eyes of company outsiders, was the product of nearly a year of planning. Labatt had originally approached US brewer Anheuser-Busch with the intention of licensing the Michelob brand for sale north of the border. Positioned as a super-premium in the States, Michelob could be brewed in Labatt's plants and marketed as a premium-priced import in Canada, the thinking went.

Labatt Breweries president Don McDougall, who led a delegation down to St. Louis to push for the Michelob scheme, was quickly disappointed. Anheuser-Busch had no intention of allowing another brewer to make its premium product. The Anheuser-Busch marketers had a counter-proposal, though. Would Labatt be interested in brewing Budweiser? A-B, which at this point had grown into the undisputed brewing leader in the United States, was harbouring as-yet unannounced international ambitions, and Budweiser was intended to be the company's global brand. McDougall's skeptical team was led to the office of August Busch III, an "aggressive, relentless workaholic," as described in the 1991 book on the Busch dynasty *Under the Influence*, who'd ousted his father in a palace coup and taken over management of the family-controlled company as chief executive officer in 1975. The US brewer pushed the idea of Labatt making and marketing Budweiser in Canada, which at the time was not sold in the great white north because of trade restrictions. McDougall left unimpressed and promised lamely that Labatt would "think about it." However, as McDougall recalls, "We came home and we thought about it, and then we thought, 'If we can do the right kind of deal, it might not be a bad way.' We saw the globalization of brands and thought being ahead of everyone else might be a good idea."

The next step was to invite Busch and his top executives to the London, Ontario, headquarters and brewery, where he could get a glimpse of Labatt's operations and discuss the pros and cons of a licensing deal. The Anheuser-Busch team, headed by Busch himself, flew to London secretly and was whisked to the boardroom where the A-B lawyers, production people, and marketers sat across from their opposite numbers at Labatt. Trying to make the meeting less confrontational, McDougall arranged that he and Busch would sit side by side at the head of the table.

As McDougall recalls, the spirit of openness that characterized the initial meeting in St. Louis was missing. Anheuser-Busch execs would answer simple questions with a clipped "yes" or "no," or would claim not to have ready answers to questions about things like where the brewer obtained its famous beechwood chips, said to give its flagship brand its distinctive taste. "So finally there was some stupid question that I couldn't believe the guy wouldn't answer, and I turned to Mr. Busch and said, 'Do you want to answer that?' He looked at me and said, 'Don, I'm not going to answer a damn thing until I know what that is,'" pointing to a bulky, fabric-covered object sitting in front of the two men. McDougall lifted the cover – a tea cozy – to reveal a tea pot. The room erupted into laughter. "They thought they had come to Canada and we were taping everything," said McDougall.

The two companies proved to be a good match. Begun just five years apart, 1847 for Labatt and 1852 for Anheuser-Busch, both were accustomed to setting the rules in their respective markets, and both had pushed their respective businesses to the point of owning the top-selling brands. While the Busch family still controlled A-B into its fourth generation, the London-based Labatt clan's control had ended in the 1960s with the ultimately unsuccessful sale of Labatt to Schlitz.

Labatt Breweries, solidly number three in 1964 with a 24% market share, well behind Carling O'Keefe's 40% share (or Canadian Breweries as it was known at the time), suffered an abrupt change of control early in that year when Milwaukee-based Jos. Schlitz Brewing Co. announced it had bought much of the Labatt family's controlling stake in the company. Schlitz acquired about 750,000 shares held by the family, and acquired nearly one million more shares from public shareholders, giving it a 39% stake, or effective control over Labatt's fate. It was described then as "the first foreign takeover of a major Canadian brewer" by the Financial Post.

Labatt's professional management team, headed by Jake Moore, did not publicly state an opinion; however, the company's action spoke for it. A week before Schlitz's offer was to expire, the company brought in Power Corp. of Canada to try and wrestle the company away from Schlitz, keeping it in Canadian hands. In one week, it attempted to do what Schlitz did over a period of six months: win over the 75 family stockholders, the scattered descendants of John Kinder Labatt in Europe, the United States, and Canada – "the Cronyns, the Graydons, the Russells, the Jarvises and Scatchards, and, of course, the Labatts," as the *Financial Post* described it. Although it pledged an identical $23 per share for the brewer, Power Corp. lost out in its bid.

While Schlitz quickly won control, it would soon become apparent that keeping it would be the difficult part. Control of John Labatt Ltd. by the US brewer became the subject of a competition investigation and lawsuit – not by Canadian regulators but by the US Department of Justice. The antitrust suit claimed the acquisition would give Schlitz a dominant position in the US Midwest, and a court order forbade Schlitz's exercise of control over its new northern asset. Through the US court proceedings, Labatt's management, which had worked so hard to find an alternative to Schlitz, was publicly neutral, arguing that the issue of control was now up to the courts.

Schlitz lost the antitrust case, and an appeal before the US Supreme Court in late 1966. Nearly two years after it had made its successful bid for Labatt, Schlitz would have to sell its shares. In the spring of 1967, when an aging Toronto Maple Leafs team won a surprising Stanley Cup, control of Labatt was bought back. In a complicated deal, Brazilian Light & Power Co., a Canadian company despite its name, purchased one million Labatt shares from Schlitz. Investors Mutual of Canada Ltd. bought 300,000 shares and Jonlab Investments Ltd., which included members of Labatt's management team, bought 400,000 shares, giving the three investors a combined 39% of the company.

While the Labatts were long departed from the business by the time the brewer sat down with Anheuser-Busch, Labatt still had some brewing royalty who could talk with August Busch III on a more or less equal basis. With the purchase of Nova Scotia's Oland Breweries in 1971, scion Sid Oland had joined the Labatt organization as a market research analyst. He rose quickly through the brewer's ranks, having literally grown up in the beer business. "I had been around most of the brewery work," recalls Oland. "Most of the other people were specialists in either marketing or production. I had done plant work, marketing work, negotiated a union contract, spent time with [sales] reps." Oland was McDougall's right hand during the Budweiser discussions, and succeeded him later in 1979 when McDougall, then president of Labatt Breweries, left the company.

Oland, whose family brewery had been founded in the same year as the Confederation of Canada (1867), personalized the discussions with Busch. Without the Nova Scotia brewer, Busch would have faced only a roomful of specialists, marketers, and managers. "Sid had more conversations with [August] then I did," said Peter Widdrington, then president of the John Labatt Ltd. holding company. "As far as I could figure out, they would spend hours talking about the beer business. Sid was a member of a brewing family; August was a member of a brewing family. People like myself were professionals. We didn't come from a brewing background and that makes a difference."

Though both brewing royalty, Oland and Busch were vastly different personalities. Driven to work and outdo the successes of his father, August "Gussie" Busch, Jr., August Busch III was macho, and as comfortable with plant workers as he was with head office executives. Oland, tall and physically imposing, was more withdrawn. But the two of them hit it off. "August was a different person but I liked him," Oland recalls. "I could talk plant talk because I had worked at the plant. Neither of us were lawyers or accountants, so we just always got along. Part of it was personal background and partly we sort of liked each other."

Oland's role in the initial meeting with Anheuser-Busch in London was as head of the "defensive" team at Labatt. His group was responsible for trying to convince the Americans how difficult it would be for A-B to attempt to make and market Budweiser in Canada without a domestic partner such as Labatt. The offensive team for Labatt detailed the company's various strengths and laid out the reasons why it made sense for the two sides to craft a licensing arrangement.

Unfortunately, the meeting quickly bogged down in details and arguments from A-B lawyers about how difficult it would be to get the groundbreaking agreement approved by US antitrust regulators, and how many other legal roadblocks were standing in the way. As Mike Hurst, Labatt Breweries' head of marketing at the time, remembers, "August listened for a while and stood up and said, 'Excuse me guys, I think you are misinterpreting here. Don [McDougall] and I have decided that we are going to do this deal, so I would think that what you should concentrate on is how we are going to do it, not on all the problems. While you are doing that, Don and I are going to take a look at the plant.'"

On the brewery walkabout, Busch quickly demolished any efforts to keep the visit secret, recalls McDougall. At home in the plant, Busch enthusiastically began discussing how the Labatt production system operated with brewhouse workers, asking questions like, "So how are you going to handle my beechwood chips?" All the same, the head office, in the form of the John Labatt Ltd. holding company, was unsure. Besides the risks of a flop, getting into bed with North America's – and the world's – largest brewer might be dangerous. Peter Widdrington, the John Labatt CEO who eventually gave his blessing to the licensing deal, knew Anheuser-Busch's effectiveness all too well from the time he unsuccessfully tangled with the company as general manager of Labatt's Lucky Lager brewery on the US West Coast. Deciding it was better to have Anheuser-Busch, the unquestioned US market leader, on its side in the event that Canada-US trade barriers fell sometime in the future, Labatt's directors finally gave their approval to the deal.

It was during this period that Tom Errath was handing in his resignation as vice-president of marketing at Schlitz Brewing Co. of Milwaukee, a brewery that had been in a decades-long, see-saw battle with Anheuser-Busch for market leadership until August's father wrestled away the crown once and for all in 1957. Informing Schlitz chairman Frank Sellinger that he was moving to Canada to become vice-president of marketing for Labatt, Sellinger mentioned that he knew the Canadian brewer had received a shipment of rice for test brewing. Sellinger, an Anheuser-Busch vice-president before being lured to try and right Schlitz's sinking ship, noted, "There's only one company in North America that uses rice and that's Anheuser-Busch."

While Errath was coming from a market where Budweiser truly was the "King of Beers," with the top market position, the marketers at Labatt who would soon be reporting to him had been busily working to figure out how to overcome Canadians' instinctual dislike for American suds. What they discovered both surprised and reassured them. Thanks to spillover advertising from US professional sports broadcasts, beer drinkers were already well aware of America's most famous brand of beer. They knew about the Clydesdale horses pulling the beer wagon, the brewing tradition, and the macho marketing message. A decent percentage of drinkers had even sampled Bud either on a cross-border trip or on a winter vacation to Florida. Research found that drinkers liked the American imagery Budweiser carried; they just weren't crazy about the "weak and watery" taste.

In its many rounds of research, both before and after Labatt decided to link up with Anheuser-Busch, marketers asked if drinkers' perceptions of Budweiser would change if Labatt brewed the beer and if its alcohol content were raised from the "weak" American standard to the 5% alcohol of mainstream Canadian beers. "When it was explained to those same beer drinkers that US Budweiser had 4.85% alcohol versus 5%, which was the standard for Canadian lager brands, and the 0.15% was undetectable, most of the resistance went away," Errath remembers. To make sure, for the first few years, all Budweiser TV commercials zoomed in on the label and the 5% alcohol listing, followed by the on-screen graphic "Brewed by Labatt's." Not exactly subtle, but what beer advertising is?

Speaking more than 20 years later, Labatt executives generally describe the launch of Budweiser as a brilliant strategic move, which it was. But the tentative pace of the rollout – just the provinces of Alberta and Saskatchewan that first summer – showed that Labatt was unsure of Budweiser's appeal, despite the research. The following year, Labatt introduced the brand to the other key provinces, Ontario, Quebec, and British Columbia. In Quebec – as distinct a market as it is a society – the spring introduction of Bud is described by Labatt executives as the most successful new product launch in the province ever. Labatt quickly experienced stock-outs, and neighbourhood grocery stores were accepting "reservations" on future deliveries.

In Ontario, the most profitable beer market in the country for a number of reasons, the sales pace was similarly frantic. Labatt's CEO Peter Widdrington, in the audience at the annual meeting of Brascan Ltd. (the controlling shareholder of John Labatt Ltd.), was forced to the podium so a persistent Brascan shareholder could learn when he would be able to buy Budweiser again. Right out of the gate, Bud became a 6- or 7-share brand (6% or 7% of total national beer sales) with each share point worth between $10 million and $15 million at the time.

Labatt was more optimistic about Budweiser's prospects than its rivals or the stock market analysts, but the shortages were proof that Labatt was unprepared for Bud's success. The first of the licensing deals between American and Canadian brewers, the Budweiser agreement remains the most lucrative, with a profit split brewing sources say remains heavily weighted in Labatt's favour.

According to Labatt Breweries president Don McDougall, the contract's uneven profit split was set up to protect Labatt from cannibalizing the sales of its own brands, the thinking being that Blue as the market leader had the most to lose from Bud. If Bud picked up two share points, the profit from the first point went to Labatt, while the second was split with A-B after Labatt's marketing costs were extracted. But even though Bud's marketing costs were relatively light, due to Labatt's reliance on US advertising spillover, A-B's profits on Canadian Bud sales were modest.

While the lopsided arrangement proved in later years to be an annoyance to August Busch, the licensing deal was good for both sides. At the time, A-B was still rolling over rivals in the United States, and was more interested in tackling Coors Brewing Co. in the California market than attempting to bash down the tariff walls to enter a California-sized market inconveniently split into ten provinces.

The King was a hit in Canada, and looking back, no one should be surprised. "At that point the Canadian drinker had not been offered many new things," recalls Sid Oland. "It was still the stubby bottle, fundamentally still the same brands. We hadn't given much. The only innovation really of the late seventies was light [beer]."

Labatt, which prided itself on its leading-edge role in the beer business, knew by the close of 1981 that it had a hit on its hands with Budweiser. The Budweiser effect altered the balance of power in the Canadian beer industry, putting Labatt ahead of its rivals for the rest of the decade. While Bud's sales ate into Labatt's brands somewhat, the American brew's success put Labatt back on top in national market share, a position it would not relinquish until Molson took drastic action in 1989.

. . .

Budweiser not only cemented Labatt's status as the industry leader in the business, in terms of both market share and momentum, it also firmly placed Carling O'Keefe in the number-three position in Canada. Molson was keeping up with the pace, a short distance behind the makers of Blue. Unlike Labatt and Molson, Carling's major weakness was that it had no big national brand that could take advantage of the synergies of national advertising.

The two Johns, Molson and Labatt, are promoted by each brewery, understandably, as founding fathers of the beer business. There would be no Molson today had John Molson not started a brewery in Montreal on the shores of the St. Lawrence River in 1786. John Labatt bought a stake in an existing brewery in London, Ontario. Both businesses, however, were only strong regional breweries until the mid-1950s when they similarly moved to build huge breweries outside their home provinces.

For a company that predated the founding of Canada, Labatt took its time making its mark. Family owned, it kept a low profile for its first century. Most of the fame it achieved in that span had to do with the bizarre three-day kidnapping of John S. Labatt, grandson of the company founder, in 1934. Returned unharmed, John S. was something of a recluse the rest of his days, living his life behind bullet-proof glass. Labatt became a public company in 1945, using the proceeds to buy a brewery in Toronto, and doubling its beer-making capacity. From that point, Labatt's beer operations grew quickly, with purchases of brewing companies in Winnipeg (1953), Vancouver (1953), and Saskatoon (1960), and the building of new breweries in Montreal (opened in 1961) and Edmonton (opened in 1964). By 1971, when it acquired Maritime brewer Oland and Sons Ltd., it had created a national brewing company.

The "father" of the modern brewing business was in fact not a brewer at all. E. P. Taylor was a hard-nosed businessman who saw opportunity in the incredibly fragmented beer business of the 1930s, and quickly began buying up small rival breweries. Unlike most who were brewers first and businessmen second, Taylor built a financial empire in the 1930s by buying up and consolidating the small, unprofitable breweries that were common in the industry at the time. More often than not, Taylor closed the rival brew houses, killing all but their biggest brands. His actions were so brazen that he became the subject of a federal competition investigation in 1955, which confirmed that Taylor's brewing operation had embarked on a predatory buying spree to knock out competitors. All the same, the commission report that found Taylor's company guilty of predatory actions ruled nothing should be done. The commissioners noted that Molson's construction of a large, modern brewery in Toronto and Labatt's subsequent plans for its own brewery in Molson's home town of Montreal ensured a healthy competitive market. By the mid-1950s, Molson and Labatt were preparing to enter the void created by Taylor's onslaught. The two family-owned brewers built huge, new breweries in each other's key "home" markets of Montreal and Toronto, and went about building or acquiring breweries across the country, striving to achieve Taylor's rank as a national brewer.

If E. P. Taylor had not cleared the playing field, Molson and Labatt would most likely have been forced to do it themselves, a process that would have dramatically slowed their expansion first into each other's home provinces and then across the country. As it was, Taylor's company, which was to become Carling O'Keefe, showed how it was done and, when its former powerhouse brands fell into decline, proved to be a pretty irresistible takeover target itself.

E. P. Taylor may have assembled through takeovers hostile and otherwise the biggest brewing company in the land, but what he wound up with was a collection of regional brands that lived and died on a province-by-province basis – Extra Old Stock in British Columbia, Red Cap and Black Label in Ontario, O'Keefe Ale in Quebec. The arrangement worked fine in the fifties and early sixties, when Carling O'Keefe accounted for an incredible one-half of beer sales in Ontario. Its brands prospered because the brewer ran commercials for its beer on US telecasts of National Football League games, but that dominance soon began to slide. Part of the decline was caused by Molson and Labatt, which introduced brands like Export, Labatt 50 ale, and Blue – beers that became the country's first truly national beer brands, thanks to steady advertising and sales efforts. Carling's slide into number-three status was also caused by its complex management structure. A creature of acquisition, Carling O'Keefe was a three-headed hydra operating three separate companies, Carling, O'Keefe, and Dow Breweries, each complete with its own presidents, marketers, and profit-and-loss lines. Rather than cooperating in the effort to keep Molson and Labatt contained, the three companies under Taylor's Canadian Breweries umbrella more often than not were competing with each other for investment capital and market share. According to Bill Bourne, who joined Carling O'Keefe in the 1960s as a manager for the O'Keefe brand, company salesmen got more satisfaction from knocking a sister company's brand out of a tavern tap than eliminating a Molson or

Labatt offering. He developed a good sense of what was in store for him when each of his first three paycheques at the brewery had a different company name on it.

Number three and sinking fast, Carling O'Keefe looked to Labatt's success with Budweiser as a relatively quick and cheap way to give itself the national brand it had always lacked. It was quickly decided that Miller High Life, a strong-selling beer in the United States in the early 1980s, would be to Carling O'Keefe what "Bud" had been to Labatt. Carling proved to be a desperate competitor. With Miller, it was willing to blow apart the cozy little understanding in place since 1962 that domestic beer would be sold in the familiar squat, compact bottle, the "stubby."

Carling knew first-hand just how powerful packaging could be as a competitive weapon. In 1970, the brewer launched Heidelberg ale in a keg-shaped bottle, complete with a screw top. Consumers, starved for variety after nearly a decade with the stubby, embraced the packaging innovation. Despite the fact that ales were suffering a steady decline in relation to lagers, Heidelberg captured a quick 10% national share. Molson and Labatt were furious, claiming Canadian Breweries had broken a standard bottle agreement dating back to the introduction of the stubby in the early sixties, and soon enough provincial liquor bodies and environmental groups were muttering about a US-style profusion of different-shaped bottles.

Unfortunately, the Heidelberg bottle proved to be a nightmare for Carling O'Keefe. When rivals found the squat bottles, dubbed "hand grenades," in their cases of empty returns, the bottles mysteriously "disappeared." Because the stubby was a standard package, it didn't matter whose label was on the bottle; it would be cleaned, refilled, and a new label would be affixed. The Heidelberg bottles were only of use to Carling and rival breweries had nothing to gain by ensuring the keg-shaped bottles sent mistakenly to them were passed on to their rightful owners. The relatively low return rate for the keg bottles was one of the reasons given for its quick demise in the market.

The fight over the bottle also threatened a bottle standard that had always kept foreign brewers in check. So-called industry standard bottles, which remain an issue even today, were one of the quiet, non-tariff barriers Canadian brewers have used to keep sales of imports to a minimum. While the US breweries sell the majority of their product in aluminum cans, which can be melted down and recycled, the Canadian industry has always argued a standard bottle, cleaned and reused, is less wasteful. (No mention is made of the cost of transporting empty bottles, their storage, or the hot water and chemicals used to clean them.) Carling eventually caved to the threats and pressure and put Heidelberg in a stubby bottle, consigning the brand to oblivion and leaving the brewery with more than $1 million worth of useless keg-style bottles.

The Heidelberg experience was still a vivid and gloomy memory when Carling launched Miller High Life in 1983. Budweiser, first into the market as a mainstream US licensed brand, could afford to launch in a stubby. The number-three brewer had to do something to make Miller stand out in the crowd. Miller, it was decided, would go in a tall-necked bottle of the same proportions as the US Miller bottle. Unlike its clear-bottled southern cousin, however, the Canadian version would be packaged in a brown bottle. Depending on who one speaks to from Carling at that time, the decision to go brown was taken either for marketing reasons (Canadians wouldn't accept a beer in clear glass) or because Carling was unwilling to risk government rejection of the sunlight inhibitors, perfectly acceptable in the United States, that Miller needed to put in its beer to protect it from light because of its clear container. Ultimately, a tall, non-stubby shape was judged far more important than the colour of the bottle. "It would have been just another brand," said Bill Bourne, Carling's marketing vice-president during the Miller introduction.

After all the prelaunch jockeying, everything seemed to go Carling's way with Miller's introduction. The summer of 1983 was hot and dry, a beer salesman's dream, and the tall new bottle stood out in the stubby crowd. The US marketing gods even deigned to cooperate. Miller Brewing that year launched its "Welcome to Miller Time" advertising campaign, which couldn't have been a better, or cheaper, way to introduce Miller in Canada.

That long hot summer was Miller's time. It quickly gained a 7–8% share and Carling O'Keefe couldn't produce the stuff fast enough. Former Carling executives fondly remember tales of customers staking out beer store parking lots awaiting the arrival of delivery trucks and a fresh supply of Miller. More so than Budweiser, the launch of Miller shook up the Canadian beer business. Labatt took a far more conservative approach with Budweiser and rolled the new brand out slowly. Carling, desperate for a big win, pushed hard with Miller High Life, hoping the American brew would become the big national brand that it had been lacking.

The responses from Molson and Labatt were predictable. In their industry groups, both complained that Carling had once again broken the stubby bottle agreement, a competition-limiting document that would have had a tough time standing up in court. Labatt's case was pretty weak given it had unveiled its own tall glass, a lanky green bottle for the premium brand John Labatt Classic, weeks before Miller appeared on the Canadian scene. Molson, which preferred to let the other breweries take the chances and risks of innovation, publicly proclaimed it would not get into this US beer-licensing game, while Labatt, the innovator behind light beer, mixed cases, and the US licensed-beer category, went away to quietly plan for the next opportunity to regain the momentum from Carling.

Though an unprecedented success for Carling, Miller speeded the brewer's eventual downfall. While Carling correctly understood that Miller High Life's success stemmed from consumers' thirst for a difference, it failed to realize that Miller's great run stemmed from the tall bottle, rather than what was inside it. Not understanding that fact, and underestimating the other guys' capacity to react, especially Labatt's, Carling embarked on a massive capacity expansion to ensure in future summers that it wouldn't run short of Miller. What it never did was ensure people would continue drinking the beer.

5

Goodbye Stubby

Carling may have owned the summer of 1983 with the Miller block-buster, but within a year, Labatt had once more firmly established itself as the country's leading brewer. Blue remained the dominant brand while Budweiser continued to grow. While Labatt's marketers fretted about Miller's success, their studies suggested its growth seemed to be coming out of Molson's sales. Powered by the Miller launch, Carling's share jumped to 29% of the market while Molson started the year with 32%. Molson, the country's top-selling brewer just four years before, had been on a steady losing streak since then as Miller and Bud ate away at its position. Carling suddenly had momentum and, just as importantly, it had an honest-to-goodness 10-share national brand with Miller – meaning 1 in 10 beers pur-chased in the country was a Miller. For a brief period, Carling's Miller was a full share point ahead of Molson Export, and was clos-ing on the Blue monster, which accounted for 15% of the country's beer sales.

Although it was back to the number-one position it was accus-tomed to, Labatt continued to act as if it were trailing badly. The innovator that introduced light beers, mixer packs, a domestic pre-mium beer, and re-introduced the tall bottle wasn't finished yet.

Labatt had enjoyed the "golden age" of the 1970s as much as any brewer in North America, prospering as the baby boomers came of age and gravitated to beer as a rite of passage. But Labatt's marketers, demographers, and predictors of changing tastes saw the boomers' bulge flattening out in the coming decade. That was the spur behind the pursuit of Anheuser-Busch, which had turned into the launch of Budweiser. Sensing that the golden age was over and the 1980s were a no-growth, zero-sum game, Labatt's response to Miller was particularly harsh. With little to lose, Carling had broken the unwritten rules with its tall Miller bottle, and Labatt intended to gain whatever advantage it could while simultaneously teaching Carling a lesson.

As in love with code words as anyone in the brewing industry, Labatt executives spent the first few months of the new year whispering the terms Project Smokey and Project Czar. Back in 1982, Carling had dubbed its plan to bring Miller into Canada Project Northern Elk. It did the job, and confused friend and foe alike. "One of our [sales] reps had heard the project name," said Carling marketer Blair Shier, initially worried that the secret had leaked out. "Then he said, 'You've got to be kidding. Somebody has it on good word that we're bringing out a brand called Northern Elk and if we are, I'm quitting.'" A year later it was Labatt with its intertwined Project Smokey and Project Czar, the former an elaborate deception to protect the latter. When the smoke cleared, Labatt brought out a genuine product innovation that is taken for granted today, but more than anything else shook Molson out of its complacency and further weakened Carling O'Keefe.

Thanks to Carling's spectacular success with Miller in a tall bottle at popular prices, the stubby was doomed. It was one thing for Labatt to introduce an expensive niche brand like John Labatt Classic in a classy green bottle, but Miller plainly showed what marketers at all three companies had known for years: beer drinkers were starved for something different. At the breweries, the marketing experts were only too happy to throw the stubby over the side. The squat bottle hailed from a time when bean counters and production guys had made most of the rules. The stubby was a plant manager's

dream. It had a low centre of gravity so it sailed through the production line, you could pack vast quantities of them on pallets and
trucks, and they were tough. Oh, were they tough. Designed to last
15 or 20 trips through the filling, sale, use, cleaning, relabelling, and
refilling cycle, the unattractive bottles were proving nearly inde-
structible. Years after their disappearance, older beer drinkers speak
of their durability, providing apocryphal tales such as using the
squat bottles to hammer in tent pegs when camping. "Some of the
stubbies were lasting double their lifetime," said Dick Walker, a
packaging executive at Labatt who was chairman of a brewing
industry packaging committee at the tail end of the stubby's reign.
"They were going through 30, 40 trips and they looked like they
had come through wars." The grizzled veterans were easy to spot.
The heels and shoulders of the bottles were so beat up from their
travels through miles of bottling lines, many of them were scarred
white. Labels refused to adhere to a bottle's belly because it too was
no longer smooth.

The primacy of the plant managers and accountants was coming to
an end. Miller had made that obvious. The questions were: What
would follow Miller, and who would make the first move? Labatt,
long a believer in first-mover advantage, did not disappoint. Early in
the spring of 1984, the brewer launched a TV ad for Labatt's Lite in
Alberta, promising "Here's something new," and depicting a stubby
turning into a tall bottle, modelled on the John Labatt Classic bottle.
The company then purchased one million of the tall amber bottles,
which, like the John Labatt Classic and Miller containers, had a standard finish, meaning they required a bottle opener. The TV ad and
the bottle purchase made up the Project Smokey deception plan.
Molson, which prided itself on its role in the industry as a fast follower, preferring to let others assume the risks of failure, took its cue
and made a massive order for tall glass, determined to get its major
brands out of the stubby for the battles of the summer.

Just a few weeks later, the folks at Molson realized they'd been
had. Labatt aired another version of its Labatt's Lite ad in Alberta,
with the same jingle again promising "Here's something new," but

this time the commercial started by flinging away a silver "church key" opener, unveiling a tall bottle like it was the obelisk from 2001: *A Space Odyssey*, and then closing the spot with a hand twisting off the bottle cap with ridiculous ease. The head fake ad and the follow-on payoff twist commercial were both produced by Enterprise Advertising, a small Toronto sister shop of J. Walter Thompson created as a place to park business potentially in conflict with some important piece of business at the big agency. Enterprise got the job to advertise the twist because it "got" the importance of the twist-off. JWT's perceived indifference to a year's work at one of its top clients contributed to the push for an advertising review for Blue, even as the brand was powering ahead of its rivals, according to Labatt's John Diakiw. Labatt took the twist-off cap seriously.

Graham Freeman, executive vice-president of John Labatt and number two on the Labatt corporate food chain, was in charge of Projects Czar and Smokey. If they had seen him, stout and bursting out of his suit, telling a boardroom full of brewer marketers that the project was damn important and they'd better impress that upon their ad agencies, JWT might have acted differently. To maintain the secrecy surrounding Project Czar, Labatt's stable of agencies was given just one week to come back with ideas, recalls Diakiw, who was promoted from Labatt's Lite to the flagship Blue brand shortly after the launch. "J. Walter Thompson, who had the largest piece of our advertising at the time, sort of came back and said, 'Well, we don't really think it is that big a deal.' That was a bad response."

Inside Labatt, Project Smokey, which inspired Molson to follow Labatt down a blind, non-twist alley, was seen as payback for all the times Molson and Carling had quickly imitated Labatt's innovations. The deception was intended to help Labatt keep its twist-off monopoly for as long as possible, and it succeeded brilliantly. Molson had just spent tens of millions on tall, non-twist glass while Carling was awash in Miller bottles that were not as tall as Labatt's and definitely not twist-offs. Labatt's initial order for non-twist glass probably cost it no more than $150,000 and those bottles could be used on the Labatt brands that did not use twist caps. "They deked us and we fell for it," said Molson's Norm Seagram, then president of Molson's Alberta operations. "It was beautifully executed and it worked perfectly."

Carling and Molson's immediate public reaction was to deride Labatt's twist-off packaging innovation. It was a gadget doomed to failure, executives at the brewers told the press. People would put foreign objects in the bottles and reseal them; the threads on the bottles would not last, and the beer would go flat; the crowns would chip. To be fair, much of what they were saying to the press was what they were being told internally by their own production people, the same guys who were so wedded to the endangered stubby. The production folks confidently assured executives at Molson and Carling that the twist-off would prove a costly failure, and a humiliated Labatt would be forced to go back to the standard finish.

The pessimists were in pretty good company. Shortly after the launch, Molson executives visited Golden, Colorado, to meet with their opposite numbers at Adolph Coors Co. to discuss plans to bring Coors and Coors Light into Canada under a licensing deal the following year. (With Budweiser and Miller already taken, Coors at the time was the only logical US drinking buddy left for Molson.) Over lunch, Molson Alberta president Norm Seagram told the Coors brothers, Peter and Jeff, that Labatt had introduced a returnable twist-off bottle, something that was not sold in stores in the States. None of the Molson people had thought to bring one of Labatt's bottles to Colorado, Seagram recalls, but they were given a reassuring response from their American partner. "They said, 'Don't worry, it won't work. They'll have all sorts of problems. They'll have all sorts of lawsuits because the glass can't take the constant pressure of the crimping of the twist-off and they're going to have claims from consumers from drinking glass.'" Glass in bottles was a nightmare for any brewer and could occur in capping even standard bottles at the time. The Coors folks' comments were especially reassuring because they had a well-deserved reputation as brilliant engineers having developed the aluminum beverage can. The Coors family also had a well-deserved reputation for stubbornness as evidenced by their devotion to the old-style dual-press tabs, which many consumers found impossible to open. Still, reassured by the Coorses, Seagram and the other Molson executives flew home confident in the superiority of their standard-top bottles.

If Molson had more fully understood the effort Labatt had put into Project Czar, they would have been a touch more concerned. Over an entire year's worth of work, Labatt did a remarkable job keeping Czar secret, especially given the fact that it had to install new equipment at all its major plants, develop and test a new crown, and work up a series of TV and radio ads prior to the launch. With the chattiness of production people throughout the breweries and the porous nature of the ad industry, it is nothing short of miraculous that Czar never leaked out. Weeks before the launch of the twist in late March 1984, the brewery ordered 430 million new tall bottles and prepared to junk more than 300 million compact bottles, which would be gradually rendered obsolete as Labatt shifted its portfolio of brands into tall vessels. (Labatt says it named the operation Project Czar because a consultant had told the brewer it would take an executive with the power and authority of a czar to push the massive project through to completion.)

Czar – both the twist and the tall bottle – represented an expensive gamble on a business that John Labatt's directors had for a long time viewed as a cash cow. Sid Oland, president of Labatt Breweries at the time, recalls, "I was going in there and I'm saying, 'I'm offering you a one-time write-off of $60 million and new costs in the business for about $70 million but it's going to be fine and we're going to make money.'" Most of the write-offs were for old bottles and equipment, while the increased operating costs represented the downside of the stubby's disappearance: taller beer boxes, less life on the bottles, sharply higher sorting costs. Considering the brewery was only making between $150 million to $200 million annually at the time, Oland was proposing to reduce the brewery's profit by up to one-third unless Czar produced dramatic market-share gains.

With memories of Carling's Miller stock-outs still fresh, Labatt worried its new bottles and twist-off caps would foul up the production system, generating embarrassing shortages of their own. "One of the scarier calls I ever got was from Montreal saying, 'These god-darned machines that you've installed in here, we're running at 60% of our previous capacity and get your bloody butt down here,'" said Dick Walker, who was director of creative services at the time, responsible for the new label and packaging designs. Walker and John Dunwell, the brewer's vice-president of production, soon found themselves in a boardroom at the Montreal plant, hearing a litany of complaints about the tall bottles and new equipment, and about how they should be running flat out for summer. "I turned to John and said, 'Can we find out how they are doing in Toronto? They're doing better than this.' He kind of winked at me, left the room, made a call, and came back and said, 'You know, Toronto is running at 107% of their efficiency.'" After a brief huddle, the Montreal staff grudgingly said they would do their best. "We got a call two days later that they were running at 110% of efficiency," Walker remembers.

Project Smokey may have been aimed mostly at Molson – Carling didn't have the immediate capital to make huge bets on new bottles, having invested millions to increase production of Miller – but Czar was clearly sighted on Carling's US import. Miller High Life had pulled Carling ahead of Molson in market share, giving the amalgam of regional breweries its first true national brand, even if it was a Canadian version of a US beer. The introduction of a tall twist-off had been identified early on by Labatt as a Miller killer. An internal briefing document for the twist-off's Ontario launch stated that Labatt's own research found 70% of Miller drinkers picked it because of the tall bottle. The Miller franchise would soon find itself "under severe pressure" from the twist-off and from Molson's switch to the tall bottle for its brands. The same document predicted Labatt's share would rise by almost two share points, from 37.02 to 38.86, following the introduction of Blue, Blue Light, and Budweiser in the twist-off. (Brewers are one of the few consumer goods makers to measure market share to two decimal places.) The company predicted the lion's share of the gains would be enjoyed by Blue, far and away the country's top-selling brand at the time.

If anything, Blue's marketers were conservative. Just as they did when Carling introduced Miller, beer drinkers bored with the stubby and those coveted 19-to-24-year-old entry-level quaffers gave the new packaging the two-fisted embrace. Blue's share shot up 5 share points following the launch of the twist-off. Even non-Labatt drinkers sampled the brewery's new innovation, and Labatt's share rose to over 39% during the summer. Molson Canadian had dusted itself off, shedding its "Dad's beer" status with its revolutionary rock video-style ads, but the "Dancing in the Street" summer that Molson had hoped for would have to wait. Molson Canadian didn't come with a twist-off. The consumer had spoken in the summer of 1984. The twist was a consumer-friendly innovation and a real point of difference in a brewing industry with little product differentiation.

Molson's response was typical of a company caught off guard by genuine innovation. It tried to muddy the waters. That summer it rushed aluminum cans to the Ontario market and priced them at a 45-cent discount from the price of a six-pack of the heavier, old-style tin cans, the kind that featured a seam down one side. The aluminum can had been around for years in the United States and had gained wide acceptance in a market dominated by six-packs, whereas in Canada cases of 12 and 24 bottles led beer sales. Molson didn't usually want to start a price war that would shake up the stranglehold the three companies had on the market, so its attempt to fight on price showed how seriously it took Labatt's twist-off.

Carling, meanwhile, had little cash to spare on marketing or price sparring. Much of its capital was being devoted to a $175-million expansion of breweries in Ontario, Alberta, and British Columbia, and its key plant in Toronto was soaking up about half that spending to boost capacity to produce Miller. It didn't help that a good portion of the Carling marketing budget was tied up by a rich $33-million, three-year sponsorship deal it had recently signed with the Canadian Football League. Carling at the time owned the Toronto Argonauts of the CFL (in 1983 the team ended a 30-year championship drought by winning the Grey Cup), as well as the upstart Quebec Nordiques of the National Hockey League. Lacking the marketing guns of the other breweries, Carling sat back and nervously hoped for the best, keeping all its other brands but Miller in the quaint stubby bottles. As Labatt's research had predicted, most of its gains came at the expense of Miller. Carling slid three share points to a 26 share after the summer of 1984.

Carling's sneak attack with Miller was proving to be a one-year wonder. Easy drinking taste aside, Canadians still harboured a smug superiority about their own brews compared with US beers, even one brewed at home under licence. With the other guys out in a tall bottle and Labatt even better in a twist-off for Blue and Budweiser, the fickle Miller drinkers were switching once again. Unwilling to make a massive equipment investment after expanding to the peak of its capacity, Carling made stopgap efforts to turn the tide on Miller. The brewer attempted to match the convenience of the twist-off cap by introducing a "rip" cap to top its bottles. Still used in some developing countries, the rip cap was made of a softer metal than a standard cap and allowed the user to pry the top off by tearing up the centre of the cap. It was hardly an ideal solution, though, as it left the consumer with a piece of sharp metal. The rip cap lasted just one season. "It didn't work shit with the consumer so we said, 'Okay, we have got to go with a twist-off.' Budweiser was on a roll again, and they had a twist finish," said John Barnett, a senior Carling executive at the time. Carling unhappily followed Labatt's lead. Three years later, and too little too late for Miller High Life, Carling adopted a Latin American bottle design that had a twist-off cap and an indentation in the heel of the bottle to grip a cap for easy turning. Carling had been planning to use the unique bottles for the launch of a new niche beer, but Miller's plight was so dire that it got the innovation. The "bottom bottle opener" was hardly an elegant solution, since you needed two bottles to make it work. But it was seen as a way around what Carling viewed as the difficulty drinkers had with opening Labatt's early version of the twist-off cap. Beer drinkers, however, saw the bottom bottle opener as a gimmick and took a pass. Miller's sales continued to slide.

In 1985, two years after Carling's "Miller Time," Roderick McInnes, Carling's president, chief executive, and chairman, started talking hopefully about how aluminum cans would be the next big thing in the market. He suggested that beer sales in Canada would become a lot more like sales in the United States, though only about 10% of Canadian beer sales came in metal at the time, compared with about 60% in the States. Carling had lots of canning capacity thanks to their recent expansions, while Labatt had limited ability to pump out cans and Molson had little appetite to play Carling's game. What Carling didn't have much of, though, was brand appeal compared to Labatt and Molson. Miller was on the wane, Miller Lite failed to excite drinkers, and its only other brands of any note had limited regional appeal.

After more than a year of attempting to counter Labatt's twist-off cap, Carling decided to bite the bullet and adopt the tall twist-off bottle, taking a one-time asset write-off of nearly $12 million. It was a move Molson continued to resist because it had bought a huge float of tall, non-twist bottles just a year earlier.

Molson had been suckered into a loser's position thanks to Project Smokey, but making and marketing beer was Molson's main business. By this point, Carling O'Keefe, was operating as a 50.1% holding of tobacco company Rothmans Inc., which was, in turn, owned by Rothmans International plc of Britain. Predictions of a market share turnaround by Miller chief executive Rod McInnes would have to compete with the increasing volume of rumours forecasting the impending sale of Rothmans' beer holdings. In the days before class-action consumer lawsuits, tobacco companies were in business to make steady, predictable profits without much fanfare. That was something Carling had also done until the nice quiet Canadian beer business turned nasty, unpredictable, and expensive after Miller and the twist-off showed up.

The twist-off summer of 1984 saw Labatt on a roll, Molson stuck figuring out what to do with its new tall but obsolete bottles, and Carling churning out little but market-share losses. The rumours were also true. Carling was being shopped around, and eventually even Carling's McInnes admitted it. He complained in one newspaper report early in 1986 about the profusion of tall bottles of different

styles that had halved industry profits and suggested again that cans –
a Carling specialty – should become the new industry-standard container. McInnes neglected to point out Carling's lead role in sparking
the bottle wars with the launch of Miller. Labatt and Molson were in
no mood to be charitable, and by the end of the year, McInnes had
left Carling.

Labatt and Molson were not just being stubborn or cheap. They
had a very good reason for keeping the sales of beer in aluminum
cans to a minimum. The big US brewers, the southern bogeymen
that the industry always feared would flood Canada with discount
suds, were geared for cans. Aluminum was easy to work with; the
lightweight cans were more efficient to ship and store over a long
period, and in the end, they were easy to throw away. Best of all, US
brewers could point to the ease of recycling the cans when those
environmental types got too pesky.

Glass bottles, and the elaborate system put in place to collect them,
wash them, and reuse them, proved to be perhaps the best defensive
weapon that Canadian breweries had against potential Yankee
invaders. Lobbying materials produced by the brewing industry
north of the forty-ninth parallel frequently boasted about the environmental benefits of the returnable bottle system. Of course, the
industry's stories never mentioned the energy expended hauling
used bottles back to the breweries or the energy and chemicals used
to clean and sterilize bottles before they were used again. But
actively promoting the increased use of cans over bottles would simply ease Canadian drinkers' acceptance of the prevailing US package
at a time when second-tier American brewers were trying to swamp
the market with cheap canned product. (The top-tier brewers,
Anheuser-Busch, Miller, and Coors, were already in Canada thanks
to licensing agreements.)

Besides being McInnes's year to depart Carling, 1986 marked
Carling's launch of Australian lager Foster's in Canada as a brewed-
under-licence product similar to Miller High Life. It didn't expect
the runaway success it had enjoyed with Miller, but Foster's soon
had a lot of things going for it. The Aussies wowed visitors to

Expo '86 in Vancouver, and then there was the launch of the sleeper hit *Crocodile Dundee*. A low-budget flick backed by an Australian public offering, the movie raked in more than US$175 million in the United States, largely on the charm of its star, Paul Hogan. It didn't hurt that the very same endearingly befuddled star was the official spokesman for Foster's and also appeared on the US airwaves shilling Australian tourism.

So for Carling, the good news was that Foster's came ready to market, complete with pitchman. Even so, the Foster's brand did not get off to an auspicious advertising start. The original batch of Carling's commercials featuring Hogan suffered from poor sound quality. It sounded as if Hogan were mumbling, and people had a hard time making out what he said, recalls Blair Shier, a Carling marketer in charge of the Foster's launch. "Thank God the movie hit about the same time and helped us along," said Shier.

Foster's quickly proved it was no Miller. Despite a big-league advertising budget – estimated to be about $5 million – Foster's was a pooch that wouldn't get off the porch. In Ontario the Aussie brew attracted about 2% of the market, well below the 4–5% threshold deemed necessary for staying power. Shier said the Carling commercials misused their Hollywood star. The brewer positioned Hogan in a number of upscale social situations in the early stage of the campaign, as if he were pitching Heineken rather than a made-in-Canada Aussie beer sold at regular prices. UK ads for Foster's depicting Hogan as a bloke in the pub were far more effective, and Foster's proved to be successful there. The movie star from the outback also made life difficult for Carling's marketers. He exercised veto power over scripts, junking lines or entire ideas that didn't fit with the *Crocodile Dundee* image. "He would say, 'Yah, yah, yah, no, this one's not going.' We knew on the radio stuff he was going to be throwing out 25% of them," said Shier. "You would overwrite for them so you would get six or eight."

By the end of its first summer, Foster's settled out as a 3–3.5 share brand in Ontario, where Carling had the greatest need for a big win. The Aussie brew wasn't going to do it. Foster's could hardly blame the competition. Labatt brought out slow sellers such as John Labatt Classic Light and Michelob in Quebec (having finally succeeded in garnering approval to launch the brand from Anheuser-Busch). Labatt's introductions hardly moved the sales needle while Molson, having launched Coors Light and Coors the year before, was also quiet on that front. The performance of Foster's in Ontario was "pretty good," Shier grudgingly acknowledges. "But within the Carling portfolio," he recalls, "it was another 3 share brand. We had [Old Vienna], we had Carlsberg, Carlsberg Light. We didn't need another 3-share brand. We needed a 10-share brand, which it wasn't going to be."

Surprisingly, Foster's suffered from authenticity. Australian brewer Elders IXL insisted the brand be brewed strictly to the Australian recipe and procedures, and Carling complied. The only problem was that few people were drinking it. Norm Seagram, the Molson operations executive who had to investigate Foster's tepid reception a few years later as part of a submission to the federal Competition Bureau, sums it up best: "Foster's had a wonderful launch. Awareness was extremely high, especially among beer drinkers, and trial was extremely high. But the actual switch was very low. Why? They didn't like the beer."

The disappointing response to its flagship brand in Canada infuriated and perplexed Elders' executives. Years later, when Molson and Elders developed corporate ties, a perplexed Aussie brewmaster, can of Foster's in hand, accosted Molson executive Barry Joslin, who was clutching a can of beer containing one of Molson's brands. "Why do you people drink that shit?" growled the brewmaster. "Because we like this shit and we don't like that shit," retorted Joslin, waggling his can, then pointing to the Foster's.

Though a marketing disappointment, the Foster's launch did get the Australians thinking about the Canadian beer business, the joy of duopolies, and the possibilities that came with being right next door to the world's largest beer market.

Part Three
Beer Wars and Weddings

6

Mergers

There are a number of ways one can judge the health of a company, particularly a public one such as Carling O'Keefe. The vitality it gained through the launch of Miller in the summer of 1983 was quickly sucked out by Labatt's launch of the twist-off. As early as the following year, Carling's sales were down, market share had shrunk to alarming levels, and profits had evaporated. The company's troubles were apparent off the balance sheet, too. Even before McInnes's departure, Bill Bourne, who directed the marketing effort for Miller High Life, had left, winding up at Labatt. Carling also lost its chief financial officer, Ralph Beatty. Denials aside, Carling was in trouble as the twist-off became the industry standard, and the company had been put on the auction block.

Even with a pale 23% share of the Canadian market, compared with 42% for Labatt and 32% for Molson, Carling remained a valuable commodity. Its existence kept the other two breweries from being as profitable as they could be. Having an unpredictable third player in the game could also cause chaos in what had traditionally been a well-ordered market. Molson and Labatt just had to look at the introduction of Miller and the still-raging bottle wars to confirm that.

In fact, Labatt did more than simply fret about Carling. Even though Carling was refusing to publicly admit that it was for sale, the number-three player had entered into exploratory sale talks with the country's top brewer. Labatt's interest in Carling was straightforward. For a relatively cheap price, it could eliminate a competitor and liquidate a glut of excess production capacity. Due to long-standing federal-provincial regulations designed to foster provincial growth, brewers had to operate plants in provinces in order to sell in them. The result was that breweries in western provinces barely broke even, or often lost money, while plants in Ontario and Quebec were highly productive cash cows. Eliminating the less profitable breweries would cut annual costs significantly, even if Labatt failed to retain much of Carling's market share.

Convinced their scheme had merit, Labatt's executives trooped to Ottawa. In a series of meetings with the Competition Bureau, the company made the case that Carling was a failing enterprise, one of the situations that would make a takeover palatable to regulators. By gobbling up Carling, Labatt's people said, they would simply hasten the brewer's disappearance, which was inevitable. Like a prospective son-in-law asking for the daughter's hand in marriage, Labatt wanted the Bureau's blessing. But in the end, the Bureau did not buy the tale of Carling's imminent demise and said it would block any Labatt-led takeover of Carling.

"That's a tactical error we made," admits Bob Vaux, Labatt's former chief financial officer. "They say, 'Come and talk to us and get pre-clearance,' but the very fact that you show up and talk to them, they say, 'These guys obviously have a problem or they wouldn't come and talk to us.'" In hindsight, Labatt executives say they would likely have succeeded in making a deal for Carling acceptable to its shareholders and presenting the competition watchdog with a *fait accompli*. Considering the competition authority's past fascination with the brewing industry – in particular the lengthy court case involving Carling's E. P. Taylor–led forerunner Canadian Breweries and its penchant for swallowing smaller rivals – that confident prediction seems unlikely. A Labatt-Carling combination would have had 65% of the beer market, slightly more than double Molson's share. Even discounting the discrepancy between the two survivors of the bottle wars, Labatt and Molson would have had a stunning 97% of the market.

As it was, the Competition Bureau's refusal just stretched Rothman's control of Carling by a couple of years at best. Early in 1987, in a move that was a surprise to the public at least, Australian conglomerate Elders IXL agreed to buy Carling from Rothmans for $392 million. Few Canadians had heard of Elders, but the company was well known in brewing circles for its acquisitions. Headed by John Elliott, a charismatic Aussie in his mid-forties, Elders had started small but had world-class ambitions. Elliott and a group of Australian investors had created Elders when they'd bought jam maker Henry Jones IXL, and Elliott rose to brewing prominence a decade later when he orchestrated the purchase of Carlton & United Breweries, which owned Foster's. Renamed Elders, the brewing operation in Australia just about split that market with beer baron Alan Bond, whose best-known brand was Swan Lager. While Canada had three players to Australia's two — a situation that could certainly change — the two countries did have some things in common. Chief among them was a depressingly steady decline in beer consumption as people grew more health-conscious or switched to other forms of alcohol.

Elliott, whose chain-smoking belied his Australian Rules football background, was described as "rough-edged" and "street smart" in a Canadian newspaper following his play for Carling. Elliott certainly didn't back away from a fight. A year before making his play for Carling, he'd taken a run at British food and liquor conglomerate Allied Lyons plc, a company twice Elders' size. Rebuffed, he turned around and bought Britain's Courage brewing outfit and its chain of 5,000 pubs for £1.5 billion.

In making its play for Carling, Elders said it wanted to focus on boosting Carling's share and profitability, leaving others to speculate about it bringing other Aussie brands to Canada, or using Carling as a springboard into the United States. As one senior brewer notes, it didn't take Elders long after they'd taken possession of Carling to fig-ure out it would take a lot of time and money to turn the brewery around. Soon after Elders' acquisition became official, the Australians worked to figure out how to maximize profit by selling part of the business or merging it with another Canadian brewery, thereby creating a comfy duopoly just like at home.

Not long after acquiring Carling, Elliott and a couple of senior Elders executives paid a visit to Molson's Toronto headquarters, located at that time near Pearson International Airport. Norm Seagram, president of Molson's brewing operations, ushered them into the executive room. "Molson, always being the good Boy Scout, had long decreed that there would be no smoking in our head office," Seagram recalled. John Rogers, who became chief executive officer of the holding company, was an avid runner and outdoor type, while Jim Black, who would soon retire from the top job at Molson Companies, was a vehement antismoker, as only an ex-smoker can be. "Within 30 seconds of entering the room John Elliott pulls out his cigarette case and says, 'You don't mind if I smoke?' – signs blazing all around. Everyone says, 'Not at all, oh no.'" Norm Seagram, the most junior executive in the room, who a decade later would be CEO of Molson Companies, went on a frantic search for an ashtray. Good hosts, the Molson executives endured the smoking of Elders' top brass, forging a relationship that would get decidedly warmer in the coming months.

Not long after that initial meeting, Seagram flew down to Melbourne to meet with the Elders executives operating directly below John Elliott. From that meeting came a Molson proposal to buy Carling's western Canada operations. The logic was straightforward: both brewers were taking a beating there because of excess capacity. Molson's proposal was almost immediately turned down because Elders was unwilling to take what would be a hefty writedown to its Canadian asset so soon after the purchase. Elders had its own idea. "They came to us with the right idea. They came to us with the idea of putting the whole thing together," Seagram said.

The Aussies' plan to merge with Molson creating a Down Under–style duopoly would have to overcome some hurdles first. Labatt Breweries vowed through its president, Sid Oland, that it would "do whatever is necessary" to keep on top. "Whatever" did not stop short of luring Carling executives away in the aftermath of the Elders' takeover. Labatt knew that the contract struck between Carling and United Breweries Ltd. of Denmark in the early seventies had an out clause. The Danes could break the licensing deal they had struck with Carling to brew Carlsberg in the event of a change of control, say, in the case of brash Australians coming on the scene. Shortly after the Elders purchase, Sid Oland flew to Copenhagen to make the case that Labatt should now handle the Carlsberg brands in Canada. "We had the deal wrapped up in two or three days," Oland remembers.

The loss of the Carlsberg brands was a cruel blow to Carling, which learned of the planned shift as its share edged down another notch to 22.5 share points. As early entrants into the brewed-under-licence game, Carlsberg's and Carlsberg Light's best days were behind them but they still retained a loyal following, especially in Ontario – every brewer's most-profitable market. In that province, it had about a 4 share of the market. Carlsberg would cost it 2 national share points, which it could ill afford to lose, and what may have hurt the most for long-serving Carling staffers was that Carlsberg Light, a draft powerhouse in cities such as Toronto and Ottawa, was a made-in-Canada Carling creation.

Labatt had its early win on the Aussies but fumbled the transition. The Danes and their new partner opted to give Carling the contract-required one-year notice that it was losing the brand, rather than spending some money and buying out Carlsberg's long-time Canadian brand manager. The second option would have given Labatt control of the brand for the Canadian market in three months. "In retrospect we should have offered to help Carlsberg buy the brand out [from Carling-Elders], we could have done it in three months," said Oland. "Carling sort of had to have a year's warning, so they just left the brand alone. They didn't do anything bad like sabotage it physically, but they left the brand alone and it lost a chunk of share." When the time came to hand the brand over to Labatt, the old partner announced the changeover with full-page ads and carton inserts that stated "Carlsberg is Changing" and that Carling would no longer be making Carlsberg and Carlsberg Light. The ads and inserts thanked drinkers for their patronage while suggesting they might want to try other Carling O'Keefe brands. On the surface, it looked like a classy, high-road exit. Simply by distributing the ads, Carling was alerting consumers, who had been satisfied with things the way they were, of the changes.

The public face would also undergo some alterations. Carling and its advertising agency ensured that the intellectual property created by Carlsberg's TV and print ads was owned by the old licensed brewer, Carling O'Keefe. The long-running ads featuring the beer being poured into ice carvings would end with the changeover. Labatt would have to develop a new campaign whether it wanted to or not.

Elders found itself in a lengthy and arcane legal battle over the value of Carling O'Keefe preferred shares that had been sold prior to the company's acquisition. Elders offered to repurchase the preferred shares at a set price but a group of affected holders led by Bay Street equities analyst Michael Palmer refused to sell and held out for what the shares originally sold for, not their present value. Elders simply shrugged and went ahead with its takeover, transferring the holdouts' preferred stock over to the new Carling. That action gave the holdouts the ammunition needed to argue that their rights had been trampled. The new Carling, they said, was not the same company since the Australians had loaded $400 million worth of acquisition debt onto the brewer – a perfectly legal tactic that kept the debt off Elders' ledgers, freed up capital, and made takeovers pay for themselves.

The objectors, including Bay Street financier Brent Belzberg, had anticipated Elders' actions and purchased a large chunk of the preferreds, hoping they could eventually force Elders to buy them out at a big premium. Belzberg knew Carling well. His merchant banking operation had successfully acquired Mother's Pizza and tried and failed to take over Carling as a financial bidder. In a heavily regulated industry like Canada's beer business, a financial bidder could do as well as a strategic bidder – another brewer, in other words. That was because the rules of competition, pricing, packaging, and distribution had already been formalized, either through regulations or industry agreements. Belzberg's thinking was shared less than a decade later by the country's best-known financial bidder, takeover king Gerry Schwartz.

Belzberg and his partners, along with a group of activist shareholders, had the time and money to make Elders miserable. First they went to the Supreme Court of Ontario, arguing their rights as shareholders had been suppressed. Though they ultimately lost the first round, they promptly appealed and received a more sympathetic hearing to the case. In the end, the ruling was that Elders, in buying Carling in a leveraged buyout with little of its own money at risk, had treated Carling as a private company and ignored its shareholders. After 18 months, the holdouts had apparently won, though Carling wasted no time appealing that judgment, which was rejected some months later.

The case created legal precedents, creating a new oppression remedy for shareholders in similar situations and setting some ground rules for future leveraged buyouts. It also marked Sheila Block of Tory Tory as a rising star in the legal profession. "She literally won this thing for us," noted Toronto lawyer John Butler, who began the legal action working for Belzberg and ended it at Tory Tory alongside Block. "There wasn't much in the preference share conditions that gave us an argument," Butler said. "The second thing was we were such terrible plaintiffs. We were basically for all intents and purposes simply trying to profit from this situation." But Block became a thorn in the side of Elders far in excess of the ultimate $43-million judgment. She sparred in cross-examination with Ted Kunkel, a tough Aussie of the John Elliott school, who'd been parachuted into the top Carling job. "[Block] is the best in the country, not even close," said Butler, who, years later, still delights in clipping photographs of Kunkel from the papers, drawing moustaches on them, and sending them off to Block. "She is just the most persuasive litigator I have ever, ever heard. She uses the fact that she is a woman to her complete advantage and yet she is way smarter than any of the men that she has to deal with." The legal battle over the preferreds would not be the last time the Elders gang would wince when they saw Block walk into a courtroom.

For Labatt, which had been happily leading the industry pack during the court case, the decision proved to be a tripwire of sorts, warning that the industry was once again changing, and decidedly not in its favour. The day Carling's holdouts were given their victory, just weeks into 1989, trading in Molson shares was halted prior to the close of the exchange, a sure signal major corporate news was about to be released. Executives of Carling and Molson were nowhere to be found and unavailable for comment, leaving the *Financial Post* to run the front-page headline "Bay St. Tips Molson to Swallow Carling." With no confirmation of a corporate deal between the brewers, the paper could only write that one was expected soon and settled for a picture of a grinning Michael Palmer, the outspoken and always quotable beer analyst, who'd launched the original suit against Carling in 1987.

The public, investors, and Labatt would not have to wait long for an answer from Molson and Elders. The day Palmer's mug graced the front of the *Financial Post*, the companies held a joint press conference announcing a 50-50 merger of their Canadian beer businesses that promised thousands of layoffs and the closure of 7 of 16 breweries across the country. Labatt executives were stunned. They had had nary a sniff of the impending merger, an accomplishment that surpassed the secrecy Labatt had managed five years earlier with the twist-off bottle. Elders and Molson had plenty of reason to keep their intentions secret, of course. Besides shielding themselves from Labatt, there were the companies' shareholders to think about, as well as the Competition Bureau. They would not repeat Labatt's misstep of a few years earlier.

A small cadre of senior executives from Elders, Carling, and Molson had met, incredibly, in secret for eight months before John Elliott and bureaucrat-turned-executive Marshall "Mickey" Cohen held their first joint press conference. From the start, Carling had considered a merger with Molson a long shot. Molson was conservative, based in Montreal, and family owned. Culturally, a deal with Labatt was thought to be a more natural merger; it had already tried to buy Carling and the two companies fit. "The first choice was Labatt," said John Barnett, the cheerfully profane former accountant with Rothmans, who prospered under the Aussies' rule at Carling. Stout, loud, and personable, Barnett was the Englishman's version of John Elliott – another chain-smoking workaholic with a street fighter's mentality. Given the raft of senior departures at Carling prior to the Elders takeover, Barnett, who had risen to the role of president of Carling Canada before the merger, provided an important bridge between Elders and Molson, and was the repository of the company's institutional memory. Barnett was most definitely a "beer guy" and had that hard-to-define, but easy-to-recognize status. Some could spend their entire working lives in the business and never be granted the elusive title, but the moniker suited Barnett.

"When it became apparent that we weren't going to be able to do a deal with Labatt, that is when we started talking to Molson," said Barnett. "Frankly, it seemed a long shot. I mean, here is the family business, it has been in the family a couple of hundred years, family controlled through the voting, non-voting share structure." Carling's proposals were not dismissed out of hand during initial discussions with Norm Seagram and Stuart Hartley, Molson's chief financial officer, so the two brewers decided to assemble senior brewing, financial, and management executives to consider the details of a merger. With topmost secrecy, they had a law firm book some conference rooms at the Bristol Place Hotel under a numbered company. Lawyers rented the brick-like cellular phones of the era for the meeting participants, and the two sides relied on fax machines in their cars to send correspondence rather than using the normal office systems. The executives even refrained from ordering Molson or Carling products for meetings, Barnett recalls. "That's why when we announced the bloody deal most people were quite surprised within the company, certainly within Labatt."

The working groups figured out the bare bones of a Molson-Carling merger remarkably quickly. Both sides knew their strengths and weaknesses – wish lists of underutilized breweries to eliminate, and underperforming brands to either kill off or let die slowly by neglect. Combining the two companies' lists gave them a very accurate picture of how much the merger would cost, how many plants and workers would be axed, and how much money would be saved in annual costs. That exercise proved to be the easy part.

The negotiations quickly bogged down over the issue of control of the merged company. John Elliott had said from the start, and maintained throughout the negotiations, that Elders would either be an equal partner or it would take its marbles and go home, ensuring that Carling would continue to be a disruptive force for Molson and Labatt. On the other side of the table was Molson's management, a group who valued their patrician image and often reminded themselves they were working for a company more than two centuries old. "The issue was control. There was no way we were going to cede control to these goddamn cowboys," said Norm Seagram, president of Molson's brewery operation. The two sides had a half dozen, or so, issues to resolve, such as who would do what in a merged management structure, how much money would Elders need to throw into the pot to equalize the different values of the two companies, and how would the merged company be capitalized. Elders, with dreams of becoming the largest brewer in the world, wanted to maximize the cash flow from the merged company as soon as possible while Molson, content and hardly acquisitive, was ready to leave capital in the brewery. "I remember writing a note to one of my colleagues as this debt debate was going on," Seagram recalls, "something about 'the problem isn't with them, the problem is with us because we have nothing within the greater Molson Companies, no strategic plan that really needed cash to execute,'" Seagram recalled. "We were just bumping along. We still had some various diversified interests, most of which we'd got rid of. We had nothing that was sort of a growth plan that would require investment." That "problem," like the issue of control, would soon be solved.

The Elders-Molson log-jam that had gone on for months received a sharp shove when Molson hired Mickey Cohen as its new chief executive officer in the summer of 1989. Mickey, 53 at the time, was hired out of the offices of the Reichmann brothers' Olympia & York Enterprises Ltd., where it had become very clear that Cohen, not a Reichmann family member, would never end up running the company. A New Jersey–born Torontonian who resisted the pressure to become a doctor for the fascination of tax law, Mickey seemed a logical choice to run a business that depended so much on the good graces of government. Cohen carried no beer baggage. He knew none of the immutable "laws" of the beer business and was not part of the beer-belly culture, but he did share the mindset of Molson executives. Mickey also would never be a "beer guy." He famously shunned the amber liquid, preferring wine.

With logic that would have made any lawyer proud, Mickey picked apart the Molson case against a 50-50 partnership, which had derailed the merger talks. Norm Seagram recalls: "Mickey really said, 'Who cares if it's 51-49? It doesn't matter, because you are not going to be able to do anything together unless you agree. As soon as one guy who theoretically is in a control position decides something that is against the wishes or would normally be vetoed by the other guy, the partnership is over.'" Molson's new boss also successfully argued for a five-year no-divorce period. No matter what happened, the two companies had to stick it out and make it work.

After that, the other "contentious" issues quickly fell by the wayside. Mickey would have say in the brewer's operations as non-executive chairman of the new entity, even though he wasn't that interested in beer. Ted Kunkel, the New Zealand–born 20-year brewing veteran, was interested in beer and became chairman of the merged company, named Molson Breweries. John Carroll, a Molson man with a packaged-goods company background, was president and chief executive for Canada. John Barnett, Elders' loyal Canadian scout and guide, was rewarded with the post of president and CEO of the new Molson US operations. Eric Molson, great-great-great-grandson of the founder, the controller of the diverse Molson family's shares, and a brewmaster to boot, had no direct involvement in the brewery's operations under the new organizational structure.

Mickey, the clever tax lawyer, also barred the taxman. The new 50-50 Molson Breweries was set up as a partnership instead of a limited company because partnership income was taxed differently. Molson Breweries was established with an April 1 year-end, one day after Molson Companies' March year-end, which allowed the parent company to keep approximately $80 million in profits from the merger that normally would have been paid out in taxes. That year, certainly, Mickey earned the $1-million base salary that so many in the business community clucked about.

Mickey, who had worked with the federal government in Ottawa and with the Reichmanns, was suddenly a corporate celebrity. Prominent, positive articles on Mickey were everywhere the first couple of years of his reign, a marked contrast to just a few years later when things went sour and he became a virtual media recluse in the wood-panelled elegance of Molson's corporate offices in Toronto's Scotia Plaza. At the time, with all the positive attention, Mickey took credit for his immediate impact on Molson. "The deal was almost dead when I got here," he said. "If I hadn't arrived, it would have died."

In those heady days following the 1989 merger, his assessment was pretty much universally shared by Molson people. "There is no question in my mind that the deal would not have happened without Mickey," said Barry Joslin, senior vice-president of corporate and public affairs, who later became Mickey's gatekeeper with the media and investment analysts, "because guys like [Stuart] Hartley were just stuck on how can we enter into a partnership with these guys when we have twice the market share that they have." Although Joslin prospered under Mickey, he wasn't sold on the deal either. At a "victory party" weekend in Florida following the deal, he loudly proclaimed the merger "a bucket of shit," an opinion he modified after the corporate combination soon began to work smoothly.

Mickey quickly moved Molson to first-class accommodations. One of his early decisions was to relocate the executive offices from near the Toronto airport brewery to sumptuous digs in the Scotia Plaza. (That decision didn't sit too well with the suburban-dwelling staff now forced to fight traffic to reach the heart of Toronto's financial core.) And the new configuration did make its mark. The merger was well executed, and within three years the combined profit of the new Molson Breweries had doubled to $310 million over what had been earned by Molson and Carling together in the year before the combination. Operating breweries was hardly on Mickey's mind, however. "I'm not going to visit the breweries or the factories much. What would I tell them? To keep the machines clean? I'm in New York, in London, in places where things are happening," he famously told *Report on Business Magazine* months after the merger.

Like lovestruck teenagers, Molson and Carling had carried out a secret romance and professed their undying devotion for each other. Unfortunately they still had to obtain the blessing of an influential authority figure, namely the Competition Bureau. On the plus side, the two brewers had already avoided Labatt's mistake. They were looking for the Bureau's blessing, not permission as Labatt had. Molson's strategy was the same: it set out to convince the competition cops that Carling had been a failing enterprise on its way out. The strategy was to be friendly and solicitous, and if the investigators asked for facts and figures, they would be supplied. As one of the Molson executives later said, "Our strategy was to bury them with information."

Molson also brought out the Economics 101 argument, claiming the merger would allow it to shutter breweries, merge head-office staffs, and consolidate buying – efficiencies that would ultimately mean lower prices for the consumer. Unlike provincial governments such as puritanical Ontario, which wanted prices kept relatively high, Ottawa's competition watchdog considered price a powerful argument. Six months after the merger announcement, a Molson contingent led by Mickey trooped up to Ottawa to met with the Bureau's director, Calvin Goldman. "He sort of folded his file and said, 'Okay, do it,'" says Norm Seagram. He recalls that Mickey made a dusting-off motion with his hands and said, "Well, we sorted out the beer business."

The feds gave approval to the deal but talked tough about reserving the right to modify it over the next three years if it didn't like how competition evolved in the Canadian beer industry in the wake of the merger. Labatt, now in the unaccustomed role of number-two brewer, had said publicly it hoped the Bureau would force Molson to sell off some of its brands. In the end, the Bureau never made a move against the pumped up Molson.

The merger allowed the new Molson Breweries to reduce its annual costs by about $225 million and briefly gave it close to 53% of the market, compared with Labatt's 42% at the time. The share gap seemed huge but Molson's new market status would prove virtually impossible to sustain. Carling brought breweries and cost savings to the table, not brand power. Its portfolio consisted of brands such as Black Label, Old Vienna, and O'Keefe Ale, and recent disappointments such as Miller High Life and Foster's. Molson had Canadian, which was fast overtaking Blue, a quiet success story in Coors Light, and the solid, if shrinking, Export. Molson decided that it couldn't spread its marketing budget to support Carling's old brands and still keep backing its own successful portfolio. The best Molson could hope for was that the majority of the share of the Carling brands, once stripped of marketing spending, would go to Molson brands rather than to Labatt.

The folks at Labatt, once they got over the shock of the biggest merger in the industry, were thinking the same thing. Labatt Breweries president Sid Oland saw only opportunity from the merger. "Shortly after I got the call from Ted Kunkel, telling me what was happening, I said to [John Labatt CEO] Peter Widdrington, 'I can't believe our good luck.'" Labatt had pretty much run through its stock of new product ideas and packaging and marketing gimmicks and looked forward at the start of the nineties to having a competitor that would be internally focused for a few years at least.

"I told the analysts at the time that they were going to look very big for a while and they were going to scoop up a lot of the low-lying fruit in terms of cost savings and things like that. But then they would stop supporting as many brands, they were going to start closing plants. All those things were going to start chipping away at their size," Oland recalls. "I said specifically this is not going to happen right away. This is going to happen three and four years out. [The analysts] were all nattering at me six months out. Sure enough, in three or four years' time, we were right on their heels."

7

All Hands to the Border

As Labatt discovered in its failed attempt to gain the Competition Bureau's blessing for a Carling-Labatt merger, handling government agencies is an essential beer maker's skill. Operating in a highly regulated industry, just like Bell Canada or the cable companies, government relations are as important as brewing good beer and marketing it to the masses. The threats for Molson and Labatt went well beyond the day-to-day battles with one another. Some of the major challenges to their existence rested in the hands of government officials and bureaucrats: the border with the United States, importation of brands from overseas, taxation, and distribution. Through their history, Labatt and Molson have done a masterful job dealing with the various levels of government that control their fate. "The real heroes in this business are the government-relations people, not the marketers," says Jeff Carefoote, a former Molson executive. Carefoote should know; he spent years at Molson, mainly as a marketer. Although Carefoote could have been speaking of myriad successes large and small in areas ranging from taxes to packaging restrictions, the breweries' best work was seen in the fight over the border, which went on for many years.

When the Canada-US Free Trade Agreement came into effect on

January 1, 1989, the beer business was the only major industry to be exempted from the deal until five years later when a new round of negotiations was to begin. Through their lobby clout, the brewers convinced the Mulroney government that the industry was horribly inefficient, and that interprovincial trade restrictions dating back to before the turn of the century had forced them to operate a scattering of small breweries in each province. That was when the feds gave provincial governments the power over the making and selling of alcohol. Concerned about "jobs, jobs, jobs" even then, the provincial governments forced beer companies to brew the stuff in the provinces they wanted to sell it in, thereby maximizing employment. In the United States, the big brewers started out as regional entities, and then grew by shipping their beer across the country by rail and later by truck. As a result, the United States is dominated by three companies that operate a few breweries, which are huge by Canadian standards, to serve the US market. Coors' main Golden, Colorado, facility, for example, makes the equivalent of 25 million hectolitres of beer annually, more than Canada's entire consumption. By comparison, the biggest Molson or Labatt facility would pump out four to five million hectolitres. Should the borders fall overnight, the argument went, US beer companies would immediately flood Canada with cheap suds swamping Labatt, Molson, and Carling.

Once the industry was granted its temporary reprieve from free trade, it quickly began shedding excess capacity. With the 1989 merger of Molson and Carling, the companies managed to shed 7 of 16 breweries and 27% of their workforce. They probably should have closed a few additional breweries. John Morgan, president of Labatt Breweries, who found himself suddenly running the less-efficient, second-place brewer, grumbled that his rivals used the merger "as a cover to take a significant amount of capacity out of the operation." Labatt was operating at a disadvantage compared to both its potential US competitors and the new Molson, unable to carry out one massive downsizing as its competitors had done. But Morgan, and Ontario president Hugo Powell, embarked on a continuous process of cost-cutting that brought Labatt to the point of being more efficient and profitable than Molson. "The difference is we put a marker down saying it is never over, and [Molson] said it was over [with its merger]," says Hugo Powell.

While cost-cutting was the number-one priority for Labatt internally – ahead of its more public drive for market share – the company consistently fought to keep the regulatory status quo. Labatt opposed the effort to drop interprovincial beer barriers before and after the 1989 Molson-Carling merger, and took a hawkish stance on the negotiations with the Americans designed to create a lasting trade agreement. Its "man the ramparts" strategy was in direct opposition to Molson's strategy under Mickey Cohen. In his term as president of Molson, Mickey saw protectionism as futile, consistently working to reduce the company's exposure to the Canadian beer business and move Molson into other areas such as retailing and specialty chemicals. For him the merger accomplished two things: it significantly increased the profitability and competitiveness of the brewery, and it also reduced Molson's ownership position to 50%. A few years later, Molson and its Australian partner sold 20% of the brewery to Miller of the United States. Once again Molson was taking money out of the beer business to use elsewhere and reducing its risk in the new market context.

Labatt's outlook was far less fatalistic and in essence amounted to the belief that the brewers should do everything possible to retain Canada's extremely profitable duopoly. "Mickey and I had a long fundamental disagreement," said George Taylor, president and chief executive of parent company John Labatt at the height of the "beer wars" between Canada and the United States. "He was a free trader, live or die. I said, 'I'm a free trader for everybody, Mickey, I believe in free trade for everybody, except for my business.'"

Drinkers in Ontario got a taste of an open border in the summer of 1989, just as the "Blue Zone" was gearing up to hit college campuses, Canadians were dubiously eyeing the $1 "loonie" coins, and provincially run liquor stores began selling six-packs such as G. Heileman Brewing Co.'s Lone Star brand. The cheap US suds, which sold as low as $4.30 a pack, or $2 per six-pack less than

Canadian brands, quickly grabbed 9.5% of the market. Regional brewers such as Wisconsin's Heileman Brewing, losing enormous amounts of money in the United States, looked upon the high-price, high-tax Canadian market as potential salvation and benefited from the lack of a minimum price for beer. But Heileman and others should have known that something as un-Canadian as cheap beer was too good to last. Under heavy lobbying by the domestic brewers, the province made it a one-summer wonder by increasing the warehousing and distribution costs for American brewers. Imports plunged to 3% of the market the next year.

The summer of 1990 also brought the early, ill-fated election call of the Peterson Liberals and the shocking majority victory of Bob Rae's New Democratic Party in September. Ontario residents and businesses, so used to the middle-of-the-road politics of the Tory governments of Bill Davis, were in for a rude shock. Rae's crew were socialists in a hurry. Not entirely prepared to govern and suddenly faced with the machinery of the biggest provincial government, they acted early on as if they would be a one-term government.

For the brewers, it was just a new batch of people to lobby, and as it turned out, a socialist Ontario was a pretty hospitable place. "The best government ever for the brewers was Bob Rae's," one former beer lobbyist said. For Molson and Labatt, in battle with each other and with Americans intent on crashing the party with their cheap beer, the NDP was the right government at the right time. During the Rae years, the two companies each operated two breweries in the province, complete with unionized workforces, and Molson was not shy about casually mentioning how difficult it was to keep both of their beer factories operational. Ideologically, the Rae government was more distrustful and hostile to US interests than its predecessors, and they also had a jaundiced view of the Free Trade deal and the Mulroney Tories who had served it up. So the NDP were quite willing to listen to the brewers' accusations of cheap-beer dumping by US competitors.

. . .

The lengthy beer wars between Canada and the United States came with a bewildering series of administrative terms and acronyms such as GATT, US Section 301, NAFTA, and the MOU. Some, like GATT (General Agreement on Tariffs and Trade), kept coming back, again and again, to enrich consultants and lobbyists while confusing consumers who only wanted to know when the cheap beer was coming back. The "beer wars" began when the US government, on behalf of some of its brewers, went to GATT to complain about what they saw as Canada's arcane and archaic provincial pricing and distribution practices. A GATT panel found in favour of the United States while a subsequent GATT panel found in favour of Canada after the northerners served up evidence of similar practices in the United States.

In between, there was the infamous environmental levy, a retaliatory 50% tariff on Ontario-brewed beer, and a counter-retaliatory 50% levy from the Ontario government on beer brewed by pesky Stroh Brewing Co. and Heileman. Along with all the levy slapping, the two sides were hurling insults. Stroh's Ontario-born chief financial officer called Ontario's beer retail system an "unbelievably inefficient and greedy oligopoly" that was "raping" the consumer. In turn, Marilyn Churley, Ontario's minister of consumer and commercial relations, accused the United States of "acting like a trade outlaw."

The bad behaviour could be traced back to the NDP's 10-cents-a-can "environmental levy," put in place over apparent fears that the pristine province was going to be littered with aluminum if Ontarians stopped returning used cans for that increased 10-cent refund. It didn't trouble the government, or Canadian brewers for that matter, that soda pop makers, the biggest users of non-refillable containers (who incidentally offered no refund on returns), were not part of the environmental levy. With the vast majority of domestically produced beer sold in bottles, the only brewers really hit by the new tax were US-based imports, the likes of Stroh and Heileman.

"The US guys went ape," recalls Molson's government point man Barry Joslin, the brewer's public face as senior vice-president of corporate and public affairs. "Their intention was to flood the Canadian market with cheap canned beer, so instead we canned cheap beer."

The environmental levy was intended to be GATT-friendly and it proved to be just that. Since it discriminated against everyone in the beer business, even if not equally in the broad sense, it has withstood international scrutiny. That doesn't mean its underlying message was missed by anyone.

Two months after the introduction of the environmental levy in May 1992, the United States slammed a 50% ($3 per case) tariff on Canadian beer shipped south; Canada slapped a similar duty on beer headed north. Amazingly, beer drinkers on both sides of the border saw no change in price. Wanting to preserve market share, Molson and Labatt decided to swallow the tariffs and keep their beer flowing south, even though they were losing money on every sale. Stroh and Heileman had no choice but to absorb the tariffs, since the government-controlled liquor stores of the province said they would stop selling their products if the price rose, claiming US brews were particularly price sensitive. (In Ontario, the key battleground, cheap US beer had not yet broken into the Brewers Retail distribution system.)

With brewers north and south being hit and no apparent spirit of compromise from any level of government, the stalemate looked like it might drag on indefinitely. That all changed in January 1993, when Molson and Elders (now called Foster's Brewing Group) sold a 20% stake in jointly owned Molson Breweries to Miller Brewing of Milwaukee. Stating "Intense competition is just around the corner," Molson Companies president and CEO Mickey Cohen structured a deal that would see Miller handle US advertising and promotion of Canadian-made Molson brands. Molson suddenly had a pressing need to reopen the border.

"From a Molson perspective, we ended up with a four-cornered negotiation," recalls Barry Joslin. Any lasting beer deal had to satisfy Ontario, which would set the pattern for the other provinces. The federal government, which had larger trade worries than beer, also wanted input on any agreement. A deal also had to accommodate Stroh's interests. (Heileman had now disappeared from the scene, subsumed in its own financial difficulties.) Finally, Molson hoped for industry backing on a deal, but Labatt, true to form, was hostile to any sort of pact that would bring down the barriers at the border. "Labatt had no interest in opening up the border," said Joslin. Labatt had been far less successful in the United States and it recognized an opportunity to stick it to its archrival.

Labatt played hardball, though, demanding a relatively high minimum price for beer in the province, thus putting the low-price-dependent American brewers at a disadvantage. Molson, more willing to appease Stroh for the sake of its expanded US business, played some hardball of its own. "They basically went in and completely undermined [Labatt]," said one beer executive who was in on the negotiations with the Ontario government. Molson effectively shot down Labatt's argument for a higher beer floor price. "They came in and basically said, 'Nope, it's going to be this level, and if you don't do it we are going to close the plant in Barrie,'" an argument that carried weight with a provincial government already reeling from a slumping economy.

Once Ontario was on side, the approval of the agreement came quickly. New US President Bill Clinton met with the also newly minted Canadian Prime Minister Kim Campbell at the G-7 summit in Tokyo, and when he returned to the United States he told trade negotiators to get the issue resolved.

The new border agreement finally gave US brands access to the Molson- and Labatt-owned Brewers Retail Inc., and lowered the minimum price nearly 9% or by $2.15 for a case of 24 bottles. US brewers were also charged lower fees by provincial liquor boards and Ontario's BRI. The Ontario government, which was nearly as hard-lined as Labatt through the three-year border battle, got to keep its 10-cents-a-can tax. "It's a minor victory for the Canadian consumer," Stroh executive Chris Sortwell unenthusiastically told *The Globe and Mail*, adding he was concerned other provinces might not follow the deal.

When the dust settled, US brewers got access to the 460 Brewers Retail outlets, but were strictly limited in the use of the one competitive weapon they had: pricing. Just prior to the settlement of the border dispute, Labatt and Molson introduced, respectively, the Wildcat and Carling lines of discount beers. The new beers, sold at the minimum for domestics, were priced only a dollar more per case than US-price brands and effectively capped their growth. "That is the other thing that [Stroh] didn't appreciate. You give Canadian consumers a choice between regular Canadian beer at a discount and regular American beer at a discount and they'll take the Canadian beer every time," summarized Barry Joslin. The discount market has since ballooned to about 20% of Ontario beer sales, but US brands such as Stroh's Old Milwaukee account for only about one-quarter of that total.

Notably silent in the border wars were Anheuser-Busch, Miller, and Coors. The three US beer giants were contractually tied up with long-term licensing deals that would have precluded them from coming to Canada in any big way even if the border and the existing unfair distribution system had disappeared the next day. Anheuser-Busch worked with Labatt and had signed a 99-year licensing deal for the Budweiser and Bud Light brands. Coors and Miller were both brewed under licence by the now-merged Molson for the domestic market. The contractual handcuffs on the big brands of the top three US brewers emboldened Labatt in its opposition. "Even if the borders open, what are they going to come in with? Their secondary brands to try and beat us up?" Labatt's George Taylor would ask Mickey. Licensing was not a one-way sucker's deal. US brewers entered the Canadian market in an extremely low-risk, low-expense fashion, while their Canadian partners benefitted by launching well-known brands without development and introductory advertising costs, which typically ran between $8 million and $10 million.

For Ontario consumers, and Canadian beer drinkers in general, the border wars failed to provide much price relief. For the cost-conscious, a discount category did emerge, but mainstream prices stayed the same. Worse, no Ontario government has ever had the stomach to take on Brewers Retail (now renamed The Beer Store), a government-endorsed beer monopoly − accountable to no one other than Molson and Labatt − which, combined, own 99% of the entity. The government did at least exercise control over pricing through the province's Liquor Control Board of Ontario, but that arrangement was jettisoned in the spring of 1996 when the free-market Harris government decided to grant control of pricing to the province's brewers themselves.

Ontario, historically the most profitable market for the big brewers in Canada, has evolved into a dream jurisdiction for the two big beer companies. They own the main means of distribution in the province and set the ground rules that smaller competitors are forced to follow. They have also forced virtually all other brewers in the province to use the 1994 industry standard bottle, an updated version of the twist-off originally brought out by Labatt a decade earlier, which saves Molson and Labatt as much as $50 million each per year, and they have control over pricing. When the minority Peterson Liberals suggested selling beer in the corner store, killing the Brewers Retail monopoly and sending their distribution costs skyhigh, the big brewers warned of the dangers of underage drinking. Worried moms and dads got the message: the vintage "beer stores" with the "In" and "Out" signs for confused customers would keep beer away from little Johnny until he reached legal drinking age. The Harris government approved Sunday openings of The Beer Store, which proved a boon to the big guys and a swift kick in the sales to microbrewers, small craft brewers that had prospered as the baby boomers aged and sought out beers brewed outside the mainstream. The microbrewers, until the advent of Sunday beer store openings, were doing brisk sales on Sundays out of in-brewery stores.

Ontario has evolved into a place where everyone is happy – except the microbrewers and the beer consumer. Molson and Labatt are guaranteed steady profits. If they need more, they can just pull the pricing lever, while the government continues to get its fixed percentage of tax revenue. Both sides satisfied, the breweries never complain about high levels of taxation on beer, and the industry faces less scrutiny than south of the border. Before the mid-1990s, brewers had to petition regulators before putting through a price increase and provide reasons why they needed more cash from drinkers. Today, Molson and Labatt just give a couple weeks' notification of a price change, which allows them to increase prices in lockstep. There are no US-style health warnings on beer, and American beer companies can only dream of an industry-owned retail chain such as The Beer Store operation in Ontario.

Based on industry price records for Ontario that go back to the early 1970s, at least one-half of the price increases for beer from that time until 1992 were due to tax increases by the federal and provincial governments. Since the time of the 1989 merger, however, when Molson suggested to the Competition Bureau that lower prices could result from one more-efficient brewer, the price of a case of 24 bottles has risen 50%, or $10.40. Just $1.15 of that increase can be traced to tax increases. In the six years following the Ontario government giving Molson and Labatt control over beer pricing in 1996, prices have risen 18%, or about 2.4% annually. The increases have not been dramatic – 50 cents here, 75 cents there – but the cumulative effect has been substantial. Price increases are pure profit for businesses that have continued to close plants following the merger. After watching Hugo Powell close breweries in the mid-1990s, Molson followed suit, and today barely half the plants it operated following the merger remain, down to 5 from 9. Molson and Carling combined had 16 in 1989. Labatt, which ran 12 breweries across the country when Molson and Carling merged, today runs only 8. As the brewers have become more efficient, they have, of course, wrung more beer out of fewer plants and more profits out of consumers.

The most telling measure is profit per hectolitre, the be-all and end-all measure for breweries. In 1990, Jacques Kavafian, then brewing analyst with McNeil Mantha Inc., estimated Labatt made $15.53 in profit per hectolitre while Molson earned $10.76 per hectolitre. (One hectolitre equals 12.2 cases of 24.) With the exception of Anheuser-Busch at $15.11 per hectolitre, both Canadian companies were miles ahead of US rivals such as Coors and Miller in that crucial measure. Molson and Labatt today make as much as $130 per hectolitre on their big national brands such as Canadian and Blue, or roughly a $10 profit on a case selling for about $31.50 in Ontario. Both make less when they sell a case of a licensed brand such as

Budweiser or Coors because they split the profits with their US partners. In Molson's situation, with brands such as Heineken and Corona, profits are slimmer given that they only act as Canadian sales agent; however, they spend far less to advertise these foreign brands than they do their own.

8

The Silly Season: Dry, Draft, and Ice

Labatt Breweries president Sid Oland could afford to feel confident in his prediction to the analysts that his company would regain its market-leading postion once the effects of the Molson-Carling merger of 1989 were fully played out. Labatt's problem, however, was that its innovation tank, always seemingly full of gimmicks designed to push that all-important share up another notch, seemed to be empty. Before Molson and Carling dropped their bombshell, Labatt could afford to be a tad complacent. It had taken Molson years to recover from the twist-off and its share seemed stuck in the low 30s, while Labatt, vampire-like, grew stronger as Carling weakened.

Amidst all the talk of brewery closures, layoffs, and cost-savings at the start of 1989, Molson marketers had developed what was a rarity for the brewer at the time – an honest-to-goodness product innovation. Well ahead of the traditional first sign of spring in the beer business, the start of the Stanley Cup playoffs, the brewer rolled out Molson Special Dry, which it described as a new style of beer copied from what Japanese brewers had developed a few years earlier. (Molson in fact had been brewing dry beer for some time in its Vancouver brewery on a contract basis for Kirin Brewery. Unwilling to sail the stuff all the way across the Pacific, the Japanese brewer trucked the Canadian-made Kirin into the States and sold it as an import, which it was in name if not truly in spirit.)

Whether Molson truly thought Special Dry was the next big thing in brewing or not, the company acted as if it was (and often that is half the battle with consumers). Special Dry launched in a unique tall bottle, another one – beer executives and bottle sorters no doubt sighed – which featured a ceramic label rather than the old-fashioned paper one. Special Dry also featured more kick, 10% more alcohol than regular beers at 5.5%, and was priced at a premium, meaning drinkers could feign sophistication as they opted for the high-test hooch. Best of all, despite the extra alcohol, Special Dry was supposed to have less aftertaste, a benefit for those who liked the effects of beer if not the taste.

Reacting to the launch of Molson Special Dry, Labatt confidently predicted it would bring out its own dry beer in a month's time. When "Project Dusty," Labatt Dry, was unveiled, those following the industry wondered why Labatt had bothered. Late to market, Labatt's version had the standard 5% alcohol, was regularly priced, and lacked a snazzy bottle. Challenged about its weaker offering, Labatt uncharacteristically played the Boy Scout. "We're also not sure it's socially acceptable to have beers with more alcohol these days," Rick Shaver, a Labatt marketer, told the Financial Post.

The beer drinker quickly decided it wasn't socially acceptable to buy Labatt Dry. The brewer could hardly blame them. It was inexcusably poorly positioned, considering the company had the luxury of a month to fine tune its brew. Consumers turned their noses up at the latecomer and paid the 10% premium for Special Dry. The Molson beer's winning ways were confirmed in the fall when Labatt launched Labatt Dry Light, which industry observers immediately saw as an attempt to flood the marketplace.

"We had all done the research on [Molson Special] Dry," said Blair Shier, who started the year with Carling's marketing department and ended it with the new Molson. "[Dry] blew away Molson's expectations. All the research said it would make out at 2 [share] and I think it hit 4 to 6 in the first summer." With an authentic market hit on its hands, Molson's main concern was getting enough of the ceramic-label bottles to meet the demand.

Labatt, ever the scrappy competitor, would not abandon the field to Molson, which had created a legitimate brand for itself. Now number two in more ways than one, Labatt cranked up the alcohol content of dry beer to 5.65%, a relatively easy task for a big brewer, and started hammering the consumer with new advertising. The Toronto office of trendy California-based Chiat\Day\Mojo was hired to put Labatt Dry back in the public's consciousness. The agency did not disappoint. The year following the disappointing rollout, it introduced a trio of ads playing off Labatt's name. The "La Dry" ads featured a world-weary narrator and quirky humour. One of the more memorable ads showed a full pitcher of beer with the onscreen caption "La Pitcher" followed by a hand clutching an empty beer glass and "La Catcher." The language of the ads soon became part of the public's vernacular, a sure sign they had struck a chord. The *Toronto Sun* played on the concept for a front page political cartoon following Bob Rae's surprise election victory in 1990. The Donato cartoon depicted Rae, David Peterson, and Mike Harris with the captions "La Winner," "La Loser," and "La Goof." Chiat\Day\Mojo came back the following season with nine more ads. By the next winter, though, truly the cruellest season for anyone associated with the brewing industry, Chiat was summarily fired. People may have connected with the advertising, but the sales needle was barely moving. Clearly the advertising wasn't the problem, but the agency was shown the door regardless.

Ira Matathia, Chiat's president who had been imported from the United States to build the business, did not go quietly. He criticized Labatt's strategy of hauling in new ad shops and continually pitting agencies against one another. "We are looking for marketing partners who embrace our process for developing great advertising. It is clear we will not get the kind of relationship we need with Labatt to continue to produce breakthrough advertising," Matathia complained to *The Globe and Mail*. Labatt was at rock bottom at the time. Marketing saviour Dave Barbour, named executive vice-president of marketing, was cleaning house in his department, while Blue, handled by J. Walter Thompson once more, continued to lose share to Canadian.

Labatt would soon regain the momentum but it would be no thanks to Dry. After Chiat's departure, it no longer spent millions to promote the brew. Unable to cut into Molson Special Dry's market-share lead, all the advertising did was legitimize the segment that Molson owned. From then on, Labatt borrowed the strategy of US partner Anheuser-Busch and attempted to kill the category. It flooded the market with the likes of Blue Dry (6.1% alcohol) and the discount-priced Wildcat Dry (5.9%). After three years of banging its head against the wall, Labatt Dry was renamed Labatt Extra Dry, and its alcohol content and price were bumped up to Molson Special Dry's levels. Today, Labatt Extra Dry is sold as a discount brand, as is Molson Special Dry in Ontario, a telling indication of how successful the brewers' efforts were over the long term.

"[Molson] had Dry and they were really kicking our butts," said Glen Cavanagh, who ran Labatt's new products division in the 1992–96 period. "What was happening was that Canadian was just contin-uing on its roll, their advertising being light-years ahead of ours, and that they had captured a significant share of the younger market."

Labatt learned its lesson from the dry beer fiasco. Barely into March, a week before it fired Chiat in fact, it introduced Labatt Genuine Draft, a non-pasteurized, "cold-filtered" brew modelled upon similar beers that had been selling briskly in the United States for a number of years. This was dry all over again, except Labatt insisted that the players would be reversed. Labatt made no bones about its intentions. Its early launch date was designed to pre-empt an anticipated Canadian introduction of Miller Genuine Draft by Molson. At the Labatt Genuine Draft press conference, which counted more brewery marketers and public relations people than reporters, the Labatt people were smug. They had beaten Molson to the punch and would set the ground rules this time.

Molson could have been first to jump on the "genuine draft" beerwagon the season before, but they'd had little reason to. The brewery was on a roll, Special Dry was doing well and Canadian continued to gain share. Brewing Miller's product would have required costly new equipment – Labatt spent $98 million in 1992 on new hardware, mainly to make the unpasteurized draft – and there was the concern about Miller's clear bottles at Molson. Labatt, after what was by brewing standards superficial research, decided consumers wouldn't care about authenticity and went with a tall brown bottle.

Nevertheless, when Labatt introduced its Genuine Draft, Molson was furious. It dismissed the brew as "a copycat product" even though there was no other such product in the market; its intentions were no more than rumours at the time. LGD, as Labatt staffers liked to call it, was intended to be a Canadian killer. It was skewed young, in the marketing parlance, aimed at those 19-to-24-year-old drinkers Canadian owned and Blue just couldn't attract any more. LGD was advertised early and often with strong use of the youthful imagery Canadian relied upon so heavily. Molson's first response was to call in the lawyers. Molson and Miller Brewing Co. applied to the Federal Court for an injunction against Labatt, claiming it had copied the US brand's packaging and advertising. A week later, about a month after LGD hit the market, Molson came out with its own brewed-under-licence version of Miller Genuine Draft.

The summer of 1992 became the first real silly season in the beer industry. It had taken a couple of years, but both sides now seemed to realize that poor old Carling was no longer around to poach share from and the gentlemanly rules no longer applied. In the beer world at least, bikini briefs competed for attention with legal briefs that summer. Molson and Labatt filed a paper blizzard of claims and counterclaims as Molson tried to get LGD pulled from the market. Not content with its own multi-million-dollar ad campaign and the slow pace of its legal challenge, Molson ran a consumer promotion called La Copycat Contest that asked beer drinkers to find similarities between the two draft products. Less a public service intended to train the youth of the day for careers as copyright lawyer than a publicity stunt, it had the desired effect. Labatt promptly applied for a court injunction to stop the contest and was turned down. Molson, having gotten millions' worth of free publicity in media coverage from the ploy, grandly said it was ending it a few days in. Trailing LGD badly in the market, Molson would now rely on the guys with the thick briefcases.

Molson's statement of claim, which alleged Labatt was trying to deceive consumers, noted that LGD bore a striking resemblance to Miller's US draft product down to the five colours used on the label, or "get-up," and used similar labelling. Labatt's defence countered that its get-up had a mountain on it, theirs didn't; LGD's label was square, theirs wasn't. Also, the Labatt version didn't use the same recipe and came out in a brown bottle rather than the clear bottle used in the States. In July, smack in the middle of beer-selling season, Molson lost its bid for a temporary injunction against LGD.

In court, Labatt could have argued that if it was ripping off anyone, it was ripping off itself. "Not a lot of people realized this but there used to be a Labatt brand called Genuine Draft that was launched in 1967," said Cavanagh, who had routinely perused the brewery's product archives looking for inspiration. "It was a non-pasteurized bottled beer and it just died a very quick, painful death. That concept that Miller was running with was not a new one, they just figured out a way to do it well." The legal battle over LGD, as much a marketing tactic as a legal stand, was soon abandoned.

Labatt owned the summer. LGD was a hit, although its staying power would remain a question mark after just one year. Blue also seemed to have caught its breath, though J. Walter Thompson remained wary. It was an open question whether advertising was the driving force behind a strengthened Blue, given the winning season of the Toronto Blue Jays that culminated in the first of two World Series victories. Regardless, the results went directly to the bottom line that explains why both sides take the marketing wars so seriously. Labatt's sales rose 6% for the year, a remarkable performance given that the beer industry as a whole shrank nearly 4% because of lousy summer weather. Labatt singled out LGD in its annual report and reported that its share reached a record 43.7%, up 1.4 share points from the year before, and brewing profit grew 22% to $218 million. Molson's financial report for the same year showed what a zero-sum game beer had become. Its share in a year fell whopping 1.8 points to 50.2% and the amount of beer it sold slumped 7.2%.

The summer of 1992 graphically illustrated what a good offence could achieve, and Labatt, its innovation mojo apparently working once more, was determined to keep up the pressure. Labatt Breweries' ambitious new president, Hugo Powell, also had something to prove. The credit for the development of Labatt Genuine Draft was claimed by John Morgan, who was Labatt Breweries' president at the time of the launch. Hugo, who had been president of the brewery's Ontario division for 18 months before replacing Morgan, was keen on something the development people were calling ice beer.

The idea for ice beer came out of the realization that the consumer had changed. A brewer could not simply slap a new label on a bottle, create some catchy advertising, and expect it to sell. The recent successes, dry and genuine draft, were types of beer existing elsewhere and could point to unique brewing processes that the beer drinker seemed to accept. In consumer research, Labatt tried to understand the growth of the microbrewer segment that had sprung up in Canada in the mid-1980s and found beer drinkers commonly complained that micro beers had more taste but that they could drink only one or two of them. The challenge was thrown back to the research and development group at the London brewery to figure out how to make a more flavourful beer that retained the "drinkability" of the mainstream beers produced by the big guys.

As much as beer snobs may look down on Molson's and Labatt's offerings, there was little money to be made by the big guys in spending millions to create another John Labatt Classic – as Molson learned with its short-lived Signature Series of micro-style beers. Cavanagh and the Labatt product development group went into new rounds of consumer research, firing names at beer drinkers. "One of the names that we had thrown out was ice beer," said Cavanagh. "Ironically one of the solutions that our R&D people brought to us in trying to accomplish this high-taste intensity combined with smoothness and drinkability was this low-temp brewing process that would cause, in technical terms, all the unwanted proteins and tannins to precipitate out of the beer at a much faster rate and a much more complete rate." The process, just like cold-filtered draft, would require more capital investment. It also promised a smooth-tasting, high-alcohol brew, delivering the marketing department's demand for a point of difference it could sell to the public. As an added bonus, Labatt could boost its efficiency by brewing the ice suds faster than with regular processes.

By the fall, Labatt had adapted technology bought from a Dutch company to brew what they wanted to call ice beer. Now it had to figure out how to position it, package it, and market it. Given how crucial first mover advantage had proved to be in the skirmishes over dry and genuine draft, the company was obsessed with even greater levels of secrecy than usual. With the battle over genuine draft still being waged, Labatt was already thinking Ice, the product that would provide the one-two punch to Molson. In November, the time brewers begin thinking about the next summer, Labatt called in a senior group from Scali McCabe Sloves. Agency chairman Gary Prouk, flanked by his president Steve Graham and associate creative director David Martin, were greeted at Labatt by Cavanagh, the new products director, and Bruce Elliot, the newly minted vice-president of marketing who replaced Dave Barbour. The visitors were presented with and signed a six-page confidentiality agreement that put the agency men into Labatt's inner sanctum. Although Scali had been fired from the flagship Blue brand, it had loitered on the brewer's roster of agencies, and remained a useful pinch-hitter to be called in for projects precisely like this one.

Labatt anticipated that it would create an entirely new category of beer, like dry or genuine draft. It also wanted to own the category, not following Molson or tactically pre-empting it. "We wanted to be the ice beer," Cavanagh told Marketing magazine, which in an article in the ice beer summer breathlessly called Labatt Ice "one of the most successful product launches in Canada's beer history." Unburdened by worries about how Blue was doing − it just handled the niche Carlsberg brand − Scali was a good choice to handle the business. The creative minds that won Blue in a shootout with the industry's best were still at the agency, and Prouk was hungry to prove the beer company had erred in firing it from the biggest beer account in the country. Listening to Labatt's plans for Ice, the Scali people were infected by the company's enthusiasm for the new product.

Scali would be part of Ice's development to a degree unheard of in the consumer-products business. Beyond the obvious work on the ad campaign, Scali would take part in focus groups, packaging design, and product positioning. It even created an Ice Beer vault in the agency, a locked room containing all the research and concepts being developed for the brand. Unless agency staffers were in on the secret and had signed the confidentiality agreement, they were not part of the slowly growing group allowed to enter the vault.

With a later than usual launch date in mind – the thinking was Labatt wouldn't have to rush the product to market in March because Molson had no inkling of ice beer – Scali had its creative concepts ready as the new year rolled around. With such an evocative name as Ice, Scali had little trouble coming up with grand ideas and was using the working ad tag line "Welcome to the Ice Age." One idea involved a giant meteor slamming into the earth and starting a new ice age. In another, Scali created a heavy metal ice kingdom. Its third idea used a tough-guy spokesman; the agency wanted Rutger Hauer, who played a killer android in the sci-fi cult classic Blade Runner.

Scali and Labatt, continued at what was a relatively leisurely pace for a beer launch, late spring or not. They took the concepts to focus groups that loved the meteor idea, and the special-effects wizards at George Lucas' Industrial Light and Magic were tapped for the project. Then disaster struck. Late on a Friday afternoon in March, Prouk received a call from an ad industry source that told him that Molson was currently shooting its own ice beer commercial and that it was using the "Welcome to the Ice Age" line. Four months' work had gone up in smoke, or melted away, Prouk thought. Scali and its client quickly rallied. Molson may have picked up the germ of Labatt's idea from a focus group or disloyal person with some knowledge of Ice, but there was no way its rival could have the brewing process and compelling product that Labatt believed it was bringing to the consumer. "We actually had developed a process that had required extensive capital investment in new equipment, and the equipment had to be made because nobody was doing what we were doing," Cavanagh recalls. (One former Molson executive has said it was trash-picking bottle and can collectors, and a quick-thinking Molson sales rep at an Ontario beer store, who gave Molson an idea of what Labatt was up to. According to the Molson exec, Labatt had designed mock-ups of the cans, then simply thrown them in the garbage.)

Its June 1 launch date out the window, the brewer was forced to scramble to get Ice to market two months ahead of plan. Just one of four Ice plants was in operation after engineers installed the pilot brewing system in the Montreal factory. That plant began pumping out Labatt Ice day in and day out until the other breweries' ice beer systems came on line.

With the luxury of time gone, Scali junked the two special-effects-laden ideas. It decided over that weekend after the tipoff phone call that it would have to feature the spokesperson – the one creative concept that could be turned around quickly. Within days, the agency had hired Rutger Hauer as the spokesman, agreeing to pay him the princely sum of $400,000 for what amounted to two days' work. Only a movie tough guy, the agency figured, could get away with spouting ad lines like: "The world was born of fire, but purified by ice," and "Labatt Ice Beer. It's here. It's real. It's the only one. Believe it." Scali met with Cavanagh and marketing vice-president Elliot in Hugo Powell's offices, along with Labatt's lawyer and a brewmaster. Within half an hour, Scali was given the go-ahead. "When Hugo trusts you and he thinks you are good, Hugo will let you do pretty much anything," said Prouk. Music was a key part of the dark, nearly apocalyptic tone of the Ice commercials and Prouk wanted to use the ominous opening drone of The Smiths' club hit "How Soon is Now?" Hugo, who knew as little about club music as Prouk did, okayed the expense. (The agency, staffed mainly by "old" fogies just like Labatt, originally wanted to use the Rolling Stones' "She's So Cold" for the initial ads until 22-year-old account director and amateur cool hunter Chris Nanos suggested the alternative rock song.) When Scali launched a brand extension to Ice, Prouk called Hugo and said he wanted to use another decidedly non-mainstream song, "New World Order" by Ministry. "I played it on the phone to him and he said, 'How much is that?' and I said '$100,000 US.' He paused and then he said, 'Okay.' I loved Hugo for that."

Two days after the go-ahead, Scali descended on Vancouver with Toronto director Richard Radke and US cinematographer Michael Givens, who arrived with his own lighting crew to shoot the Ice commercials with Rutger Hauer. The location was dictated by the requirement that they work around the Hollywood star's busy schedule. Disaster once again struck when Prouk and his team met with Hauer that evening in his hotel room. The German actor said he wanted to look over the scripts for the weekend shoot. The next morning Hauer had changed the scripts, reportedly replacing the agency's work with lines more to his liking. Hauer wanted to end the ads with the line, "Big Deal. Ice Brewing." Labatt and the requisite liquor boards had already approved the scripts; Scali did not have time to go through the exercise again. Hauer had just written himself out of the part.

"He walked away from $400,000 for two days' work because he wanted to rewrite my commercials," said Prouk, with a tone of amazement nearly a decade later. "We were all lined up. We had a crew of 60 out in Vancouver. A big-league US cameraman, and no Rutger. We had 24 hours to find someone." Cavanagh led an emergency talent-search team to the local video store. Desperate agency types descended on the action-adventure section, pulling the likes of Christopher Lambert, Dolph Lundgren, and Christopher Walken from the shelves. They also walked away from the store with the Bruce Willis vehicle Die Hard that featured Russian ballet-dancer-turned-actor Alexander Godunov in the role of a crazed German terrorist. Well past picky, they were in luck. The actor's agent promised he would be on a plane to Vancouver the next morning, and be there in plenty of time for the scheduled filming.

Godunov looked the part, with his long blond hair and piercing blue eyes. In appearance at least, he may have been an even better choice for the commercials than the difficult Hauer. "Little did we know he couldn't speak English," said Prouk. "But he was a sweetheart. We had to work with him syllable by syllable." Scali and Labatt also didn't know Godunov was an alcoholic, which if uncovered during the run of the campaign would have been yet another disaster for the star-crossed ice beer. More tragic figure than tough guy, Godunov, the premier dancer of the Russian Bolshoi Ballet, defected to the United States when on a tour there during the height of the Cold War. At the age of 29, he was separated from his Bolshoi soloist wife as she was packed onto a plane bound for Moscow when he defected. He tried to bring her to the States for a year before they divorced in 1982. Two years after the Labatt Ice campaign ran, Godunov, 45, died at home. His death certificate listed chronic alcoholism as the cause of death, complicated by hepatitis. Few at the time knew the sad, dark side of the man who looked like a modern-day Viking.

Godunov patiently soldiered through his scripts, and knowing that some sort of ice beer was coming from Molson, Scali added a new tag line for him to mouth: "If it's not ice brewed, it's not ice beer." The camera zoomed in to the 5.6% alcohol warning carried on the label, and then Godunov mumbled that Ice was "uniquely easy to drink," a message to Labatt's more youthful drinkers.

Labatt didn't have to wait long to see what Molson would do. The day the shooting wrapped up, Molson ran a teaser ad for its new beer during the March 1993 Juno Awards telecast. (Rushing to market also, it had a label but as yet no beer to sell to the public.) Labatt, braced for the worst, was relieved. Called Molson Canadian Ice Draft, the brew was a line extension of its flagship brand and was labelled "Draft" to boot, lumping it in with last year's beers. The brewer also described the process as "ice filtered." Judging by its positioning, Molson clearly didn't think much of ice, and its initial ad and follow-on spots confirmed its ambivalence. Prouk dismissed the effort as "stock footage and some tabletop." The generic beer imagery included blue skies, mountain streams, ice, and sweaty bottles, accompanied by a Hendrix-like electric guitar playing the first few notes of "O Canada." After viewing the teaser, Cavanagh later told *Marketing* he was "reassured, like I had just stepped into the ring and saw that my competitor was a 90-pound weakling."

If anything, Labatt could have been accused of over-thinking Labatt Ice. Scali had spent weeks working on little details – the colours of the packaging, for example. After much research he settled on black and silver, which professional sports teams such as the Los Angeles Kings had switched to. (The black and silver Kings jerseys had become favoured colours of some urban gangs in the United States, which the agency felt didn't hurt Ice's image.) Initial Labatt Ice packages also included a diagram earnestly explaining Labatt's patented process. Again, Labatt didn't want to educate beer drinkers; it just wanted to convince them it had something the other guy didn't. Molson did acknowledge using a much simpler process to make ice beer. While Labatt partly froze the beer and "gently removed" the resulting ice, Molson claimed its process started to freeze the beer then thawed it without doing anything else to it.

Only the most addled drinker would have had difficulty telling the two brewers' ads apart. The dark, gloomy Labatt Ice ads avoided all the rules of beer advertising. There were none of the pour shots breweries liked, and the ads had no images of the target group having fun – those "beer sociability" scenes as the industry calls them. Beach-blanket bingo was replaced by *Die Hard*. Godunov and his monosyllabic delivery also broke the mould. He was, well, old. Nearly two decades senior to the 19-to-24 target age group, he was foreign, had a thick accent, and was famous in the minds of that beer-drinking demographic for getting killed by Bruce Willis.

Dark and odd, the ads had a *Saturday Night Live* aspect to them, almost as if the brewer were poking fun at itself. "It had a lot of talk value. People were imitating him in bars. It was pretty funny," Cavanagh said of the campaign. CBC's *Royal Canadian Air Farce* joined the parody parade, creating its own mock version of the commercials. Labatt literally watched "Iss Bee-Air" sweep across the Canadian consciousness. The two breweries each spend more than $1 million a year just to track what people remember about beer ads and beer brands. The who's hot, who's not research found people were aware of Molson Canadian's advertising, for example, but they had trouble describing a single ad. In the case of Blue, people would often mention the balloon, which had been shot from the skies more than a decade before. But focus group participants noted the Godunov ads. "People would complain that they didn't understand what Alexander Godunov was saying, and then they would turn around and start imitating him, word for word," marvelled Cavanagh.

Labatt Ice got out of the gate slowly, owing to production bottlenecks, while the more widely available Canadian Ice received a decent consumer trial. It was soon joined by Molson Black Ice. In the first year, both sides were claiming ice superiority, stating they were each grabbing about 6% of the market. Later, Molson would add Carling Ice to its Carling discount-priced family of brands, a tacit admission that it would rather it had never heard of ice beer – at least in Canada. Molson also subtly altered its labelling for its ice products, substituting "ice brewed" for the original "ice filtered" or "slow brewed," which adorned its packaging. That was cited prominently in a $10-million lawsuit launched by Labatt, which sought to take Molson's ice brands off the shelf permanently. (Molson fought back and the case was settled by the two brewers in private.)

Even the normally staid *Globe and Mail* couldn't ignore the initial fuss over ice beer. It put Labatt's last-minute search for a spokesman on its front page and subtly mocked executives of both companies, quoting them as they talked sternly about their efforts and those of the other guys.

Labatt, for one, did care. Ice was Hugo's baby and he harboured the same ambitious plans for it as he did for himself. A master salesman, he seemed to have convinced his boss, John Labatt chief executive George Taylor, that ice beer would put the company over the top. His goal of overtaking Molson in market share within sight, Hugo took the luxury of promoting Labatt's new technology and brewing process around the world in hopes of licensing it. Disappointingly, there were few takers. He did manage to convince the engineering-inclined people at Adolph Coors, Molson's partner, to sign up. Coors produced one ice brand, which promptly disappeared. Labatt's biggest disappointment was with its old ally Anheuser-Busch. A-B was treated to the deluxe sales pitch and given a detailed description of the process. The St. Louis company promptly turned around and entered the ice fray on its own.

As Labatt failed to protect its use of the term "ice" in the United States, Hugo's efforts to license the technology across the globe fizzled. "It became a joke," concedes Cavanagh. "Within a year there were 38 ice beers in the US alone." When Labatt complained to the world's largest brewer about its decision to launch ice beers in the United States without making a deal with its Canadian partner, A-B did not shrug its collective shoulders or say it was sorry. Instead, the Anheuser-Busch lawyers were called to launch a lawsuit in the U.S. District Court in St. Louis in what the brewery described as an effort to shield itself from legal action by Labatt.

Anheuser-Busch claimed it sought legal relief after Labatt's lawyer fired off a letter to the St. Louis-based brewer warning A-B "will be accountable for any harm" to Labatt's ice brewing trademarks. A-B asked for US$13.5 million in damages; Labatt asked for a jury award of US$61 million, stating that was triple the amount of money it lost as a result of A-B's introduction of its own ice beers. Anheuser's lawyers argued that ice beer was a generic term that had existed for years and that Labatt had made "injurious falsehoods" against A-B through Labatt advertising claims that it brewed the only real ice beer. Lawyers for the US brewer showed up one day with about 40 different alcoholic products from all over the world, beer and otherwise, that used the word "ice" somewhere in their name. After just over a year, the jury found Labatt at fault and ordered it to pay US$5 million in damages. Labatt later appealed to the Supreme Court but it refused to even hear the case, and the Toronto brewery was eventually forced to hand a cheque over to A-B.

For the 10-year period beginning with the launch of Miller High Life, through the twist-off bottle, to ice beer, Molson had worked largely from a defensive position. The industry's "fast follower," it took the lead on dry beers, but was otherwise content with what Molson executives liked to call a "block and tackle" strategy. Labatt might gain share, but Molson was determined to make its opponent's growth as slow and expensive as possible. Molson raised its game to a new level in the fall of 1993 when Labatt was poised to launch a high-test version of ice beer called Maximum Ice, with a hefty 7.1% alcohol content. Learning of the impending launch through legitimate channels (both brewers gave advance notice of new brands to the jointly owned Brewers Retail stores in Ontario), Molson began to lobby government officials and alcohol-abuse lobby groups. Its efforts were rewarded with an article in The Globe and Mail critical of the new high-alcohol beer. The report quoted the director of Mothers Against Drunk Driving (MADD), who angrily denounced the introduction of Maximum Ice, which carried 40% more alcohol than regular beers. The lobby group's comments appeared the same day Labatt launched its product, and press coverage of the launch and subsequent reports all took note of the opposition to Maximum Ice from anti-alcohol groups.

Publicly, Molson took the stance that it was willing to break its solidarity with Labatt and other brewers in their efforts to limit regulation of the industry in order to curb the growth of high-alcohol beers. From the day of Maximum Ice's launch, it was Labatt that was on the defensive. It was forced to pull an ad for the high-strength product, featuring Canadian actor Michael Ironside, after just three weeks and found itself bogged down with hearings on the matter. Eventually Ontario's beleaguered NDP government ordered the industry to adopt a voluntary code of guidelines, and if it failed to comply the province would look into higher prices and marketing restrictions. Five noisy weeks after the launch of Labatt's 7.1% Maximum Ice, Molson unveiled its own version of high-powered hooch, Molson XXX (or "triple X"), with 7.3% alcohol by volume. The two brands still exist today and are sold in huge cans and bottles, the Canadian equivalent to US malt liquor.

Depending on one's viewpoint, the ice wars were either the high-water mark or low point in the new product skirmishes between

Labatt and Molson. With Labatt Breweries president Hugo Powell looking beyond the Canadian borders for accomplishments, later product introductions certainly generated none of the excitement, reckless spending, or industry bitterness. The forgotten fallen that have come after ice include Molson's Red Dog, Labatt Classic Wheat, and Labatt Copper.

Of the three new segments developed by the brewers in the new product wars, Molson Special Dry ultimately proved the most successful. Notable as the unofficial beer of the gay community, Molson Special Dry continues to sell at a good pace, particularly in Quebec, more than a decade after its introduction. And both Labatt Genuine Draft and Labatt Ice did well as long as the company lavished heavy advertising support upon them. When it decided to concentrate its efforts once more on Blue, with the "Out of the Blue" campaign and its NHL promotion, the two brands sank like a stone. Today, Labatt Ice is a discount brand and Labatt Genuine Draft is a pale shadow of what it was during its glory years.

Labatt's experience with ice beer showed life is often unfair in the jungle that is the US beer business. By the time Labatt lost its legal case against Anheuser-Busch in the United States, American brewers had quickly rolled out their own ice beers. The American consumers quickly labelled ice a fad. Most galling for Labatt, ice beers that didn't use expensive technology, as Labatt had, ended up leading the American market for a couple of years, including Molson with its Molson Ice import.

Part Four

Labatt by Leaps and Bounds

9

Labatt Fills Its Plate

Beer companies by their very nature are followers of fashion. Middle-aged men, mostly, who make it their business to be hip and happening with the moving youth target. Decades ago, the top minds running both Labatt and Molson also took on the corporate fashion of the day, diversification. Fuelled by the steady profits of their respective brewing empires, the two built huge, unwieldy conglomerates during the seventies and eighties. It all seems quaint and almost prehistoric now, when business leaders are all talking about focus and streamlining. But at that time, the breweries and lots of other businesses operated a bit like self-contained mutual funds. Some of this, some of that, assembled in an effort to smooth out the financial peaks and valleys that less prudent, less diversified companies would experience.

Of the two, Labatt was the most diversified. At the peak of its diversification diet in the mid-1980s, Labatt had gobbled up pasta maker Catelli, Laura Secord, US frozen food maker Chef Francisco, Omstead Foods (the world's largest processor of freshwater smelt), juice maker Everfresh, Chateau-Gai wines, dairy company Ault Foods, US dairy company Johanna Farms, grain processor Ogilvy (the world's largest producer of wheat starch and wheat gluten), and

The Sports Network. This list does not even include partly owned businesses, the most notable being the Toronto Blue Jays. Labatt proudly described itself as "the most diversified beverage company in Canada." Were the Labatt of 1985 to emerge today, through some miracle of time travel, brokers and analysts would recoil in horror.

At its bloated height in 1989, Labatt had sales of $5.4 billion and a profit of $135 million. The new Labatt had become what looked like a fun company. It sold beer in Canada, the United States, and Europe, and also owned TSN, the Discovery Channel, and 90% of the Toronto Blue Jays. John Labatt was also doomed as an independently owned company, a corporate dead man walking that would not last another year and would never get to publish its 1995 annual report.

In the late sixties and throughout the seventies, Labatt began using its excess beer profits to buy what it thought of as complementary businesses such as Ogilvy Flour Mills, which included Catelli-Habitant Ltd. and Ault Foods Ltd. Laura Secord Candy Shops Ltd. was also "repatriated" when Labatt purchased it from a US company. Labatt decided upon its diversification course in part because business professors advising the company predicted beer companies would become heavily regulated utilities, churning consistent profits but with little flexibility. Besides, Molson was doing the same thing with its purchases of chemical companies and firms involved in the oil and gas business.

While beer was producing most of the money, John Labatt Ltd. was in danger of becoming a dull food conglomerate. That soon evaporated with the appointment of Peter Widdrington as president and chief executive officer in 1973. Widdrington was only 43 when he was named to the top spot and was by then a legendary figure in the company. Immensely popular in the organization, he regularly played hockey with the Labatt workers in London. He was good looking and a flamboyant dresser, and wore his blond hair unfashionably long for a Canadian chief executive. A 1983 magazine article describes his unique CEO style: "$500 tailored suits with black earth shoes and a silk tie that appears to have a pattern of small diamond jewels on it; on closer inspection the triangle forms turn out to be jock straps." Widdrington also had a reputation as a ladies' man, which was only heightened at a summer investment meeting when he grew annoyed with a repetitive string of questions posed by a roomful of Bay Street analysts. Intent on trying to find out what Labatt might buy next, one analyst asked Widdrington what his "immediate" plans were. "My immediate plans if I can get out of here, is to get laid this afternoon," Widdrington recalls saying. "And the meeting broke up in about five seconds."

Widdrington stories also abounded within Labatt, not surprising considering he started with the company in 1956 as a salesman, and the tales were told with a mixture of affection and admiration. Widdrington was the master of the unexpected telephone call, dialing up managers at all hours saying he was in so-and-so bar and "Why didn't they have any goddamn Labatt Lite?" He also had his pet peeves, and would often ask staff if they had air conditioning in their company cars, an expensive option for an outfit such as Labatt with a large corporate fleet. "He used to ambush his employees," said Richard Walker, the company design man. Walker recalls being invited to take the trip from Toronto to the London head office in the back of Widdrington's limousine. "The next thing you know he hits me with questions about why from a marketing point of view were we increasing the colours on the Labatt 50 label from four to six. And what were the economic justifications and all. I'm thinking, Jesus Christ how does this guy know all of this?"

Widdrington was not just a beer guy, having acquired some polish before Labatt. Born in Toronto, he'd been educated at Pickering College, a private school, then went on to Queen's University and Harvard where he earned an MBA before joining Labatt as a beer salesman. But as an executive, Widdrington's mind was not always thinking about beer, as the contribution of profits from brewing dropped from 85% of the company's total to well less than half that amount by the end of his tenure. Increasingly, he had to concern himself with such things as gluten price futures or the oft-troubled Laura Secord operation, which dulled Labatt's profits in the mid-1970s after the opening of a new candy factory in Scarborough, just east of Toronto. Visits to Laura Secord's candy plant were memorable. "Here's this huge belt with Turtles moving along it and scads of women on either side of it, packaging the Turtles," Widdrington recalls. "The only problem was the belt was moving about three times faster than the women were packing. At the end of the belt there was a huge pile of Turtles on the floor. It must have been four or five feet high. I said, 'I'll admit I don't know much about the candy business, but even I know that's not right.'"

Laura Secord also included a retail business. At that time, John Labatt was perplexed by what it thought was the unusually high "shrink" at the candy stores. Brewers knew all about shrink, that tiny percentage of beer that never made it out of the tanks and into the bottles. Less than a percent, the minuscule figure added up to a huge amount of beer over time. In the case of Laura Secord, store shrink was running at about 5%. Candy was vanishing into thin air, the ledgers said. It turned out the kindly grey-haired ladies in the smocks behind the counter got to be knowledgeable about the candies by tasting them. "So we quit calling it shrink and started referring to it as marketing expense because it was obvious those grey-haired old ladies were very well thought of by the buying public," Widdrington said. Laura Secord was sold, after 13 troubled years, in 1982, well before Labatt's drive to undo its diversification. Labatt took a loss on the sale.

Under Widdrington, the company decided to make a play for ownership of a major sports franchise, rather than contenting itself with the marketing rights to various sports and teams. Labatt's initial foray ended in failure: in 1969, Labatt was turned down by the National Hockey League in its bid to buy the Oakland Seals hockey team and relocate it to Vancouver. A decade later, in 1978, just a year after Labatt entered the world of Major League Baseball, the company went after the biggest sports prize in Canada, the storied Montreal Canadiens, a team that seemed to own the Stanley Cup.

The bleu, blanc, et rouge, as much a part of Montreal as Molson itself, had ended up in the hands of Peter and Edward Bronfman. The 1971 sale of the city's most important sports team (some would say cultural institution) split the Molson family and ended an association spanning five decades. Ownership of the club and the Forum it played in had been sold by family patriarch Hartland Molson, known simply as "the Senator" to employees and family members, to three brothers from another branch of the family tree. The three Molsons bought control of the sacred Canadiens and the team's shrine, the Forum, in 1968 for $3.3 million. The trio, who saw their future in the stock market, took the team public and within three years was collecting dividends that were six times greater than when they began. With a new capital gains tax looming, the brothers sold the team and the arena company to the Edward-and-Peter side of the Bronfman family for $13.1 million, or about four times what they had paid for it. The Senator was furious and felt betrayed. He released a rare statement to the media in which he said the Canadiens were a "trust" he had sold to the brothers, not just a hockey team or a business. He went on to say that he "couldn't understand the reason for the sale and was bitterly disappointed by this move on the part of David Molson and his brothers," as stated in the biography The Molsons. After 15 years, eight first-place finishes, and six Stanley Cups, the team was no longer in Molson hands. The sale split the family and would end up costing the company substantially. The cost of the television rights for hockey broadcasts increased by half a million dollars the next year. The Senator, who was on holiday when the sale was announced, soon returned and removed a photograph from his office, which showed him with David, Billy, and Peter on the day they purchased the Canadiens, according to the 1983 book The Molson Saga.

About the time Guy Lafleur was leading the Habs to a third-straight Stanley Cup win in 1978, Labatt executives had heard the rumours that the Bronfmans had grown tired of their sports holding. Until that point, Molson seemed to have always owned hockey in Canada due to its long association with television sports broadcasts. Viewership peaked in the spring with the playoffs, the same time that brewers were introducing new brands and ad campaigns, and drinkers were deciding – consciously or unconsciously – what brand they would be drinking all summer.

Seeing an opportunity to upstage Molson in its home market by securing the marketing rights to *Hockey Night in Canada*, Labatt went into action. The brewer's first step was typical. Labatt Brewery president Don McDougall simply called Canadiens' general manager Sam Pollock and found out that, yes, the hockey club and its various holdings were indeed for sale. The Bronfmans hoped to create an auction for hockey's most famous franchise, but as the deadline for bids loomed, no serious bids had yet been put forward. With the deadline for bids just days away and Labatt's $20-million offer formally presented, McDougall and Widdrington were ready to become Habs fans, at least in Quebec.

At this point, the Bronfmans informed the former owners that the Habs were on the block and that Labatt was poised to be the new owner. "They decided at the last minute that because they'd bought it from Molson they should tell them they were selling it to Labatt," McDougall recalls. "It was a pretty shrewd move. Molson called everybody who was anybody in their senior group together and two days later they put together a much more complex but enriched deal." Molson offered $20-million for the team, but agreed to an option on the Montreal Forum and later purchased hockey's holiest shrine. This would not be the last time Labatt would have a brush with the Bronfmans. With the sale of the Habs, the duo of Peter and Edward moved their base of operations from Montreal to Toronto and not long after ended up as the largest shareholder of Labatt.

On the sports front, Labatt had better luck closer to home, landing a new Major League Baseball franchise for Toronto, which entered the American League along with Seattle in 1977. Labatt took a 45% stake in the new club along with businessman Howard Webster and the Canadian Imperial Bank of Commerce. The partnership put up the sum of US$7 million to buy Canada's second baseball franchise. The brewer initially became interested in the idea of a Toronto baseball franchise because of the weakness of its Labatt Blue sales in southern Ontario. Blue might have been the country's most popular brand, but its share was underdeveloped in the heavily populated Golden Horseshoe around Lake Ontario, where drinkers had moved on from Red Cap and Black Label to Molson's Canadian and Export brands.

Labatt promptly put its stamp on the club, naming the team the Blue Jays. (The joke at Labatt, which held a name "contest" for the infant team and received more than 4,000 proposed names, was that people could call the team anything they liked as long as it was "Blue.") Labatt's latest marketing vehicle – people did drink beer while watching the boys of summer, after all – made money right out of the gate by virtue of a modest team payroll and near-league-high attendance. That first year more than 1.7 million fans made their way to windswept Exhibition Stadium, dubbed by fans the Mistake by the Lake, undeterred by the team's miserable 54–107 record of wins and losses.

Within a few years, however, the sinking Canadian dollar would turn the Blue Jays from a money maker to a money loser, as the spectre of Quebec separation grew by the end of the seventies. By 1983, the first year the Jays got a sniff of a pennant race, the fast-shrinking Canadian buck had become the biggest issue for Blue Jays vice-president Paul Beeston, a colourful cigar-chomping executive who had been a chartered accountant with Coopers & Lybrand. Beeston's job was to make the Jays' financial difficulties tolerable because for Labatt, if not for the other two owners, the Jays' worth went far beyond gate receipts and end-of-year profitability.

The Jays also formed the foundation for an ever-growing entertainment company, a business that had little to do with beer but would eventually get Labatt into exotic locales such as backstage with the Rolling Stones. With the Blue Jays and Labatt becoming synonymous in the minds of baseball fans, the company turned its attention to the broadcasting side of the sports business, which was lagging in relation to similar enterprises south of the border. The brewer held discussions with the new ESPN all-sports channel in the United States and considered buying a stake in the company, John Labatt CEO Peter Widdrington said, before deciding to build a Canadian version. It created The Sports Network, one of the Canada's first specialty pay-television channels, hiring CBC veteran

Gordon Craig to run the venture. A former cameraman who'd risen through the ranks, Craig's most significant achievement at the CBC as head of TV sports was the broadcast of the 1976 Montreal Olympic Games, which set a new standard internationally for quantity and quality of coverage.

Getting into the all-sports broadcast business made sense. Labatt already owned a piece of the Jays and had sponsorship rights to other sports properties. Viewers would be predominantly 18-to-49-year-old males, approximately the same group who made up Labatt's major consuming audience. Naming the specialty channel the Action Canada Sports Network in their application to the Canadian Radio-television and Telecommunications Commission, the broadcast hopefuls were lectured by the CRTC about not abusing their brewing connections. In granting the licence, the CRTC secretary-general noted the new channel promised that "fair and equitable advertising policies and practices [would] be maintained" and TSN would "ensure that no preferential treatment will be given to Labatt products." In the end, business fundamentals took care of the CRTC's concerns. The three big breweries all advertised on the all-sports channel, although it did not quickly degenerate into Suds TV. In fact, the single biggest advertiser in TSN's first year was General Motors, not Labatt.

Winning its broadcast licence in 1984, TSN's early years were driven by the success of Canada's two baseball clubs. Its programming core included 40 Blue Jays games and another 40 Montreal Expos games – hockey would come later – and the newest sports network would ride the 1985 pennant run and first playoff appearance of the Jays for all it was worth.

The first specialty channel to appear in Canada along with Much Music, it's not accurate to call TSN a pay channel like the movie channels appearing at about the same time. TSN took in advertising revenue, although it was heavily dependent on subscriber revenue and the cable companies, which acted as intermediaries between TSN and potential subscribers. TSN attracted 600,000 subscribers in its first year of operation, about half of those coming from the Blue

Jays' home base in Ontario. The broadcaster predicted a doubling of that figure to 1.3 million subscribers, TSN's forecast break-even point, by 1987. "We don't expect that we'll achieve much more than that," Gordon Craig said in a 1985 newspaper interview.

Labatt sank $20 million into TSN initially to build a staff, buy programming, and create an infrastructure. In the four months from receiving the CRTC's approval, recalls Peter Widdrington, to the network's launch in the fall of 1984, "We had some rough times. We lost about $25 million after the first two years. One night I had dinner with Ted Rogers at the York Club [in Toronto]. He said he might take half of TSN off our hands. That is when I knew we had something. After that we had much better access to cable. TSN became profitable, very profitable."

TSN can thank the CRTC for its rapid turn to profitability. Initially, TSN was granted a discretionary licence (which meant that people had to consciously decide to pay extra to get the channel). Then, TSN was moved to the basic tier for television subscribers. Cable TV viewers would suddenly get TSN whether they wanted it or not. TSN's subscription base told the tale. Subscriptions went from 1.6 million in February 1989, in keeping with the channel's most optimistic initial predictions, to 5.3 million households by October 1989. When Labatt was forced to sell off its TSN holdings a decade later to a management group headed by Gordon Craig, the broadcast jewel went for $605 million, a remarkable return on an initial $20-million investment.

Labatt was caught up in the go-go eighties, using its steady brewing properties to fuel further expansion. Unlike its earlier purchases under Widdrington and prior management groups, though, the acquisitions were far from the wheat, gluten, and pasta purchases of the sixties and seventies. Along with the launch of TSN, Labatt was fast building an entertainment element to its business as well as boosting its beer holdings internationally. In the same year it launched TSN, Labatt signed a deal with rock concert promoter Concert Productions International and sponsored 42 concerts that summer. Like Molson and Carling, Labatt had come to the conclusion that its customers weren't just sports nuts, they enjoyed music, too. Labatt decided that promotional deals weren't enough and bought a 45% interest in CPI in 1988. It was renamed BCL Entertainment Corp., the initials "BCL" representing partners Bill Ballard, Michael Cohl, and Labatt. BCL, like the Jays, provided Labatt's small army of beer salesmen with added ammunition. At the time, the Jays were a hot ticket, particularly after the SkyDome opened in 1989 and the Jays looked poised to win it all. "People had control of things that were crazy," recalls ad man Gary Prouk. "Guys who under normal circumstances would never have that kind of influence in the world or their own country [suddenly had access to] everything from sports teams to rock concerts. The Rolling Stones for God's sake, you name it." As head of Labatt's key ad agency, Prouk remembers requests from senior Labatt executives such as creating ads to help Blue Jays outfielder Joe Carter get voted onto the American League All-Star team.

Labatt found it cool hanging out with the Stones and other rock royalty, but the company got into the concert promotion game mostly because Molson seemed to own the medium. It was Molson, after all, that had punctured the Labatt balloon by marrying beer ads with the emerging art form of rock videos. And Molson would not be allowed to hold sway over music the way it had reigned over hockey for all those spring playoff runs. At the time, no one questioned whether Labatt should get into concert promotion, but the beer company added nothing to BCL apart from its money, which should have been a warning to the brewer. BCL's value, like that of CPI before it, was based largely on the personal connections Michael Cohl had with the elite of the rock world. He is credited with convincing the Rolling Stones to end an acrimonious split and begin touring again in 1989. Cohl revolutionized the city-based business of staging rock concerts with his winning offer to get the Stones on the same stage again: "$40 million for 40 shows" – about double what the Stones expected per show. The only problem was that Cohl didn't have $40 million, and he hadn't asked Labatt whether they would come up with the cash. In the end, Cohl found the money and the Steel Wheels tour got rolling. (Because the tour was insured by Lloyd's of London, the Stones' members had to take physicals. Even Keith Richards passed, *Fortune* reported at the time.)

Under Labatt Breweries president Sid Oland, the reserved scion of the Nova Scotia brewing family, the company took on a distinct Hollywood-North flavour. In 1987, the brewer bought half of radio and TV ad jingle house Supercorp, and, in partnership with jingle man Syd Kessler, it added the country's largest TV commercial company, Partners' Film Co., a year later. It then acquired media-buying powerhouse Harrison Young Pesonen & Newell. In the Toronto-centric advertising world, Supercorp was a dominant player and it was difficult to film a commercial, make commercial music, or buy ad space without touching it. Labatt was not only funnelling much of the tens of millions it spent on advertising each year back to itself, but Supercorp was also capturing the spending of other big advertisers.

Sadly for Labatt, Supercorp failed to live up to its name. Gary Prouk remembers how Scali and other ad firms working for Labatt were ordered to feed the conglomerate. "They would send memos to all their agencies. You have to use Labatt facilities. You have to use our production companies. They were out of their minds. We didn't, by the way." Within a few short years, Syd Kessler, a jovial bear of a man with a huge biker beard and an easygoing style, gave up running the business and sold his share of Supercorp. The grand experiment a failure, the various pieces of the ad conglomerate were sold off, in most cases to the original principals who had sold out to Supercorp.

Labatt's exit from the concert business demonstrates the preparedness of beer companies to jettison non-core assets, particularly ones that were the passion of presidents twice removed. By 1995, the employment contracts with Michael Cohl and Bill Ballard had expired, and Cohl sued Labatt for $18 million for his stake. Labatt countered with an offer for $14 million, though it is uncertain how much BCL was worth without Cohl's star power to bring in mega rock bands like the Stones. Eventually, the fight was settled out of court. Labatt was desperate to become a pure beer company, so desperate, in fact, that it would sell distractions such as BCL to anyone, even Molson. Sure enough, Molson and MCA Concerts Canada Ltd. purchased BCL in the summer of 1996 for an undisclosed price.

Labatt's altercations with the music business didn't end there. A few years later, Molson and MCA, now called House of Blues Entertainment, took Labatt to court over a series of "Out of the Blue" promotions that featured live acts such as The Red Hot Chili Peppers and Moist. Contest participants had a chance to win an invitation to an event that Labatt termed a promotion but House of Blues and Molson described as a concert. House of Blues said in court documents that BCL had sold away its rights to stage concerts for a 10-year period. Labatt countered that the live bands were giving "musical performances," not live concerts, and all the attendees of the event were contest winners rather than music fans who lined up and purchased their own tickets. Labatt was trying to sell beer, not stage concerts, the argument went. An Ontario judge didn't buy it. Labatt was eventually forced to settle, and requires permission from House of Blues and Molson anytime it wants to use live music to sell its beer during the 10-year contract period.

10
Labatt Goes Foreign

Labatt watchers, an audience made up of analysts and institutional investors, were not overly concerned with the company's forays outside of its core business. Win or lose, the entertainment forays did not affect the cash-machine beer business. The company lost overall on the Supercorp.-BCL plays, but won big with TSN and the Blue Jays, perennial playoff contenders for more than a decade leading up to their two consecutive World Series victories. While failure outside the beer business would be tolerated, Labatt's brewing acquisitions in Europe and elsewhere were judged by a higher standard. Labatt's "failure" to successfully expand outside of Canada in the eyes of its Bay Street audience resulted in the loss of independence for the proud, century-and-a-half-old company.

Labatt had all the necessary conditions to build a world-class international beer company. Like its two main rivals, it was fortunate to operate in a highly regulated, highly taxed country, where steady profits were all but guaranteed. Labatt was the most aggressive and innovative of the big three brewers and, like Molson, also benefitted from stable ownership.

Jake Moore, the canny accountant who waited out the failed sale of John Labatt to US beer maker Schlitz in the sixties, is credited with transforming Labatt from a regional brewer into a fast-growing conglomerate. He moved from Labatt's top job to Brascan Ltd., where for a decade he built the company into a $3-billion conglomerate and Canada's sixth-largest company by 1979. The brewer's controlling shareholder, with a 40% stake, Brascan sheltered Labatt from potential acquirers. Moore's reign at Brascan ended in 1979 when Peter Bronfman's Edper Equities Ltd. purchased control of the company. Labatt, which had unsuccessfully attempted to buy the Montreal Canadiens from Edper just a year earlier, would continue under the controlling ownership of Brascan, as per the agreement between Edper and Brascan. Like Molson, Labatt would enjoy the access to capital of a public company without the worry of corporate predators, thanks to Brascan's continued controlling position. With a strong parent owning 40% of the company, Labatt could take a longer-term view of business, rather than worrying that a few bad quarters would result in an opportunistic buyer attempting to win control of the company.

While Edper's takeover of Brascan meant John Labatt Ltd. would still have a strong parent company guaranteeing its future, Edper's ownership brought management strife. Peter Widdrington, the flamboyant beer salesman turned Labatt CEO, clashed regularly with the board of directors. Widdrington wanted to expand the beer business, particularly in the United States, but the Edper-dominated board of directors wasn't interested in such bold moves, Widdrington recalls. In particular, the Labatt chief wanted to buy US beer giant Miller Brewing, a holding of US food and tobacco company Philip Morris Co. Widdrington held exploratory talks with Miller, but was not supported by the Brascan directors, Widdrington contends.

The purchase of Miller would have entailed huge risk for Labatt. The price would have run into the billions and the less-than-stellar track record of Canadian companies operating businesses in the United States was hardly reassuring. Widdrington certainly knew only too well how cutthroat the American beer market was. As general manager of Labatt's California beer company in the mid-1960s, he saw the growth of Colorado's Coors Brewing Co. in the west and the unstoppable national expansion of Anheuser-Busch. One worry at Labatt was that, while Miller's corporate ties to the enormous Philip Morris entity put some restraint on Anheuser-Busch, that tendency would be unleashed should a relatively small foreigner such as Labatt acquire Miller.

Kept back from a blockbuster purchase, Labatt Breweries, under the direction of president Sid Oland, contented itself with a series of more modest and geographically scattered acquisitions. In 1987, it bought Pennsylvania's Latrobe Brewing Co., the makers of Rolling Rock, a premium-priced beer sold in a distinctive green bottle, which has never been more than a niche beer in the United States. To Labatt's chagrin the beer, which its executives say would be a strong seller in Canada, has never been sold north of the border because of a contractual restriction contained in Labatt's Budweiser brewing licence with Anheuser-Busch.

That same year, the Canadian brewer launched Labatt Lager (Blue Light under a foreign guise) in England under a deal that had regional brewery Greenall Whitley brew and distribute the brand. Not content to let others manage the brand, Labatt soon began pouring resources into the United Kingdom, a market that quickly proved to be far different from the cozy Canadian oligopoly it was accustomed to.

By 1989, Labatt's Edper-Brascan ownership decided Peter Widdrington should no longer act as both chairman and chief executive officer. Widdrington was asked to recommend a CEO. He produced a short list: George Taylor, president of Labatt's food businesses; Sid Oland, president of the profitable and growing Labatt Breweries; and Ed Bradley, Widdrington's right-hand man in corporate development and planning. "George came to me about three months afterwards and said he didn't want to be considered as a candidate anymore," Widdrington recalled. "As time went on I went to Brascan and suggested to them that maybe I should stay on another six or eight months, and try to find a guy from the outside."

In the end, it was decided that Sid Oland, who had spent a lifetime in the beer business and, like Widdrington, held an MBA from Harvard, would get the top spot. On the surface, the decision did not seem particularly controversial. In 1989, before the final decision was made, Molson and Carling merged, "Blue Zone" entered its second year, and the beer business earned $158 million on revenue of $1.8 billion, while Taylor's food side needed exactly twice the revenue, $3.6 billion, to churn out a profit of $106 million. By that time, it had also been decided that Taylor's food empire should shrink. The Catelli pasta operation and the wine business had been sold off in 1988. (Headed by Allan Jackson and Donald Triggs, Labatt's cast-off wine business would grow into Vincor Inc., today Canada's largest winemaker.) Just as enthusiastically as it had embraced diversification in the previous two decades, Labatt was now determined to build businesses in which it had the expertise and heft to be a world-class player. A quick analysis pointed to beer, and not much else.

Whether the CEO position was taken up by Oland or Taylor, the new leader's style would be a dramatic change, compared to that of the easygoing and glamorous Widdrington. George Taylor was the antithesis of Widdrington. Quiet and thoughtful, Taylor was the solid and reliable stereotypical accountant. Oland, who had joined Labatt after his family sold its East Coast brewing business in 1971, was more of a mystery. The product of one of Atlantic Canada's wealthiest families, Oland was described as very private and difficult to get to know.

When Peter Widdrington finally tapped Oland for the top job, the outgoing CEO took pains to state that he would "continue to be involved in all major decision making." It was clear, however, that Widdrington was no longer calling the shots. Meanwhile, George Taylor, the finance-based executive who was now running Labatt's non-brewing businesses, was in charge of selling.

Under Oland, Labatt increasingly looked overseas for growth opportunities, rather than to the United States. Barely into the United Kingdom, Oland decided to push onward to the Continent. In 1990, the company purchased not one, but two breweries in the European wine stronghold of Italy. Added to the Labatt empire – which now included 42% of Canada's beer sales, a US import arm, and a toehold in the United Kingdom – was Prinz Brau Brewing in central Italy and Birra Moretti in the north. Labatt told investors it made the Italian investments with an eye towards the upcoming European union in 1992. Unstated was the hope that with the two breweries it could turn a nation of wine drinkers on to beer.

Labatt's Italian play was in fact two investments, and neither looked like a good one at first blush. Bill Bourne, the former Carling O'Keefe marketer who wound up running Italy for Labatt, thought it "a disaster. We were losing a million dollars a month." Prinz Brau, Italy's number-six brewer, was a discount player in the market and was acquired more for its excess production capacity than for its brand portfolio.

Birra Moretti, the seventh-largest brewer, had real potential. Founded in 1859 and into its fifth generation of family ownership, the northern brewer's market was underdeveloped in the rest of the country. Moretti was well known throughout the country to young Italian men who, during their military service, spent much of their time in the north of the country, drinking Moretti beer. It just wasn't widely available in other parts of the country. Labatt's intention was to change all that.

Bourne, the quiet, unassuming marketer who'd done stints at Carling and Labatt, proved a fortunate if unlikely choice to head up the Italian operation. Appointed as general manager for a six-month tour, Bourne and his wife ended up staying for five years. His tenure, however, hardly got off to an auspicious beginning. Fresh from Canada, Bourne pulled up to the Moretti brewery for the first time, only to be greeted by a group of men out in front of the main building. "I was thinking, this is great. Everyone lined up to greet the new manager from Labatt," recalls Bourne. "Making our way through this mob, I asked, 'Who are these guys?'" His Italian assistant replied, "They are all creditors, *signor*."

"Signor Bourne" never did manage to master the Italian language, speaking through his assistants for five years, though Labatt's man from Canada assumed the patriarchal mantle of the departed Morettis that the brewery workers so craved. "I staggered out of there with 80% of the job done. In five years, we doubled the volume, tripled the revenue. We took it from losing $1 million a month to making $5 million a year."

Italy proved to be a consolation prize in Labatt's quest for big international acquisitions. Labatt entertained the idea of buying the beer business of Australia's Bond Breweries for as much as $1.8 billion, but in the end backed away from what was perceived to be too great a risk. It was also outbid for Spain's largest brewery, Cruz del Campo, which Guinness forked out a handsome $1.2 billion to acquire.

Thwarted in its quest for the big deal, Labatt lavished more management and cash upon its British venture. Not satisfied merely to ink a licensing arrangement with a brewer in the country, Labatt signed a number of agreements under which it essentially rented excess capacity and made its beer with brewmasters sent over from Canada. Labatt spent money as if it intended to stay, as well. Its initial £6.5-million advertising campaign for Labatt Lager was a series of television commercials starring a red-coated character called Malcolm the Mountie. More Dudley Do-Right than the polite hero of TV's *Due South*, Malcolm was depicted being tossed about by thugs, scaling walls aided by suction cups, and paddling a canoe up the Thames, all in search of Labatt's Lager. The campaign, which ran during most of the brewer's push in Britain, boasted the tag line "Malcolm the Mountie always gets his can." Done in the irreverent British style, the beer-loving Mountie landed Labatt in hot water with the ever-vigilant Royal Canadian Mounted Police. The Mounties failed to find the humour in a character dressed as one of their own, obsessed with tracking down a can of beer and, in the end, downing an alcoholic beverage in uniform. Executives were summoned to a "friendly" meeting in Ottawa where they attempted unsuccessfully to explain the British humour behind Malcolm to an unsmiling roomful of RCMP brass and their lawyers. The nation's cops asked Labatt to drop the campaign. However, since the Mounties had no jurisdiction over Labatt UK, the campaign continued. (Just a couple of years later, the Mounties signed a marketing deal with Walt Disney Co., provoking gasps of horror across the country.)

Labatt UK also went "native." Dissatisfied with its number-nine ranking among lager brands, it embarked on a pub-buying binge. In Canada, beer is consumed mostly in the home, but in Britain, most beer is quaffed in licensed establishments. Many pubs are "tied" to a particular brewery through outright ownership or hefty financial deals. Within a couple of years, Labatt assembled a portfolio of more than 500 establishments. The pub crawl cobbled together enough of a stake to occupy management time, but was not enough to really drive sales of Labatt brands in the country.

If Labatt did not have enough distractions overseas, it certainly had them at home. The brief Oland era was dogged by persistent rumours that controlling shareholder Brascan was trying to sell its 40% stake in the company to prop up the Bronfmans' Edper Group of struggling businesses. The rumours would not go away because they were true. John Labatt CEO Oland and executive vice-president Taylor were asked to find a brewer willing to swallow the Bronfmans' entire position. For a year, Taylor held talks with companies around the world, finally settling on Japan's Kirin, which was keenly interested in the brewer's strong position in the British Columbia market with its close proximity to the United States. Labatt went so far as to give Japanese lessons to some of its executives and have Japanese business cards printed for them. Then, as abruptly as Edper-Brascan had decided to sell, the Labatt stake was taken off the market.

After what Taylor describes as a "serious falling out" with the board, Oland stepped down as CEO in 1992 after just three years in the top job. Today, Oland says little about his departure. "[Brascan] said, 'You won't like what you are going to have to do, and more specifically what you won't be able to do.' And I looked at them and said, 'You're right.'" Taylor, in England on vacation at the time, got a call requesting that he come back to Canada for a "corporate emergency." "My wife was not at all pleased," says Taylor. Even though he had declared that he didn't want the job of president and chief executive a few years earlier, Taylor was thrust into the top position at Labatt by Brascan.

The reluctant president did not enjoy much of a honeymoon with the Bay Street crowd. Announced at Labatt's annual meeting in the fall of 1992, Taylor's elevation to CEO was something of a surprise, and investors always hate surprises. Far from flamboyant, the accountant now in charge of one of Canada's sexiest companies – they sold beer, after all, and owned TSN and the World Series champion Blue Jays – stuck to his knitting. The big news at the start of the Taylor era was that Labatt would be split in two, and the dairy operation he had run would be spun off into a new company, Ault Foods. The novel decision to give Labatt investors shares in the new dairy company proportionate to their ownership of the parent company was crafted as a tax-saving solution for big shareholders, including the people at Edper-controlled Brascan. Despite the fact that Labatt's shares were trading near $30 (up more than $5 in a few months) and the company had just announced a special $3-per-share dividend to shareholders, the mood at Taylor's inauguration was hardly celebratory. Small investors grumbled that the company had bowed to political pressure when it replaced the traditional maple leaf on Labatt Blue bottles in Quebec with a sheaf of wheat. Institutional investors, notable for their nicer suits and polite silence at annual meetings, decided to bide their time, confident a pure-play brewing company with a few entertainment assets tacked on would be of irresistible interest to a foreign brewer willing to pay a high price.

Although reserved publicly, the institutional shareholders, pension and mutual fund managers mostly, were unhappy with Labatt in their own way. As Labatt board member and corporate lawyer John Tory discovered when dispatched on a scouting trip to canvass big shareholders, the big money was generally hostile. The main reason was that 40% controlling stake. Investors were down on the slumping Bronfman empire during this period and were unhappy with how the financial conglomerate was dominating the direction of Labatt, making a takeover of the company unlikely due to their large controlling position. "I think George [Taylor] suffered for that," said Herb Solway, another Labatt director at the time. The institutional investors were soon rewarded for their patience, however, for after months of heated denials, the Edper-Brascan ownership group sold its interest in a $1-billion bought deal to brokerage firms. The largest such transaction at the time, a group of Bay Street firms purchased Edper's Labatt shares for $28.25, having already lined up big institutions as buyers for the shares.

Edper's Brascan managed to exit Labatt near the height of the brewer's share price, a situation that left investors with high-priced shares and high expectations. George Taylor, the financial fixer, may have been the man to shape up the company and sell off the losers acquired in the eighties. Described as a funny, compassionate CEO by former Labatt corporate staff, Taylor was reserved in public – just what people expected of a balding accountant – squinting out from behind thick eyeglasses. All the same, Taylor brushed aside the Bay Street sniping about his management and refused to make concessions such as dumping the Edper directors of Labatt's board. Although Edper executive Jack Cockwell was gone, investors wanted to remove the rest of the directors connected with the former controlling shareholder: Peter Bronfman, Trevor Eyton, and Sam Pollock, the Labatt chairman. In their place, Bay Street wanted new directors, independent of Labatt or its former owner. Taylor wouldn't budge. He considered Bronfman – an amiable and supportive billionaire – a confidant and potential ally. Eyton, the politically well-connected corporate lawyer, "provided solid, capable, and knowledgeable governance to the board on a variety of matters, and Sam quite frankly was just a good chairman," says Taylor. The issue about the directors "was an enormous red herring the market created. It created a negative view of me on the part of the funds."

While Taylor lacked the charisma of former CEO Peter

Widdrington, he harboured the same North American ambitions for Labatt. The distracting European adventures would be put aside. The UK and Italian operations would continue but Labatt did not plan to add to investments on the other side of the Atlantic. Taylor viewed the world's largest brewer, Anheuser-Busch, as an ally in the struggle to dominate the continent. With the world's largest brewer on its side, Labatt would relegate the alliance of Miller and Molson to secondary status. It was that thinking that drove Taylor to make the most ambitious and daring investment in Labatt's modern history, the $1-billion purchase of a 30% interest in Mexican brewer FEMSA Cerveza SA during the summer of 1994.

FEMSA was quite simply the largest beer acquisition in Labatt's history. The northern company agreed to spend $720 million for a 22% interest in the family-controlled Mexican brewer, with a pledge to later take its holding up to 30%, bringing the price to $1 billion. Over time, it was thought, FEMSA would sell control in the brewer of such brands as Dos Equis Lager and Tecate. For Labatt, the risks were huge but so were the rewards. This was not a deal to slowly break into the UK or Italian markets. FEMSA controlled 48% of the Mexican market, which was twice the size of Canada's. FEMSA's largest brewery at the time produced 6 million hectolitres of beer annually (or about 220 million cases), triple the 2 million hectolitres produced by Labatt's biggest Canadian brewery.

Mexico also represented the future for brewers in North America. Lucrative as it was, stagnant population growth made the Canadian beer business a zero-sum game of expensive market-share swaps and no growth. Labatt was committed to slowly growing its position in the United States, the only way to tackle the world's largest and most difficult beer market. Mexico, however, was a Latin version of Canada. A government-protected duopoly, FEMSA and Grupo Modelo, the brewer of Corona, together owned the market. Most intriguing, half the population was under 19 with their peak beer-drinking years ahead of them. FEMSA would also provide product for Labatt USA, which distributed Labatt Blue and Rolling Rock across the country at a time when Corona was the fastest-growing import beer in the States.

The risks seemed pretty obvious. Besides the sheer scale – Labatt asked to buy only 22% of FEMSA at first because of the financial strain of the deal – Mexico had just joined the North American Free Trade pact at the start of 1994. In many ways Mexico was not ready for the "prime time" of the NAFTA world. It was for all intents and purposes still a one-party state and was highly dependent on foreign investment (such as Labatt's) to rebuild its economy. By 1993, the flood of investment had begun to slacken and in March 1994, just months before Labatt finalized its FEMSA purchase, the presidential candidate was assassinated, putting the worth of the peso in question in relation to the mighty US dollar.

It took Taylor well over a year to persuade Labatt's directors to support the FEMSA investment, a span of time that was also spent convincing the families behind FEMSA that hooking up with Labatt was preferable to doing a deal with Miller Brewing. The Milwaukee company already owned a small stake in FEMSA parent Fomento Economico Mexican SA, a huge beverage and packaging concern. Labatt did not have the bucks of the boys from Milwaukee, but they had one thing going for them: they weren't Americans. "There was no way that I could compete with Miller unless I could convince the Mexican family that we were better guys, we were nicer guys, than the Americans," says Taylor. "So we spent an awful lot of time courting the family that owned the business, and that was done largely by Sam Pollock and myself."

Taylor eventually got the support of his board to do the deal, but he never convinced Labatt's shareholders that the purchase made sense. "I could never get the market to understand the Mexican transaction." Labatt did manage to upstage Molson for a brief time, announcing its FEMSA transaction at Toronto's SkyDome the same sunny day in July its archrival was holding its 1994 annual meeting just blocks away. A bold acquisition, the Mexican deal failed to win over skeptical institutional investors who still preferred the "safer"

Molson conglomerate under Mickey Cohen. Part of the problem was that while Taylor was willing to sell the sizzle of Mexico, the market's size, and the potential of all those drinkers in their prime, the strategy underlying the deal, namely the Labatt-Anheuser alliance, was not fully explained. "It was basically getting a stake in the heart of the Molson-Miller relationship and taking Miller out of Mexico." The Canadian CEO had previously approached August Busch, his Budweiser partner, for his blessing on FEMSA. "When I first met with Busch and said, 'Lookit, I'm going to pursue a very aggressive strategy to get into Mexico,' he was very angry." Taylor then asked Busch if he wanted a repeat of the marketing and new-product battles Budweiser was currently waging with Miller in the United States in the booming Mexican market, where it had a major interest in Modelo. Busch "thought about it for 10 minutes and said, 'I hope you get Mexico, what can I do to help?' He understood what we were trying to achieve in knocking both Miller and Molson out of the box."

Taylor had just pulled off the sort of stunning coup that Widdrington had dreamed about. But Taylor unfortunately didn't have the luxury of a controlling shareholder since Edper-Brascan had exited the scene. Hugo Powell, president of Labatt Breweries, was doing an excellent job of fighting the beer wars on the home front and milking maximum profits out of its main business, investors thought, but here was George risking the profits. Taylor proved unwilling and unable to cozy up to big institutional investors and the analysts that advised them. At one analyst meeting, Taylor angrily told the investors who held control of his company to "sell your shares" if they didn't like the direction Labatt was going. Fund managers, many of whom had bought in during the Edper-Brascan sell-off, were not going to take Taylor up on his offer and dump $30 shares when Labatt was trading in the low $20 range.

Whether it was true or not, Bay Street complained in the financial press that Taylor and his management group were unfocused and undisciplined. Taylor laid out his rationale for the Mexican investment and took his time with plans to sell non-core assets, trying to get the best price and pay the lowest corporate capital gains tax possible. Nowhere was that more evident than in the case of the sports and entertainment businesses, which the company had concluded had peaked in value. Labatt had as much as $1 billion worth of assets in the form of the Blue Jays, the Toronto SkyDome stadium, and its broadcast assets, including TSN, the country's most valuable specialty channel, and the newly launched Discovery Channel. But Taylor the accountant was slowed by the tax implications of cashing in on the success of its entertainment assets. Labatt had carried the businesses on its books for next to nothing, meaning big capital gains payouts should it decide to unload them.

While Taylor was working behind the scenes to orchestrate the FEMSA purchase, impatient investors were demanding that Labatt do something to unlock the value of the other assets. Pressed at a Friday analyst meeting in June 1994 at TSN's new broadcast centre in Toronto, Taylor talked about selling a large portion of its 90% stake in the Blue Jays, then taking the remainder of that interest, bundling it with its SkyDome holding and the broadcast channels, and selling the whole thing to the public in a stock offering. Analysts seized on the announcement, made two weeks before the FEMSA deal, as proof that Labatt was finally doing something to address their concerns. The reality was that Labatt had no such concrete plan to take the entertainment division public. "After [Taylor's speech], I was surrounded by all the analysts, and they said, 'Is it 30 days, is it 45 days?' They thought we had announced we were going to do it," says Bob Vaux, Labatt's chief financial officer and a Taylor loyalist. "We hadn't even started to do work on it. And then everyone kept calling me saying, 'When is it going to happen?' I was to the point of saying, 'It's not going to happen,' but it was difficult to say." Buying, not selling, was Labatt's priority at the time. It was wrapping up the FEMSA investment, not worrying about the mechanics of selling all or part of its non-brewing businesses. In a few months, after a showdown with the institutional investors who controlled its fate, Labatt's corporate focus shifted from spinning off assets to getting the best price for Labatt in a takeover executives felt was inevitable given the lack of a controlling shareholder, depressed stock price, and hostility to management among several large institutional shareholders, Vaux says.

Rather than getting smaller and more focused as investors had hoped, the company seemed preoccupied with acquisition plans in that summer of 1994. First there was the Mexican deal, then a few weeks later, it leaked out that the company was looking at bidding for Madison Square Garden, a sports holding that included the New York Rangers, basketball's New York Knicks, and a regional sports cable-television network. Labatt, which had unsuccessfully backed a bid for the Toronto Raptors NBA franchise, still held ambitions to develop a Toronto sports empire, creating one corporate umbrella for its Jays and Toronto Argonaut franchises, adding the Raptors, and eventually the Toronto Maple Leafs, along with broadcaster TSN. Madison Square Garden was the Big Apple model of how Labatt wanted to do things in Toronto, and Taylor and his executive team wanted to take a look at MSG's finances. Labatt had no intention of making a bid, it just wanted a look at the books to see how such an entity functioned. But rather than stating that reassuring fact, either to the investment community at large or privately to the key fund managers, Taylor insisted in newspaper articles that the company was interested in the New York sports holdings. Labatt soon dropped out of the MSG bidding, but the damage had been done.

Investors were furious. Here, they thought, was a company ignoring the wishes of shareholders who were only interested in ever-increasing beer profits and cost-cutting initiatives, which Labatt Breweries president Hugo Powell was delivering. They did not want the international acquisition binges that parent John Labatt appeared to be indulging in. Taylor may have gotten away with such conduct if Edper-Brascan had still owned 40%, though it is far from certain whether the Bronfman crew would have supported the Mexican gamble. The point was moot. Labatt was widely held. Those fund managers Taylor had advised to sell if they didn't like Labatt's strategy controlled the fate of the company, not the chief executive officer.

Those powerful investors found their chance to tell Taylor who was boss, and that his days were numbered, at Labatt's annual meeting in September 1994, just two months after the Mexican investment through FEMSA. Institutional shareholders such as pension plans and investment funds loathed such "poison pill," anti-takeover plans because they were seen to deter potential bidders for companies and entrench senior management. Such poison pills usually make hostile takeovers more difficult, allowing management more time to stall and search for alternatives, but they rarely beat back unfriendly bidders. Prior to the meeting, Labatt's management, with the support of its directors, introduced its own poison-pill plan. Aware of the hostility to the measure from large shareholders led by fund company Altamira Management Ltd., Labatt weakened the more objectionable aspects of its rights plan, removing some of the discretionary power of management and directors in the face of an unsolicited bid. Confident of approval, Labatt put the shareholders' rights package on the agenda at the Toronto annual meeting.

As any follower of Canadian business knows, annual meetings are usually dull, predictable rituals. Typically, the corporate auditor is reappointed, the slate of directors is unanimously elected, and the CEO, and perhaps another senior officer, deliver a speech. Questions are usually deferential, aside from the queries of one or two strange souls who seem to flit from one AGM to the next, and dissent is dealt with behind the scenes in the weeks and months before the event. Labatt's 1994 general meeting was anything but typical. Echoing the combative remarks he'd made earlier to analysts and fund managers, George Taylor spoke derisively of "third-party armchair strategists" who wanted Labatt to sell assets and buy back shares. "Over the last 12 to 18 months, we have listened carefully to the financial communities; we have heard that Labatt has no vision, no growth opportunity, and no commitment to building shareholder value. Now in the wake of [the proposed sports spinoff and FEMSA], we hear that our strategy is faulty, perhaps misguided, and too bold."

After Taylor's speech, Labatt's executives successfully elected its slate of directors including rising-star Hugo Powell and those dis-agreeable directors (in the eyes of Bay Street) Peter Bronfman, Trevor Eyton, and Labatt chairman Sam Pollock. The unhappy insti-tutions held their fire for the bigger issue of the poison pill. Management rarely loses critical votes at meetings because small shareholders typically return proxy forms blank, thereby handing the vote to management. This annual meeting was no different in that respect. A total of 2,450 shareholders "voted" in favour of the poison pill, versus just 167 against. But while the No side was low in numbers, it was high in holdings. The large institutions behind the rebuke won by 52% to 48%, and when the tally was announced, the well-dressed men, traditionally so silent, erupted. "Look at 167 peo-ple voting enough of the stock. That is pension guys that can actually vote saying, 'Not a hope in hell,'" CIBC Wood Gundy vice-president Fred Walsh said at the meeting. (CIBC at the time was Labatt's bank while Wood Gundy was Labatt's underwriter.) Scott Penman, an executive with pension fund Investors Group Ltd., said following the breakup of the meeting that the decision was more a vote against Labatt management than a statement against rights plans. "We are unhappy with the lack of focus that management seems to have."

More than anything, it was Taylor's unwillingness to court the large shareholders who were now in effect his bosses and his inabil-ity to pull the trigger on the sports and entertainment assets that led to the Bay Street defeat. "There were three issues that I had to deal with all the time with the market, on top of the business perform-ance," remembers Taylor. "'What are you going to do about the sports businesses, and the entertainment businesses?' was the first question. 'Why in the hell did you ever invest in Mexico? What are you doing about getting rid of the bad apples that are on your board from Brascan?'" Taylor successfully kept the Brascan executives on the board, although the frustration of the Bay Street moneymen with Labatt's continued interest in the sports business and terribly timed investment in Mexico proved to be rallying points. The man who built his own farmhouse in St. Mary's, Ontario, may have been the right CEO to fix the company, but he proved to be the right man at the wrong time once the Edper-Brascan group took its exit. It would take just one final piece of bad news to close out the Taylor era at Labatt.

In December, the Mexican peso began a free fall as political insta-bility led foreign investors to pull billions out of the country. Within a couple of months, the peso's plunge had wiped out half the value of Labatt's initial $720-million investment in FEMSA Cerveza. Labatt had not hedged its Mexican purchase against a possible devaluation of the peso – an insurance policy CFO Bob Vaux had decided was too expensive for what would be a long-term investment. Vaux learned of the peso crisis when he called his office from Busch Gardens, Florida, where he was on a family vacation. "I asked, 'So is anything going on?' and they said, 'Well, have you heard about the Mexican currency?'" Nine months after buying its stake, Labatt was forced to write down the carrying value of its FEMSA holding by $272 million and warned of another $110-million writedown to come if the cur-rency continued its swoon. Taylor admirably continued to talk to the business media, patiently explaining that the FEMSA purchase was a long-term investment that would recover in value over time. The only harm, his story went, was to FEMSA's immediate profit contri-bution to Labatt.

But if FEMSA hurt Labatt's bottom line, it did even more to make Labatt a takeover target. Shareholders wanted the John Labatt of old – a stripped-down, massively profitable Canadian brewery – which hadn't existed for decades. Instead, they saw a high-risk gamble in a "third world" market that, according to them, had predictably blown up in Labatt's face just months later. Stripped of its long-time corporate protector with the departure of the Edper-Brascan compa-nies, its management team under fire from powerful shareholders, the World Series titleholder Blue Jays off the field because of a league lockout, the Mexican mess proved to be the tipping point.

Labatt management knew from the day Edper-Brascan sold their control position that the company was a takeover waiting to happen.

So they were not surprised when, after the defeat of its poison pill and the peso meltdown, the company was being stalked. The pursuer was none other than leveraged-buyout specialist Gerry Schwartz. His Toronto company, Onex Corp., was somewhat unique in Canada as a firm that specialized in identifying poorly run, undervalued companies that could be acquired, stripped down, and ultimately made more profitable before being spun off at a handsome profit to public shareholders. Before Labatt, however, Onex had never made a hostile run at a company, had never gone for a public company, and had never tried to swallow an outfit as big as John Labatt Ltd. Its preferred method of approach was to gain the approval of owners and management, and then proceed. In the case of the country's largest brewer, Schwartz lined up powerful partners in the form of the giant Ontario Teachers' Pension Plan Board and South American brewer Quilmes Industrial SA. They would provide the bulk of the cash. Onex planned to throw in some capital, but its main contribution would be in orchestrating the deal and running the new beer company afterwards.

Onex's interest in Labatt first surfaced in the media in February 1995, but Taylor claims that his company knew of Schwartz's intentions well before that time. "We had a mole at Teachers [the Ontario Teachers Pension Plan Board] who was keeping us informed of what [Schwartz] was doing," said Taylor. Labatt was just one of five vulnerable companies that Onex and Teachers had identified as prey. "So we knew what was happening, we knew what was coming. I made numerous attempts actually to speak to Gerry, unsuccessfully." Against his instincts, Schwartz had accepted legal advice that talking to Taylor before making a bid would be the wrong move, that somehow Labatt would use the information against Onex. "I listened to that advice. And I was stupid," Schwartz later said. The takeover king's refusal to speak to the sheep farmer from St. Mary's made it personal and only hardened Taylor's resolve to fight any Onex-led takeover.

What Schwartz did not understand was just how receptive Labatt's management would have been to a friendly takeover. In the handful of years leading to this point, Labatt had almost sold Brascan's interest to Japan's Kirin, led the way to negotiate a new US-Canada trade deal for beer, sold off a slew of non-core assets, and finessed the FEMSA purchase. The plan to spin off the sports and broadcast businesses, a move so desired by the financial analysts, had barely begun before being put aside. Efforts to deal with its TSN and Blue Jays holdings had been abandoned in the wake of the poison-pill defeat at the annual meeting and the knowledge Onex was pursuing Labatt. "My sense was that the company probably did need a change of control," recalls Bob Vaux, Labatt's chief financial officer. "Under a change in control, the company could get restructured and the best thing for the shareholders was effectively a change in control, and I still believe that. After control changed, someone else could sell off these assets, someone could do all the stuff required."

George Taylor was ready to make a graceful exit, if only Gerry Schwartz would open the door for him. Instead, Taylor received a call in May from Schwartz saying they had to meet at the end of the day. Taylor, who controlled the Blue Jays but had no use for sports generally, was going to one of the two Toronto Maple Leafs games he attended each year, and dinner afterwards with friends. Schwartz suggested dinner, which an annoyed Taylor declined. The Labatt CEO did agree to speak to Schwartz face to face, and tracked down his hockey-loving chairman Sam Pollock at the Leafs game. The two sides eventually gathered for a midnight meeting at the Four Seasons hotel. Schwartz, flanked by Onex executive Anthony Melman and Norbeto Morita, CEO of Argentina's Quilmes, laid out his cards. He would be making an offer amounting to $24 a share at 7:30 the next morning and he wanted Labatt's public support. "I just said, 'The offer is totally unsatisfactory and you can't possibly have my support going at it this way,'" Taylor recalls saying. "'You can't make a public announcement and expect me and my board to stand up and say, "Well you know that's great." It can't happen.'" After rebuffing Taylor's suggestion to work out a friendly deal, Schwartz slapped down a hostile bid that was certain to raise the Labatt chief's ire. "Of course he was infuriated," said Schwartz. "And he worked tirelessly, ceaselessly, to find an alternative," he admitted in Peter C. Newman's book *Titans*.

The two combatants could not have been more different. Hugely wealthy and well connected as a fundraiser for the federal Liberals, Schwartz was well known for his expensive trappings of wealth: the underground garage jammed with luxury cars at his Rosedale mansion, and his friendships with Hollywood stars. Taylor, on the other hand, was noted for not being noted. He lived in an unremarkable downtown Toronto condominium during the week and travelled to his 70-hectare St. Mary's, Ontario, farm on the weekends where he and his wife raised cattle and sheep and grew cash crops. "I built my house. I built it with a hammer and saw and stuff," he said in the midst of the takeover battle. Taylor may have lost the confidence of investors with the Mexican deal and his perceived unwillingness to sell off the sports and entertainment businesses, but he was determined to find a richer alternative to Schwartz's $24-per-share takeover bid. "What Gerry failed to recognize is that we have a lot of friends in the beer business . . . I know everyone in the beer business."

Labatt already had a well-developed list of companies and contacts from the aborted attempt four years earlier to sell Edper-Brascan's 40% stake. American partner Anheuser-Busch, which Labatt considered the most logical buyer, quickly declined. As lawyers and public relations people representing Labatt and Onex fought in the courts and business press about issues of access to financial information, and about whether or not Onex's price was fair, Taylor and brewing chief Hugo Powell beat the bushes for alternative bids.

Few on Bay Street expected them to be successful. As the takeover fight went on, Taylor claimed Schwartz was trying to "steal" the company and Labatt held an analyst presentation in which it claimed the company was worth between $28 and $32.50 a share, versus Schwartz's proposed $24. Few were believers. "I came out of that meeting convinced that the stock is not worth a dime over $24," analyst Jacques Kavafian said at the time. Just two analysts accepted

Labatt's optimistic valuation, an endorsement that was key in convincing foreign brewers to consider a richer bid. "That really helped us," said CFO Bob Vaux. "If you are looking at upping the bid, and you are getting all these analyst results from so-called experts saying, 'The thing is not worth more than $22; give it to Gerry at $24,' it wasn't making our job exactly easy."

Labatt quickly narrowed its list of suitors to Dutch brewer Heineken and little-known Interbrew SA. The Belgian brewer, which was not even contacted in the 1991 attempt to find a buyer for the Edper-Brascan stake, traced its roots back six centuries and was privately owned by three aristocratic families. Its board studded with barons, counts, and viscounts, the urbane, British-raised Hugo Powell took the lead in discussions with Interbrew. "George wasn't the guy to deal with the counts," said Vaux. Europe's beer barons, literally, liked the Mexican purchase, especially since the peso devaluation had already settled out, and they also saw the value of Labatt's growing US import business. Canada was a steady profit machine for Labatt, although potential buyers worried, as did most outsiders, about the sustainability of those profits given the huge US brewers fenced off south of the border. Once the licensing deals and 1992 cross-border trade pact were explained, those concerns evaporated. With Onex poised to win control of the brewer in mere days, Labatt's negotiators took advantage of the regional rivalry between Interbrew and Heineken. "Interbrew were convinced that Heineken was breathing down their neck," says Vaux. "If [Interbrew] bid $26.50 it wasn't going to be [the winning] bid. In the end . . . like every other deal, they just looked at it and said, '$26.50, $28.50, let's get it at $28.50 and we can make our numbers work.' In retrospect, it was the best thing they have ever done. If you look at it, you would say they got it at a steal. Now they didn't, the reality is that they paid fair value for it." The $28.50-per-share, $2.7-billion acquisition of Labatt (Onex offered only $2.3 billion) catapulted the brewer of Stella Artois into the number-three position internationally. In the coming years, Labatt would provide an increasing flood of profits to Interbrew to bankroll an ambitious expansion across Europe and Asia. Just as importantly, Labatt exported much of its top management to Brussels, including fast-rising star Hugo Powell.

At the time of the takeover fight, an article in the *Financial Post* posed the question, "Why Labatt and not Molson?" It concluded that Molson had stayed true to its core beer business with the 1989 merger with Carling O'Keefe while Labatt had hared off on international forays that one unidentified analyst termed an "unmitigated disaster." The article failed to focus on the real reason why Labatt was swallowed up while Molson continued to operate unmolested. Immensely profitable and "worth more dead than alive," Labatt was essentially seeking the security of an owner since the Edper-Brascan sale three years earlier. Its Montreal-based rival had the luxury of being owned by the same family for more than two centuries. But as the Molson family learned during the nineties, that kind of stability is not necessarily a good thing.

Part Five
Mickey Diversified

11
Molson Cleans Up the World

Labatt's difficulties in the early to mid-nineties – the management turmoil, backfiring investments, and final shareholder revolt – all provided useful cover for Molson's Mickey Cohen. The outsider, the cultured corporate lawyer who didn't even drink beer, was viewed as a shrewd CEO. Thanks to the initial flurry of positive press around his arrival at Molson and the subsequent merger with Foster's Canadian operation, Carling O'Keefe, Mickey was soon cast as a far-sighted genius who overcame internal opposition to clinch the merger. It didn't hurt that the combination went off with nary a snag, despite misgivings from Molson Brewery executives about their new Carling partners.

The Molson-Carling merger was a much more calculated affair than it appeared to be from the outside. The issue of combining breweries had been studied to death – even before executives from the two breweries locked themselves up in a Toronto hotel room to hammer out the deal. The two companies produced virtually identical products, operated in the same market, and played by the same rules. With the merger, the new entity would end up with too many breweries and too many people. Deciding which plants were least efficient led to the number of production jobs that would have to go.

Making the call on white-collar layoffs in areas such as marketing, sales, and administration turned into much more of an exercise of "a Molson person here, a Carling person there."

Besides overcoming the Molson resistance to handing 50% of the new company to "those cowboys," Mickey's biggest contribution may have been structuring the new entity as a partnership and famously changing its year end to April 1 (one day after the Molson Companies' fiscal close), a move that deferred about $80 million in taxes. Mickey also sidelined the Molson family from running what was the most important business financially and emotionally – Molson Breweries. Under the new setup, Mickey was non-executive chairman of the brewing company, shutting out Eric Molson, chairman of the parent company, Molson Companies. So Eric, the Princeton-educated brewmaster, had no operational say in the brewery that had spawned his family's fortune. Ted Kunkel, the able operations man from Foster's who had been running Carling, was named Molson Breweries chairman. Below Kunkel, great care was taken to alternate executives in a Molson, Carling, Molson, Carling fashion.

The initial shock and surprise of the merger agreement, its ease of passage through the federal Competition Bureau, and subsequent cost savings of hundreds of millions annually, in addition to $400 million paid by Foster's to Molson, cemented Mickey's reputation – even though his career as a corporate CEO could be measured in months. With the merger and the corporate coffers flush, Mickey became Molson's first chief executive officer with a hint of imperial power, apparently immune to criticism from Bay Street or the company's controlling shareholder, the Molson family. "[The merger] kind of started Mickey off almost on a rocket," says Sheldon Bell, a finance executive with Molson who was put in charge of combining Molson and Carling. It may have also created overconfidence at the top. "The success of the merger, putting the two companies together almost flawlessly, created the view that mergers were easy," says Bell.

The CEO quickly put his stamp on the company. The head office near the airport was abandoned for luxurious, if expensive, corporate digs at the Scotia Plaza in Toronto's Bay-King financial epicentre. By putting Molson's top brass in downtown Toronto for the first time, the move de-emphasized the company's Montreal roots, and made it Montreal-based in name only. Mickey also lived well at a time when people were fixated on perks that seem petty now after the wealth and excess of the dot-com era. There was the million-dollar salary, the corporate jet, and the special ventilation system so Mickey could smoke his cigars at work. "He was a great believer in convenience," said Barry Joslin, who replaced Hershell Ezrin as Mickey's assistant-cum-PR man in 1992. "He wasn't a big believer in luxury per se. He believed that a senior executive's time was worth a lot of money." Early on in his new right-hand-man position, Joslin learned Mickey was more down to earth than he appeared when Joslin attempted to carry the boss's bag from the airport carousel to the limo. "I started carrying it and he took it away from me and said, 'I'm not a fucking [government] minister you know.'" Using the same logic, Mickey viewed the gorgeous wood-panelled corporate offices at King and Bay Streets as a necessary improvement over the airport accommodations because the Molson's law firm and all the accoutrements of mergers and acquisitions were right downtown.

Mickey the deal maker wasted little time looking for the next corporate conquest. Unlike his counterparts at Labatt, who were attempting to divest non-brewing businesses and expand their beer operations internationally, Mickey was down on selling suds. He had already sold 50% of the Molson family's two-centuries-old business, albeit at a substantial profit, and he quite rightly identified the Canadian market for beer as mature, if still hugely profitable. For Mickey, the future of Molson would be in chemicals, not beer, and the foundation for Molson's growth would be a little cleaning and sanitizing company the brewer had purchased in 1978, Diversey Corp. Unlike beer, the prospects appeared limitless for businesses that handled industrial cleaning for institutions such as prisons, and for service companies such as hotels, bars, and restaurants. Diversey made the cleaning chemicals, showed these establishments how to use them, and sold them directly. Even better, Diversey was, well, diversified, with operations in Canada and the United States, as well as Europe, Latin America, and Asia. The steady increase in global travel for business and tourism would only add to the demand for Diversey's services. "The world is getting cleaner," as Mickey liked to say, and Diversey would be a beneficiary of this trend. At Molson's annual meeting in 1990, on the heels of the beer merger with Carling O'Keefe, Mickey proclaimed that Diversey's business of cleaning and sanitizing was "a bigger growth business than the beer business." But Molson's executives would soon learn it was a hell of a lot tougher to make money in chemicals than in beer.

Diversey was attractive because the industrial cleaning market still had yet to be consolidated. Besides Diversey, there were just a handful of competitors with international heft. In a lot of ways, specialty chemicals was not much different from the beer business, which at the time still had strong regional players but no dominant international players like Coca-Cola or Pepsi in the soft-drink market. Mickey quickly moved to build Diversey, which would in just a few years surpass the Molson Breweries' contribution to the parent corporation's revenues. At no time, though, did Diversey ever threaten beer's status as the profit engine for the company.

In the first three years under Mickey, Molson made a total of a dozen acquisitions to buttress Diversey, the most significant being the 1991 deal to buy Cincinnati's DuBois Chemicals Inc. for $265 million. Fast growing and operating virtually around the world, Diversey's future seemed bright. In its 1992 annual report, Molson noted that Diversey's revenue had jumped 36% to $1.2 billion while profit had soared 62% to $76 million. (The beer business by contrast earned $173 million on an identical $1.2 billion in sales.)

In reality, 1992 marked the top of the roller coaster for Diversey, with the dramatic plunge still to come. While revenue would steadily increase over the next few years, profit would never again reach the 1992 mark. Far from being the future, Diversey would become a bleeding wound that threatened Molson's continued existence. People at Labatt and Molson used to say that it takes an idiot to lose money in the beer business. In the case of specialty chemicals, questionable decisions became a willing foe to corporate expansion. Diversey was about to go wrong, though it took shareholders some time to figure it out. For most, the first whiff of trouble came in Mickey's 1993 message to shareholders, in which he advised: "While the production synergies anticipated from the acquisition have been achieved, the realization of the overall benefits is behind our original plan. This is primarily because Diversey attempted to complete its own extensive rationalization program while integrating the two companies, all during a tough recession." Intrepid shareholders would have to plough through the company's annual discussion and analysis to find out what was really going on at the burgeoning specialty chemicals group. In the United States, Diversey's biggest operation, a $14-million loss was sustained compared with a $17-million profit for the previous year, while sales fell 3% to $407 million. The losses were caused by the merger of Diversey and DuBois, Molson admitted. The company had attempted closing plants at both companies, and reducing DuBois' staff while simultaneously merging two distinctly different companies had thrown the US operations into disarray.

Molson finance man Sheldon Bell, brought in by Diversey for advice on the DuBois acquisition and a little later appointed as chief financial officer at the chemicals company, describes the merger as an attempt to "Diversize DuBois. And they did it. The first thing they did was fire most of the sales force at DuBois." The reality was that DuBois (pronounced Doo-Boy) was a totally different business. "It ran almost exclusively on a sales force that considered themselves independent entrepreneurs," said Bell. "And they made like 30% commission on sales and they had 70% margins on their businesses. These were guys making a ton of dough, too. They were making $200,000 to $300,000, these sales guys. As soon as they started taking them out of the business, the DuBois business started to erode rapidly."

Molson Breweries' executives, who didn't require an annual report to deduce that they were still filling the corporate coffers at the parent company, were skeptical of Mickey's new emphasis. At a presentation to management of Molson's increasingly diverse set of holdings, held in a Toronto hotel, a relaxed and confident Mickey presented his view of the world and how Diversey would literally clean up. "The world is only going to get cleaner and beer drinking is declining," is how Jeff Carefoote, a marketing executive with Molson Breweries, remembers the presentation.

As Carefoote recalls, sitting at his table was a salesman from Diversey-DuBois' Michigan office who had recently won a top sales award of a new Cadillac. As soon as he was presented with the luxury car, he took it to a body shop where they ripped out the back seat and installed a trailer hitch so he could haul more stuff to sell on sales calls. "Here we were going from a company owning hockey teams and, you know, selling cases of beer that make $10 or $12 bucks [profit] that you basically sell through government-regulated stores, to the future of selling chemicals out of the back of your car."

Diversey illustrated Mickey's best and worst qualities as a chief executive. Few doubted his genius for corporate strategy and deal making. Specialty chemicals, cleaning up the world, at least for those who could afford it, was proving to be a growth business. But managing it was proving far more difficult. In hiring top management talent, Mickey relied heavily on a consultant headhunter, Herb Stoneham, Molson's former head of human resources. Stoneham set up his own business, but remained a master of "selling the sizzle" to Molson's board of directors. "Mickey would go out and hire some guy who we would never have heard of and give him a big incentive package and let him work," said Norm Seagram, the Molson veteran who eventually took over Mickey's role.

At Diversey, Mickey tapped Derek Cornthwaite, the chemical company's executive vice-president, to replace the retiring industry veteran John Pick as president and chief executive. Cornthwaite, armed with a Ph.D. in biochemistry from Britain's Sheffield University, was, in many respects, in the most critical position in Molson's far-flung operation. The beer business would continue to churn out steady profits, the retailing businesses appeared to be on track, and sports and entertainment holdings (basically, the Montreal Canadiens hockey club) were too small to greatly affect Molson's fortunes. Because of its size, only Diversey could actually throw Molson's financial health dramatically off kilter.

From the Mississauga, Ontario, Diversey headquarters, Cornthwaite ran a $1.25-billion North American business, accounting for more than 40% of Molson's revenue but a disappointingly smaller share of profit. Cornthwaite's goal, he said in the brief optimistic period of the early nineties, was to have the number-one, or number-two business in each of its markets. "I'm astonished Diversey is not better known in Canada," he told the *Financial Post* in 1992. He would soon get his wish.

Cornthwaite had spent 25 years at Britain's Imperial Chemical Industries plc, but, like Mickey, this was to be his first crack at taking the reins of a company. Cornthwaite's focus at Diversey was on the US business, the geographic weak spot in the international cleaning empire. In the States, Diversey found itself competing with the Ecolab Inc., a company based in St. Paul, Minnesota, that was run by a cadre of senior managers who'd spent decades in the business of selling cleaning chemicals to hotels, hospitals, and restaurants. Ecolab president and chief executive Al Schuman had started with the company in 1957 as a junior salesman, rising steadily through the ranks, and he was surrounded by subordinates with similar experience. Besides Cornthwaite, who did have a chemicals background, Diversey had US division president Don Gray and a coterie of Molson accountants from Canada headed by Diversey chief financial officer Sheldon Bell.

"You had a bunch of accountants running this global chemical business, and while they clearly had the intellect, they didn't have the depth of experience [in the chemicals business]," says Sheldon Bell. "But the individuals who were running Ecolab, I do know that every single one of them had 30 years of experience in that business, and you had Al Schuman who ran Ecolab knowing every single customer on an intimate basis." That did not seem to deter Diversey US from attempting to take Ecolab on in its strengths. Diversey engaged in largely fruitless attempts to wrestle away Ecolab's biggest accounts, such as the Marriott hotel chain, a piece of business that Diversey would have had difficulty servicing in the event it had captured it, Bell says. Because of the demand for what Diversey did, the company was adding an account here and there, but for every piece of business it picked up, Ecolab seemed to land two or three.

Then, in the fall of 1993, Diversey announced it had hired six senior sales executives from Ecolab, and set them up in a new company called Service 145. The thinking behind the new enterprise was simple: the defectors were each paid $1 million up front and the expectations were that they would hit the ground running, quickly hijacking Ecolab business and bringing it to Diversey. Service 145 was crafted with the utmost secrecy. "Literally, one day Derek [Cornthwaite] called me into the office at about 4 o'clock in the afternoon, and he said, 'I need a cheque for $6 million for Monday morning,'" recalls Sheldon Bell. "As soon as [the Service 145 deal] was announced, Ecolab was in the court minutes putting in an injunction against these guys, preventing them from working for the next year. This whole thing was being decided in a Minneapolis court about five blocks from the Ecolab head office."

Ecolab's lawyers produced some kryptonite for Diversey's new super salesmen. Ecolab's legalists successfully constrained five of the six from competing with their former company for more than a year. And by the time the five sales managers were able to approach former clients, Ecolab had replaced them all with senior sales people and shored up shaky or vulnerable accounts with new, long-term contracts.

Service 145 was an embarrassing failure, but worse still, it attracted the full, angry attention of Ecolab. "We poked the sleeping giant with a sharp stick," says Bell. "Ecolab was 5 to 10 times bigger [than Diversey US] and became a major drain on cash and distracted the company from other parts of the world where it was actually doing quite well." Ecolab's immediate response to the defections of the Service 145 group was something called "Operation Rolling Thunder." Copies of the sales presentation that were part of Operation Rolling Thunder didn't provide much useful intelligence for

Diversey, but they did confirm Ecolab's determination. "The intent was to drive Diversey into the sea," Bell remembers.

With Service 145 out of service for an entire year, the expected sales did not come and Diversey US stalled, proving to be enough of a disaster for Mickey and the board to finally address the Diversey sinkhole. In March 1994, at the end of Molson's fiscal year, it was announced that Cornthwaite had "resigned" – with a $2.7-million severance package and another $1 million in salary and other payouts – and that Mickey would take over as president of Diversey until a replacement could be found. Mickey joked at the 1994 annual meeting that the extra work from Diversey was cutting into his golf game.

Dumping Cornthwaite with no successor in the wings was a less than ideal situation. Mickey was not an operations man and, of all Molson's businesses, he probably knew the least about Diversey, which he had relied upon Cornthwaite to run. Meanwhile, the US business was proving to be a money pit. While Diversey overall had its best year in fiscal 1994, with profit rising 4% to nearly $73 million, the US unit lost $13 million on top of losses of $14 million the year before. Molson's response was to throw money at the States, about $100 million in total, to add sales staff and address delivery and service problems, which could be traced as far back as the DuBois merger.

Things only managed to get worse. All that capital lavished upon the US business just seemed to deepen the pool of red ink the following year. Diversey US lost nearly $38 million for the year ending March 1995. The bleeding was concentrated in the institutional business, the main area of competition between Diversey and Ecolab, where Diversey was losing a stunning $40 million and $50 million annually on sales of about $150 million. Ecolab had institutional sales of about $580 million and analysts figured it enjoyed profit margins of between 14% and 18%. Mickey and the rest of the team took a personal hit for the poor showing, which provided cold comfort for long-suffering Molson shareholders. None of the top executives received a bonus for fiscal 1995. (Mickey had been paid a $450,000 bonus the year before.)

Just a week before Mickey was forced to face shareholders in September 1995 and explain a third consecutive year of losses at Diversey US, Molson announced it would slash 450 jobs at the chemical unit, virtually all in the States. Mickey talked bravely about how the move would help with the goal of "doubling Diversey's running rate of operating profit" by the end of the year, but to outsiders the move was seen as cleaning the company up for a sale. Ecolab, for its part, saw the initiative for what it was, a sign of weakness, and vowed to beef up its sales force to take advantage of an ailing rival. "The only way they can get anywhere back on path is to knock off these people and cut their costs, which means more problems in the field, which means more opportunities for us," said Ecolab's Al Schuman at the time. "They change their strategy constantly."

Within a few months, Molson's end-game had leaked out: Diversey would be sold off, and once that was accomplished, Mickey would take his leave of Molson, and it of him. By January 1996, Molson announced it had sold about 70% of Diversey to the Anglo-Dutch conglomerate Unilever plc. For $780 million, Unilever acquired Diversey's industrial laundry and food business outside of North America, as well as the DuBois industrial sanitizing group in the United States. The rest of the cobbled-together company would be sold as it had been acquired – in pieces over the next few months. Near the end, Diversey found itself in "that never-never land where we were too big to be regarded as a regional player yet too small to be a national player," Barry Joslin summarized.

Analysts, at least, were pleasantly surprised at the price Molson managed to command for Diversey, and they were happy to see the distraction gone. Norm Seagram, who was not working at Molson during the sell-off of the chemicals business, was not surprised that the company had managed to successfully sell its way out of the Diversey mess. "Molson made excellent deals. When they bought something, they generally bought it at the right value – they never overpaid – and when they sold something, they sold it pretty well," he said.

Mickey, and Molson generally, fared better with the company's retail holdings, where the margins may have been skinnier, but the business was a great deal less complicated. Molson's main retail operation was the 174-store Beaver Lumber chain, which was run mainly by franchisees with a minority of company-owned locations sprinkled throughout the mix. By the beginning of the nineties, the Beaver operation was showing its age and vulnerability. Mass merchandisers were nibbling away at the business and specialty chains were taking a bigger share of the renovation business, but most worrisome, a giant operating out of the American Deep South was revolutionizing the hardware and lumber business in the United States. The rapid rise of Home Depot's warehouse chain, nicknamed Agent Orange for its corporate colour scheme and devastating effect on traditional rivals, did not go unnoticed by Molson's retail unit, Malsham Group.

Molson held preliminary discussions with Home Depot before deciding to tackle the home improvement super-centre business on its own. In one of the company's more astute moves, Malsham hired Home Depot vice-president Stephen Bebis to head up an effort to create a Canadian version of Home Depot. Short, dark, and intense – the Massacusetts-raised son of a Greek Orthodox pastor – he proved an excellent hire. "Bebis was a dynamo," says Sheldon Bell. When a newspaper reporter called Bebis a year before the first Aikenhead's warehouse store was up and running, he took the call from his car – which just happened to be parked in the lot of a Home Depot in Altanta, Georgia. "Just looking things over," he said at the time. By April 1992, less than two years into the venture, Bebis had the first made-in-Canada Home Depot clone up and running in Toronto. The once-defunct Aikenhead's hardware name, which Molson had acquired when it bought the hardware chain in 1971, only to kill it off to make way for Beaver Lumber, was resurrected to christen a new home improvement warehouse chain. Ironically, the new chain would end up giving Beaver the chop.

Aside from the healthy inventory of snow-clearing equipment, there was little to set Aikenhead's apart from Bebis' former Altanta-based employer. The gigantic 125,000-square-foot stores, which dwarfed Beaver Lumber's 30,000-square-foot outlets, were cookie-cutter versions of Home Depot locations. The stores also included huge nurseries, floor-to-ceiling racks on polished cement floors, and they copied the Home Depot site plan of 10-acre footprints near major highways. For American customers who may have strayed into an Aikenhead's store, the only difference might appear to be the corporate colour scheme: forest green for the employee aprons and signage, rather than the US chain's bright orange. But publicly, Home Depot had no plans to bring the chain to Canada at that time.

Aikenhead's quickly proved to be the future of home improvement retailing, a lucrative sector in the age of cocooning Baby Boomers intent on fixing up their nests. The business was quickly profitable and the cash flow from newly opened stores was providing the capital to fuel expansion. Even in the relatively straightforward world of retailing, though, Molson could not figure out a profitable way to usher in Aikenhead's while showing Beaver Lumber the door. Molson knew the giant Aikenhead's stores would vacuum up sales from small rivals, including Beaver. But the effect of Aikenhead's would be devastating in the big cities, where the megastores would be concentrated. The country's urban areas just happened to be where all those Molson-owned Beaver stores were clustered. The stores in secondary and rural markets would continue to churn out steady profits for Beaver franchisees.

In its 1993 annual report, released after Aikenhead's was operating three Toronto-area stores and had many more planned, Molson told shareholders, "It appears probable that full-service home improvement warehouses, which dominate the home improvement retailing sector in major urban centers in the United States, will spread to major metropolitan markets across Canada sooner than had been previously anticipated." Rather than attempt to sell the doomed Beaver outlets before starting up the Aikenhead's steamroller, Molson set about gutting its main retail business. It slashed more than 100 people from the Beaver headquarters and planned to close 30 Molson-owned stores over the three-year span beginning in fiscal 1993.

Under the direction of Bebis, Aikenhead's set out an ambitious strategy. After the first year, the company had purchased 9 additional real-estate locations, and had plans to build 28 of the gigantic stores in Ontario and the West within the first six years. Molson acknowledged in its 1993 annual report that "competition is expected to enter the marketplace" and it was doing all it could to snap up the best possible locations before the orange swarm descended.

But Aikenhead's was running out of time. Its real-estate people found themselves competing for the same land as US-based big-box retailers, including emissaries from Home Depot. The sun was setting on Canadian retailers, a point driven home with the entry of Wal-Mart in January 1994. Less than a month later, Molson announced it had sold 75% of its five-outlet Aikenhead's business to Home Depot for $217 million. The deal had the appearance of the best of all worlds for Molson. The company saved face by selling to a $10-billion competitor, which surely would have squashed Aikenhead's. Molson received a piece of the action and a healthy return on its investment to get out of Home Depot's way. "They are a very good company, and it just made more sense to join them than to fight them," Mickey said at the February 1994 press conference in Toronto to announce the sale. "I don't think we capitulated. What I think we have done is the sensible thing."

The sensible thing was hardly as profitable as it seemed. Beaver Lumber was rapidly gobbling up a $83-million provision to close stores and fire staff. The $217 million collected from the sale of three-quarters of Aikenhead's operation should have easily covered that sum but the money seemed to disappear faster than beer in a heat wave. Molson recorded a net gain of just $40 million on the Aikenhead's sale, and most of the cash went to incentive plans, transaction costs, and $35 million in severance payments to senior management – a result of Molson's penchant for loading up executives with hefty incentives. Jack Edwards, the boss of the fast-shrinking retail division, was paid $6 million in long-term incentives as a result of the sale, Molson reported. (The company never said what Bebis was paid from the deal.)

(Bebis did not last a year at what became Home Depot Canada. Bebis has stayed in retail, winding up as president of Canadian golf equipment retailer Golf Town. One of his financial backers? Mickey Cohen.)

While the non-brewing aspects of Molson provided plenty of distraction for the company's management and shareholders, Mickey the deal maker still found time to put together a corporate marriage on the beer side that would have long-lasting and profound consequences for Molson.

12

Poor Mountain Men

Even when Mickey so dramatically dusted off his hands at the Competition Bureau with the approval of the Carling merger, he wasn't finished with Molson's two-centuries-old brewing business. The deal maker with the belief in free trade was also dancing with tobacco and food giant Philip Morris Co., Carling O'Keefe's old US partner. Two weeks into 1993, Mickey held a news conference in Toronto to announce that Philip Morris' beer unit, Miller Brewing Co., was buying a 20% stake in Molson Breweries and the US import business of Molson for $370 million.

As Mickey explained it, the corporate coupling worked on many levels. Molson's growth in the States was stalled. The Molson Golden brand was strong in the US Northeast along the border, and Canadian-brewed Foster's Lager had some pockets of strength, but in total, Molson had less than 1% of the US market. Getting more market share would take the kind of distribution and marketing muscle that only Miller, Coors, or Labatt's partner Anheuser-Busch had. Molson's government relations people were doing their best to limit the damage that would be caused by freer trade in beer – and none of the big US brands already licensed for sale through Labatt and Molson could be sold outside those arrangements in Canada. But

Mickey was still worried about a flood of cheap American suds. "Intense import competition is just around the corner, and we have to be able to meet it head-on," was a standard line.

John Barnett, who was then president of Molson USA, said Miller made the first corporate approach. "It really started with Miller wanting to get a foot into the imported beer market. Miller approached Molson about taking an equity position with the import company that I was running. Miller's interest in buying into the import company then ballooned into a bigger thing. 'We're going to be partners. It's going to be one market. Why don't you buy into this business?'" was how Molson eventually pitched the deal.

Mickey had accomplished something that no other Molson executive had managed since the brewery was founded in 1786 by John Molson in Montreal. He had sold control of the company to foreign interests. When the dust settled, Foster's and Molson each owned 40% of the brewery, with Miller holding the rest. Here was the company which had a top brand called "Canadian" and was the producer of Molson's *Hockey Night in Canada*, selling to US interests, one magazine pointed out. So pervasive was Molson's influence on the country's culture that comedians Dave Thomas and Rick Moranis used the beer as a prop for their long-running Bob and Doug McKenzie "hosers" skit on *SCTV*.

The company's annual meeting in July 1993 marked the high point of Mickey's reign. The cracks in DuBois and Diversey were only just beginning to show and appeared fixable. Expansion of the Home Depot retail clone Aikenhead's was already throwing off the cash required for further expansion. The equity sale to Miller was "bound to have success" Mickey said at the meeting, predicting Molson sales could eventually grow to 3–5% of the US beer market, the world's largest. The conglomerate seemed to be running on all cylinders. Profit was up 30% to $165 million, padded by the sale to Miller and shrewd tax planning – Molson paid just $9.6 million in taxes that year compared to $60.6 million the year before because of the use of accumulated capital losses.

Even Stanley was in the house. The Stanley Cup was on display at the Montreal hotel where the annual meeting was held, a recognition of the surprise championship of the Montreal Canadiens that year. The team had even contributed a modest profit to the hockey-heavy sports-and-entertainment division, which earned $2.9 million in profit. The win was the Habs' 24th cup, marking more championships than any other professional sports franchise at the time. It was also going to be the last for a very long time, as the economics of the league were tilting against "small market" teams like Montreal. Behind the scenes, Mickey, prodded by his executives, had raised the possibility of selling the Habs, but the proposal was flatly rejected by Eric Molson, perhaps remembering how the sale of the beloved team in seventies had split the family. "Sell the team when it's hot" was the failed argument Barry Joslin recalls management using. Eric Molson's refusal to sell the team had some logic behind it. The Canadiens' financial contribution was only going to grow, it was believed, once the new 21,000-seat Forum, just beginning construction that year, was built. Labatt had its state-of-the-art SkyDome and the World Series–winning Blue Jays, Molson needed its new Forum. No one was predicting at the time that both buildings would soon prove to be white elephants for their respective owners.

Over the next few years, most of management's attention would be devoted to chemical unit Diversey Corp.'s widening financial spill and relations with Molson's US brewery partners. The initial results of the Miller sale concluded in April 1993 were encouraging, to say the least. In the first year, with Miller handling advertising, sales, and distribution for Molson brands in the States, Molson's sales soared 32% to 2.2 million hectolitres (or nearly 27 million cases). About 20% of Molson's beer production was flowing south. That number jumped another 14% to 2.5 million hectolitres the following year.

Miller was producing the dramatic sales gains not with the green-bottled Molson Golden, the long-time competitor to Heineken in the US market, but with Molson Ice, a brand that, like Golden, didn't really exist in the Canadian market. Molson was lukewarm to the idea of a big push on Ice. It still wanted to emphasize Golden, which Miller people argued had achieved about all the sales gains it could. "The Molson organization didn't really believe in Molson Ice, didn't even want it," says a former senior Miller executive who fought against more money for Golden. "You get farther from Canada and people want Mexican beer, or they want Heineken. Then you are in competition with a zillion other imported beers. Unless you had something truly new like Molson Ice which sold well everywhere, you were spending a lot of time and money on distribution with not much reward."

Molson Ice gave Miller's marketing department a new, higher-alcohol beer to run through its huge marketing machine. Miller sponsored NFL football and NBA basketball, and could slot in Molson Ice ads in the place of Miller spots to honour its heavy $270-million ad spending commitment for the first three years of the pact, a commitment that Miller lived up to, people at both companies say. With the early entrance of Molson Ice and the subsequent rollout of products from Miller, and Bud Ice and secondary brewers, the ice category exploded for a few years in the States before the inevitable fall-off, growing to as much as 5% of the market. "Ice was a wonderful plus," says the former Miller executive. "Unfortunately within two years, the premium-ness of Ice had dropped to sub-premium. Everything was cheap Ice suddenly, and that made it a lot tougher." By March 1996, three years into the Miller deal, Molson USA's sales had begun to slide, falling 8% to 2.3 million hectolitres, but Molson Ice would stubbornly hang on. Even two years after that, when Molson was sending 2.4 million hectolitres (29 million cases) south in fiscal 1995, Molson Ice remained the third-highest volume imported brand sold in the United States.

Unfortunately, the deal with Miller had some unintended and far-reaching consequences. More than a year after Molson revealed its equity sale, its Colorado-based partner, Coors Brewing Co., said that it wanted out of its decade-long licensing agreement with the Montreal brewer. Coors' announcement was a bombshell. Under the terms of its contract with Molson, Coors could give 10-year notice that it wanted out of its licensing pact, which it did, but it could also seek arbitration under the contract for damages and for an immediate end to the pact. Coors was reportedly furious because Molson had jumped into bed with Miller, one of its two bitter US rivals, and because it believed Molson had reneged on an agreement that Coors should get the first crack at any such equity deal. Molson hotly denied any breach of its deal with Coors.

Coors' links with Molson stretched back to the early eighties when, after the surprising success of Anheuser-Busch's Budweiser in Canada under the brewing and marketing stewardship of Labatt, and Carling's launch of Miller High Life, Molson sought its own licensing deal. The last to jump on the licensing bandwagon, Molson linked up with Coors. Molson had no links with Miller until the Carling O'Keefe merger of 1989. The Colorado brewer's fury over the Miller sale was understandable, said Molson USA president John Barnett, who explained the Coors mindset: "It was bad enough that they didn't sell it to [Coors], but when they fucking sold it to Miller – there's two [companies Coors can't stand] in America: the first one is Anheuser-Busch, the next one is Miller."

Perhaps most galling for the Coors clan, Miller was making more money on the flagship Coors Light brand in Canada than Coors was as a result of the sale. "It was one of the things that really irked them, and you could understand it," said one former Molson financial executive. "Let's say the marginal profitability was $80 [per hectolitre for Coors Light]. There was Miller who owned 20% of Molson, and therefore earned 20% of that $80, so Miller was earning $16 a hectolitre on the Coors brand and Coors was earning $5 a hectolitre [in royalty fees] on the Coors brand." At first blush, the royalty fees might appear to be skewed in the favour of the Canadian brewer. Molson got the benefit of a famous brand name, "free" spillover advertising from US TV channels leaking across the border, and, of course, the recipes to brew the stuff. Like Labatt's deal with Anheuser-Busch to brew Budweiser, though, the Canadian brewer was taking all the risk on the deal, doing all the work, and building the brand in the Canadian market pretty much from scratch. Coors, like A-B, would have input into what ads would make it on television and in print. But Molson, like Labatt, would do all the heavy lifting to get the brand into bars and retail outlets.

A sales phenomenon in Canada, just as it had proved to be in the United States, Coors Light had been created against all odds. It had been brewed up in secret against the wishes of the company's third-generation owners, who insisted the original Coors beer was already "America's fine light beer," as the slogan went. Coors Banquet, as the original beer was known, had always been considered a light beer. In the United States, Coors Light initially stumbled when it was introduced because beer drinkers had difficulty telling it apart from regular Coors, as both were sold in similar, creamy-yellow cans. It was only later, when Coors Light was sold in the clean, unadorned cans with the scripted red lettering, that the brand took off and became known as the Silver Bullet.

The Coors family was much more involved in the day-to-day operations of its business than the Molson family. Part of that was a function of time. Molson had been around for more than two centuries and no Molson had been president since Peter Molson, who committed suicide in 1966. At Coors, no one but a Coors had ever run the company. The US brewer had been around only since 1873, after Adolph Coors, a 21-year-old stowaway, landed in Baltimore on a ship from Germany. He later founded a brewery with a partner on the banks of Clear Creek, Colorado, about 15 miles "up the slope" from Denver. It took a long time for the western brewer to become the national force it is today. In 1948 it was the 49th-largest brewer, rising to number 5 by 1973 while still serving just 11 states. By 1985, as Canadians were having their first taste of Molson-brewed Coors, the fourth-generation Coors, Peter and Jeff, were assuming the reins of the Colorado brewing company from their father and uncle. The great-grandsons of Adolph were steeped in the family traditions of hard work and honour and brewing excellence. Jeff, the technically inclined brewer who'd formulated Coors Light, ran the operations side. Peter, the more gregarious brother, had the sales and marketing background, and was the obvious choice to be public face of the brewery.

Pete Coors, described as an old-fashioned "my word is my bond" type by Molson's John Barnett, felt betrayed by the Molson sale to Miller, as did the rest of Coors management. Even as Coors Light led the light-beer category and Molson held what should have been celebratory quarterly update sessions with Coors, the mood darkened. In 1993, the year Molson announced the sale to Miller, the Coors people asked for a renegotiation of the licensing deal, only to be rebuffed by Molson. "We've got an airtight, rock-solid licence agreement that can't be broken" was the attitude at Molson, according to one senior official at the brewery. "That is why we have no qualms about making someone else's name the largest brand in Canada if we have to." Molson's attitude was spelled out in its 1994 annual report: "The [Molson] partnership has been advised by Canadian and United States counsel that the arbitration submission of Coors Brewing Company [is] unlikely to succeed."

John Barnett, the accountant-turned-beer-executive promoted from Molson USA to run the Molson Breweries in Canada, ran the northern operation during much of the Coors dispute. He was moved north to replace Bruce Pope, the marketer-turned-president who was removed not for the disintegrating relations with Coors, but for failing to arrest Molson's plunging market share, former Molson executives say. Immediately following the merger with Carling O'Keefe in 1989, the new company enjoyed a commanding 53% share of Canadian beer sales. When Barnett took over, that share had fallen to about 47.5% and was showing no signs of a turnaround. (With each market share point worth about $20 million in gross profit at the time, Molson was down by roughly $100 million since the merger.) Pope, a marketer with consumer-goods giant Warner Lambert before he joined Molson, was in charge for three years, a span when Molson's stranglehold in Quebec was broken with the decline in popularity of ales, and Labatt had the brewery on the run elsewhere with the launch of new products such as cold-filtered draft and ice beers.

"We were losing mainstream business to Labatt," said Barry Joslin, Molson's senior vice-president of public affairs. "In fairness to Bruce, he inherited this legacy of too many brands. I would certainly argue in retrospect that if we had bit the bullet earlier on those brands, our share may have gone to 48 or 49, it would not have got down to the 45, 46 [share] levels it did."

While Molson and its Australian brewing partner Foster's were busily planning their conquest of the US market with their new partner Miller, Coors management was doing a slow boil. Requests to recast the licensing deal for Coors Light, a fast-growing brand and Canada's top-selling light beer, had been turned down by Molson. But inspiration and motivation came from an unexpected corner. "I initiated the lawsuit," claims George Taylor, John Labatt's president at the time. "I went down to Coors and knocked on the door and sort of said, 'Peter, wake up. Tell them to pack their bags and we'll do the Silver Bullet for you and we'll do a better job.'" As it had done a few years earlier when it grabbed the Carlsberg brands from Carling O'Keefe, Labatt was attempting to take advantage of ownership changes at a rival to gain key brands.

Coors had options to tackle the Canadian market. Coors Light was now established as a heavyweight brand in the north, with more than a 5% share of the market and recording steady, double-digit growth every year. If Molson didn't want to make concessions to brew and market the Silver Bullet, Labatt had already said it was willing to do what it would take to make Coors happy. Furthermore, soon after Molson had swung its Miller sale, the Canadian brewer had also orchestrated the historic border agreement for beer over Labatt's objections. Suddenly US brewers had free access to the Canadian market, access Molson was happy to grant because the US big three – Anheuser-Busch, Miller, and Coors – had their main brands locked up with bulletproof, long-term licensing deals with Molson or Labatt. If Coors could free itself from its Molson contract, it could ink a significantly richer deal with Labatt, buy or build a brewery in Canada to make Coors, or simply truck its beer across the border.

The Coors-Molson dispute, like most major feuds in the North American beer world, was carried out in the clubby corporate world of secret arbitration. Conducted in Toronto, the private arbitration panel was made up of three men with solid legal backgrounds selected to act as judges and picked from Canada, the United States, and New Zealand.

The 200-page decision of the arbitration panel, which ended the two-year legal wrangling, is still secret. Keeping the dirty linen out of sight of both Labatt and Anheuser-Busch always remained a consideration. The two sides agreed before the case started to keep all but the outcome confidential. What emerges from interviews with former Molson executives, however, is that Coors' legal experts skilfully presented a picture of a company wronged by their more sophisticated and unscrupulous "big city" Canadian partners. The Coors case was neatly summed up by Peter Bobeff, Foster's top lawyer and a member of the Molson Breweries board of directors, as the "mountain men" appeal. "He was one who would always say that their case was 'we're just poor mountain men,'" said a former Molson Brewery executive.

The arbitration pitted two of Canada's top corporate lawyers and their Bay Street firms against one another. On one side was Lyndon Barnes, a top partner of Molson's chief law firm, Osler, Hoskin & Harcourt, and on the other side of the room was Sheila Block, one of the stars of Tory Tory DesLauriers & Binnington, who had played a key role in humbling a brewery a decade ago. Block was the lawyer who'd successfully acted for Carling O'Keefe's preferred shareholders when they claimed their rights were being trampled during the Molson-Carling merger. Carling was eventually forced to pay its preferred shareholders all at once rather than pay them over a period of years, as it would have liked, to clear the way for the merger with Molson. Former Carling CEO Ted Kunkel had left Canada a few years earlier but he was not far removed from the case as the head of Australia's Foster's Group, a 40% owner of Molson Breweries.

The arbitration was more than just a showdown between Osler's and Tory Tory's top legal teams. Coors was determined to win or lose the case on the differing characters, or lack of same, of the Molson and Coors organizations. The brewers from Colorado maintained that their long-time partners from Canada had always said that if the time ever came to sell equity in the continent's oldest brewery, Coors would be asked first. No documentation existed to back up this claim, Molson people say, except handwritten notes following meetings made by Coors executives and the testimony of Peter Coors himself. It would be up to Eric Molson, whom most Molson investors would hear from only at annual meetings, and select other company executives to counter Coors' testimony.

In the final week, Peter Bobeff and Molson Breweries president John Barnett were approached by a representative of Coors, who said the brewer was willing to drop the case rather than wait for a decision. "This is awful for both of us," the Coors pitch went. "You could win; we could win. We think we have a pretty good chance. Put that aside. If you guys will go back to the original proposal, tear up the existing licence agreement, put the brand in Canada, we'll just forget about this." The two men asked for a Molson partnership meeting and urged the companies to accept Coors' deal. Reportedly, Bobeff, Foster's top legal man, did most of the talking. Bobeff "walked through the legal arguments and that sort of stuff," said one executive who attended. "This was binding arbitration. No appeal. He pointed out that you put these people in a role that is godlike; they are not bound to follow legal precedent. It is going to hinge much more on sort of commercial fairness, and I think on balance that they think Coors is more aggrieved than we are." Management of the two controlling shareholders vetoed the Coors offer, according to the executive attending the meeting.

As Bobeff predicted, the arbitration panel exercised its omnipotent powers and rendered its decision a few agonizing months later. Coors won on every major count. In the fall of 1996, the arbitrators declared that Molson Breweries' licence to make and market Coors brands was null and void retroactively from April 1993, when the Miller sale was concluded. The Colorado brewer now owned the rights to Coors Light in Canada, which Molson had so painstakingly nurtured for the past decade.

The panel ordered Molson to continue brewing Coors until its former US partner could find an alternative to supply its beer to Canada. Coors seemingly had numerous options for the Canadian market and sticking with Molson seemed the least likely at the time. The arbitrators not long after decided that Molson Breweries would pay damages of $100 million to Coors. Molson Breweries also had a $15-million bill for costs related to the arbitration case. Ordered to make financial restitution on its injury to Coors, the brewer almost added an unintended insult. The $100-million settlement cheque was made out to "Adolf Coors Company" rather than the correct "Adolph." Detected just before the cheque was to be sent to Colorado, it was hastily corrected.

Coors wrote a cheque of its own, which arrived soon after the verdict at Tory Tory's offices. "At the law firm we got a $2-million bonus from Coors," recalled John Butler. "We didn't even ask for it really. That is more American-style. Because they have that contingency system they are more used to rewarding success and we were sort of shy, retiring Canadian lawyers." After more than two years of legal wrangling, Coors had plenty to celebrate. The company had broken an ironclad, 10-year contract and was free to craft a new, far-more-profitable way to sell its best-selling brew in Canada.

"To me, Molson not only lost the case but they got fucking slaughtered," recalled John Barnett, Molson Breweries president. "This wasn't 51–49. When you strike the licence down, tell Molson to keep making it until Coors make their alternate arrangement, assess $100 million in fucking damages. That is for Coors a home run." The Molson Breweries president, who had quit smoking 10 months earlier, lit up the day of the decision, and has been smoking ever since.

Barnett had plenty to worry about while he got reacquainted with his long-time vice. The penalty paid to Coors might have been painful, but the prospect of losing Coors Light would be disastrous. Despite closing 13 breweries since the merger, Molson was swimming in excess brewing capacity. The company's eight plants running from St. John's to Vancouver could brew 13.2 million hectolitres of beer annually, yet even with the southbound shipments of Molson Ice and Molson Golden thrown in, the brewer would be lucky to sell 11 million hectolitres. (Molson made a small step toward reducing that gap when it announced the small Winnipeg brewery would close, eliminating 400,000 hectolitres of production.) At best, Molson was operating at just over 80% capacity and should have closed another brewery.

Beverage analysts, who could read capacity tables as well as beer executives could, pointed to the 2.5-million hectolitre Barrie, Ontario, plant, which happened to be just an hour away from the larger, Toronto brewery, as the logical candidate for elimination. If Molson had too much beer-making capacity on its hands before the Coors decision, it would find itself swamped in suds should Coors decide to find another way to make its brands for Canada. Coors brands represented 11% of Molson Breweries' total sales volumes. If it lost Coors Light, Molson might as well tear down two breweries – and not the midget 300,000 hectolitre operations in St. John's or Regina, either. Put another way, if Molson lost the 5.5 market share points represented by the Coors brands to Labatt, its share would fall to 41% while Labatt's would rocket to close to 50%.

Coors held all the cards and was not in the mood to be charitable. It signed on for an interim brewing and marketing agreement with Molson in the fall of 1996 and then said Molson had until the end of 1997 to conclude a new licensing deal with it on substantially better terms. The hitch was that Coors would not get back into business with Molson Breweries as long as Miller was an owner. Molson, the brewing partnership, had one year to craft a new deal with Coors. Molson Companies and Foster's had the same amount of time to buy out Miller.

Mickey Cohen, the architect of the Miller sale, didn't stick around. He left Molson in the spring of 1996, months before the arbitrators' decision. Norm Seagram, the former brewery chief brought back to Molson as president and CEO of Molson Companies, was charged with taking Miller out of the picture and putting the focus back on beer. With Diversey finally sold off, the proceeds could be used to make international brewing acquisitions, a prospect that sent shudders through analysts and institutional investors alike.

With the Coors deadline ticking, Molson proceeded on the dual goals of buying out Miller's interest and creating a new Canadian licensing deal for Coors Light. Having witnessed the fiasco first-hand as a Molson Breweries partner, Miller was ready to sell out. "The profit growth that had been in the original plan when Miller bought into Molson had vaporized," said a former Miller senior official at the time. "Suddenly you couldn't make money on Coors. If you are going to be forced to leave Canada, you might as well get the most money you can for it and just go."

At the beginning of December 1997, Molson Cos. paid $201 million to buy out Miller's interest in Molson Breweries. Australian partner Foster's paid a similar amount, refusing to allow Molson to gain ownership control of what was now the only core asset for the Montreal company. Back to a 50-50 partnership in Canada, the two companies kept the marketing rights for Miller brands north of the border but did not regain control of the US import and marketing business Molson USA. Each of the companies wound up with a 24.95% stake in Molson USA, with Miller holding a 50.1% stake. The ownership of Molson Breweries was simplified while Molson USA remained out of reach. Buying out Miller did clear the way for a new licensing deal with Coors, however, they conducted negotiations with Molson Breweries through much of 1997 while Coors Light continued to be brewed by Molson under the interim agreement.

The Coors group charged with creating a new entity to brew and sell Coors Light in Canada had a strong hand to play, but hardly kept their cards close to their respective vests. "Throughout the early stages of the process Coors kept reminding us that they were negotiating equally with Labatt, for them to [make Coors Light]," said a senior Molson Brewery executive. "Then about, let's say, halfway through it, Coors tells us its fallen through with Labatt; it won't work. Coors also told us that what won't work with Labatt is they won't go for [Coors' demand of] exclusivity around light beer." Labatt, unlike Molson, had a growing roster of light beers. The first to seriously market lower-alcohol brews in Canada, it had Blue Light, Labatt Lite, and Anheuser-Busch's Bud Light. More often the "fast follower" than the innovator, Molson was hugely dependent on Coors if it wanted to stay in the growing light segment. It had tinkered with brand extensions such as Canadian Light and Export Light, but it would take years and heavy ad spending before most beer drinkers took any notice of them.

Molson's negotiators were stunned by Coors' bald admission that Labatt was out of the Coors Light game. "When we were sitting in our own room, we were like, 'Man, why would they tell us any of that?'" said the Molson Breweries executive. "'What are we missing, what trick are they pulling that we are missing? Are they trying to make us overconfident or something?' To this day, I do remember that my own posture toward them changed in terms of becoming a bit more aggressive following that. I was quite proud of the deal we ended up with. We ended up having salvaged quite a bit for what was still our number-two brand and our fastest-growing brand. We were a fair bit off from where we were but it was like in English Canada 7 or 8 market-share points and about 10 today."

What Molson ended up with was something known as Coors Canada. Controlled by Adolph Coors, which took a 50.1% stake, the new entity managed the Coors brands in Canada and had the final say on marketing and advertising. Molson Breweries' job was to brew, distribute, and sell Coors in the country. Compared to the former, more ironclad deal Molson had inked in the mid-eighties, this one was less binding. The agreement could be terminated, without cause by either party, on two years' notice.

Coors also received a far larger share of the profits from the surging sales of Coors Light in Canada. In the first eight-plus months of the interim agreement (mid-October 1996 to June 1997), Molson Breweries' earnings fell by $15 million overall, or about 10% of the company's earnings before interest and expenses that year, because of the new arrangement with Coors. The following year, with the Coors Canada deal signed and sealed, Molson Breweries said the new arrangement cost it about $24 million in profit for fiscal 1998, and that it would suffer a similar $24-million hit to profit for the year ended March 31, 1999. Besides the $100-million cash windfall, Coors would be reaping the rewards of the arbitration long into the future. "The new arrangement with Coors will be an important factor in maintaining Molson Breweries' market position," the company stated in its fiscal 1997 information form, with typical corporate understatement.

Molson, for its part, had little choice but to take the Silver Bullet to the bottom line.

Part Six

Stealth, Discounts, and Modified Empires

13
Management Shuffle

With Miller Brewing expensively removed from the Molson Breweries partnership and a new Coors licensing contract settled, it should have been business as usual at Molson. Unfortunately, it was. There was management turmoil, enough changes in corporate strategy to make a management consultant's head spin, and continued frustration with the ownership structure of the country's largest brewer. To top it off, the old nemesis Labatt had not gone away and seemed intent on causing as much damage as possible. Now private and part of an international brewing group based in Belgium, Labatt seemed to be enjoying Molson's public trials and tribulations, much as Molson had a few years earlier when Labatt under George Taylor had been such a lightning rod for shareholder discontent.

Norman Seagram, hired to replace Mickey Cohen in 1996, was a rarity. An old-time "beer guy," Seagram was the first executive out of the brewing side of the business to run Molson Companies since the 1960s. On the surface, the appointment made sense. Molson was going back to becoming a focused brewing company, even if it was one with yet-to-be-defined international ambitions. However, Seagram soon found himself at odds with a Molson Cos. board that, quiescent for so long with Mickey at the helm, was suddenly activist. Five directors left the board that summer, including four "outside" directors who had no other affiliation with Molson. They were replaced with two directors who would have a lasting impact on the company: corporate lawyer James Arnett, and Ian Molson, a cousin of chairman Eric Molson and an England-based banker with CS First Boston.

Norm Seagram had to deal with the corporate loose ends – the loss of the Coors arbitration and licence, and the sell-off of Beaver Lumber and remaining Aikenhead's–Home Depot retail holdings – for a now impatient board. Seagram, in his second go-round with the company, was determined not to be rushed. He resisted making quick corporate deals to satisfy the board of directors and shareholders, questioning certain corporate arrangements. Seagram lasted all of nine months in the top job.

According to Barry Joslin, Mickey Cohen's long-time right-hand man and a senior executive during the Seagram interregnum, "[Seagram] had been told to do things like sell Beaver Lumber and such and the thing that nailed him was he went back to the board and said, 'You know, maybe we would be better off to hang onto this.'" Besides urging Molson to retain its Beaver Lumber holding – in direct opposition to a board of directors now intent on ending the diversification debacle – Seagram refused to sell Molson's 25% stake in Home Depot Canada. "In Atlanta, [Home Depot CEO] Bernie [Marcus] offered me a deal. I rebuffed him," said Seagram, who instructed Molson to value the company's interest. "They came to the conclusion it was worth $70 million to $120 million more than what Bernie was offering. So I had to report to the board." The board, interested in divesting the company of some of its diverse holdings, advised Seagram to take the offer. "I said, 'No, it was ludicrous.' [The bid] was way undervalued. I got horrible pressure. Six months after I left, they eventually sold it for $365 million."

At about the time of Seagram's refusals, the Molson Cos. CEO agreed to participate in what was known as a Bloomberg Forum, an audio report that featured a journalist interviewing Seagram for the benefit of Bloomberg's audience of brokers. "We are taking the 'for-sale' sign off the lawn," Seagram barked into the microphone, hunched over like a very small lineman awaiting the snap. The accompanying article cited analysts' predictions that the Home Depot stake would sell for about $200 million, far less than Molson's eventual sale price. Seagram never received credit for his refusal to sell early and cheap to Home Depot.

Seagram also conducted a quest for an international brewing acquisition. Molson Cos. had gained nearly $700 million from the sale of Diversey, and wanted to put that toward a purchase. The company was investigating developing markets for the same reason Labatt had courted FEMSA: safe places to operate like western Europe were mature, slow-growth regions, just like Canada, and too expensive. Molson also engaged in fruitless discussions to buy out its long-time partner Foster's, which had still not given up on Canada at that point.

Seagram, "a straight shooter," as Barry Joslin described him, was also deliberate. "If there was some more analysis to be done or more thinking to be done, Norman would do it." That included the work required to take out Miller Brewing as a partner. That divorce had to go through before the Coors-imposed deadline of the end of December 1997. It was a date that Seagram would not be around to meet. Molson went through two sets of negotiations to repurchase the Miller interest, an aborted attempt conducted under Norm Seagram and the later one under his successor. The delays caused by management changes ended up raising the final price, as Coors' deadline loomed. The final deal for a little more than $400 million was "far more expensive than it was under the deal we had with Norm," said a former Molson Brewery executive. "They lost a lot of ground under the two CEOs."

More recently president of the SkyDome, the stadium that's home to the Blue Jays and the Canadian Football League's Toronto Argonauts, Seagram gave some reasons for his abrupt second departure from Molson.

"If I were to list the points of difference I had with the chairman I had at the time that I left, they would be in excess of 10 important ones including the relocation of the head office to Montreal,"

Seagram says. "The basic principle that we should be moving back to being virtually or solely a brewing company, that was well established. But to operate most efficiently as a brewing company [you need to be in Toronto] because it is such a marketing-driven type of business and the core of your marketing brain through agencies and creative guys and so forth is right here in Toronto." Molson, in fact, had plenty of experience operating as a Montreal-based brewer, which made sense during most of the century, as it was a regional company well into the 1960s. In the mid-1980s, however, the shift was made to Toronto as brewing executives found themselves spending most of their time on airplanes.

Under the now-activist Molson family, the centre of the universe would move back to where it all began. In 1996, with Mickey and Diversey gone, and Seagram the new president, it was clear the days of the Toronto-centric Molson were over. That year the company held its annual meeting in Montreal for the first time in three years, and since then it has not ventured back to the country's financial capital to host its formal, once-a-year report to shareholders.

Seagram's challenges extended well beyond where to put the company's headquarters. The new chief executive wrestled with the "classic problem" of so many Canadian companies: how to balance the rights of the majority of shareholders with a controlling shareholder who owns just a fraction of the company's total equity.

Seagram was out in May of 1997 and was replaced, not by an existing Molson executive or blue-chip corporate CEO, but by James Arnett, the corporate lawyer and partner with Toronto law firm Stikeman Elliott, who'd joined Molson's board of directors just a year earlier. The second shakeup in just a year, this one proved to have more far-reaching consequences than the one that brought on the hiring of Seagram. Another two directors left the Molson board, following the five who'd departed a year earlier, and four new ones were appointed. They included two Montreal-based executives: Luc Beauregard, chairman and CEO of National Public Relations, and Francesco Bellini, president and CEO of BioChem Pharma Inc. Molson also added some international heft to its board, appointing

Daniel Colson, deputy chairman and CEO of London's Daily Telegraph, and Michael von Clemm, chairman and CEO of Boston's Highmount Capital. With the changes, it was announced that Ian Molson, 42, would become chairman of a new, powerful executive committee made up of Eric Molson, Matthew Barrett, then chief executive of Bank of Montreal, and James Arnett.

Quietly, Ian Molson had become the new centre of power at the two-centuries-old company. Eric and his brother Stephen still controlled the family's voting block, but Ian would increasingly play a central role. He made his interest in the company dramatically known a week before the annual meeting when he spent $13.6 million to buy 535,000 of Molson's class B shares. He has continued to add to his holding and today owns 2.3 million shares, or just over 10% of the class B total. In Molson, the class B shares carry most of the voting power over the direction of the company and were the way the Molson family controlled the fate of the company with just a small fraction of the total equity. The owners of the 104 million class A shares get to vote for 3 of 15 directors. Company chairman Eric Molson and his brother Stephen together control 10 million class Bs, or 44.55% of the class, giving them effective control of Molson Inc. even though they hold only about 8% of the company's equity.

Trim, blond, and boyishly good looking, the seventh-generation Molson (17 years younger than his cousin Eric and 15 years the junior of Stephen, the president of Molson Foundation charity), Ian represents a branch of the family that has not been involved in the business for decades. Ian's father, William "Billy" Molson, was one of the three brothers – along with David and Peter Molson – who bought control of the sacred Canadiens and the team's shrine, the Forum, in 1968 for $3.3 million from family patriarch Hartland Molson. Ian, who has spent much of his working life away from Canada, appears to hold little of Eric and Stephen's reverence for Molson. At the 1997 Molson annual meeting, he baldly stated that he wanted to make money from his Molson stockholding, and since he joined the board, the company's focus has very much been on increasing shareholder returns and, by result, the stock price. It is a far cry from the "guardians of wealth" attitude of Eric, the brew-master-turned-chairman and Molson family patriarch. "The results of that were pitiful," Ian said of the diversification strategy in a CBC television documentary on the family. "The company destroyed billions of dollars of shareholder value."

Getting back to beer basics became the mantra in the post-Mickey era, and that carried on even with Norm Seagram out of the picture. But returning to those brewing roots was proving to be very expensive in terms of executive compensation. The shareholder circular sent out before the 1997 annual meeting detailed the pay for two former Molson CEOs that year: Mickey was paid just over $5 million in total compensation for the fiscal year, and the short-lived Norm Seagram was paid $452,000 for his nine-month term, although the company warned it was in discussion with him "concerning the nature and amount of the corporation's obligations to him arising out of his employment." Molson Cos. also took a $7.3-million charge in the first quarter of fiscal 1998 to cover the costs of executive golden handshakes. (The following year, Molson disclosed that it had paid Seagram $2.45 million "in respect of provisions contained in a separation agreement.") At the 1997 annual meeting, with Molson Cos. still holding just 40% of the namesake brewery and Miller stubbornly negotiating to sell back its 20% interest, newly minted CEO James Arnett took a subtle shot at his predecessors when speaking of acquisitions. "We're looking for something in a stable market. If I had my druthers, I would find another Molson Breweries as opposed to something with a lot of sizzle and a lot of risk," said Arnett, alluding to Seagram's talk about emerging markets such as China, South America, and India.

While the parent company was going through more turmoil than it had in decades, things at the brewery were transpiring as they had since the Carling O'Keefe merger: badly. Under brewery president John Barnett, Molson continued to lose market share to Labatt, although at a slowing rate. One of Barnett's first moves was to decentralize the brewer's operations to better reflect the distinctly regional markets it operated in. The appointment of three regional presidents at the close of 1995 was just the latest in a succession of centralization and decentralization oscillations. The brewery also announced the departure of its top vice-president of corporate affairs, the executive running the Ontario division, and the executive in charge of personnel. A few months later, Barnett cut 165 salaried staff or about 16% of the brewer's workforce and said he wanted to cut 250 unionized workers at its giant Montreal brewery.

Barnett wanted to wield the axe even more energetically, making proposals to the Molson Breweries management board on two or three occasions to close one of the two Ontario breweries, located just an hour's drive apart by beer truck. With three, and then two owners of the brewery, its executives were unable to sell the owners on the need to close either the Barrie or Toronto brewery. The closure and subsequent expansion of the surviving brewery – be it Toronto or Barrie – would cost between $50 million and $100 million. During Barnett's tenure, the brewery held unsuccessful discussions with European brewers such as Bass and Heineken about brewing brands for the US import market in Ontario, much as it did for the Foster's brand.

Unable to deal with the small lake of excess brewing capacity sloshing around the triangle of Montreal, Toronto, and Barrie breweries by winning contract brewing deals or selling more Molson-branded beer, the company contented itself with the closure of a small, isolated plant, which was the relic of interprovincial beer barriers taken down early in the nineties. The Winnipeg brewery, about 16 percent of the capacity of the Barrie plant, was closed in mid-1997. The Regina brewery, half again as large as the Winnipeg facility, remained in operation five years longer and was not shuttered until long after Barnett had left Molson.

Meanwhile, since Interbrew's takeover in 1994, Labatt no longer had to concern itself with looking good to shareholders. Labatt's president, the ambitious Hugo Powell, had his sights set well beyond Canada. Named chief operating officer of Interbrew's Americas operation (Canada, the United States, and its minority Mexican-ownership position), Hugo had his eye on the top job at Interbrew.

The Belgian company, a privately owned business that traced its roots back to 1366, wanted to sell shares to the public. It was not that the incredibly wealthy Belgian families wanted to cash out, but rather that they wanted to dramatically expand within the beer business using the capital generated by a stock offering. Hugo, who played a starring role at Labatt, wanted to be the head of Interbrew when it went public.

The often public sparring between Hugo and Molson Breweries president John Barnett marked a low point in the already deplorable state of relations between the two megabreweries, which was characterized by public lawsuits and nasty statements. Barnett authorized the "Brewed with Pride in Manitoba" ad campaign in 1996 to highlight the fact that Labatt had closed its brewery in Winnipeg while Molson's continued to operate. The effort failed to swing sales from the Labatt stronghold, which kept its 65% share versus Molson's 30%. The campaign was still fresh when it was hauled out in the press a year later as Molson also moved to close its brewery in the prairie city.

Molson had better luck with its later effort to blunt the eastward expansion of Labatt's Kokanee brand, which had become British Columbia's best-selling beer. Positioned as "BC's beer," Kokanee moved across the west more like an avalanche than a glacier. Blair Shier, Molson's president for Western Canada, had watched the brand rumble through his territory. "[Labatt] had rolled out to Alberta and rolled out to Manitoba-Saskatchewan before Ontario," he said. "In Alberta, I don't think it hit 10 share [points] but it hit close to 10."

Ontario was, and still is, the most important province to Molson, but especially at that time when the brewer's market share had been on a near decade-long losing skid nationally, and the company was operating two big breweries at well below capacity. Worse, Kokanee was the first "stealth beer" employed by Labatt, a regional brand that was not directly tied to the parent brewer. The young core audience, who were attracted to the brand's snowboard-BC image, saw the words Columbia Brewery, not Labatt. So any inroads made by the brand would likely come more or less equally from both brewers, given the lack of identification with Labatt. Worse still, the brand was aimed right at the heart of the Molson Canadian–Coors Light demographic.

As feared by Molson, Kokanee was an immediate sensation when it was introduced to Ontario in the spring of 1997. Television advertising, which carried enough images of snow and cold streams that they could have been mistaken for Coors Light ads by some, carried tag lines such as "BC's mountain beer is here" and "glacier-fresh taste." In a few weeks, the brand had shot to over a 5 share. Molson responded quickly: it launched a mud-slinging ad campaign. "BC or BS?" was the question posed in newspaper and radio ads about a month after Kokanee's launch. The ads pointed out that "BC's Mountain Beer" was in fact brewed in Labatt's London, Ontario, brewery, in the decidedly flat heart of the city. Labatt had not hidden the fact, exactly. The beer's origin was there for all to see on the label, but in very small type. Labatt's press materials were similarly obtuse. The Kokanee press release made a single mention of the L-word, conceding that "in Ontario, it will be brewed in London by Labatt, under the watchful eyes and taste buds of Columbia brewmaster Kevin Hyrclik." There was no mention of the fact that Labatt owned said Columbia Brewery in British Columbia.

Molson's unexpectedly harsh criticisms caught Labatt flat-footed. "It's a desperate response from our competitor," one Labatt PR person opined. Trying to show there were real, honest-to-goodness people behind the attack ads, Molson took the earnest high ground: "At the end of the day, we were concerned with the impressions being left – that it was brewed in British Columbia, in the mountains," said Dave Minnett, the man on the hot seat as Molson's vice-president of marketing for Ontario. "The madness had to stop, as far as Molson was concerned." The "madness" did stop. The 19-to-24 demographic, which is far more susceptible to advertising than it thinks, learned the mountain beer was in fact southwestern Ontario beer – and made by Labatt – and the brand almost immediately lost its cachet. Rather than becoming the strong shoulder to support the ever-sagging Blue, Kokanee became yet another 2–3 share brand just like Labatt Ice and Labatt Genuine Draft.

Molson's Blair Shier, who had been squinting at Kokanee production codes in the brand's march across the Prairies to ensure the beer all came from British Columbia (it did until Labatt took aim at the huge Ontario market), felt the Kokanee attack was a turning point for the brewery. "It was a harsh response but a calculated one. The stakes were getting higher – not necessarily financially, but the battle for market share was more intense than ever. I don't know how many years of decline we'd been in and if you do the math on losing share in Ontario it is pretty hard to make it up everywhere else." Kokanee was repositioned for the province as "BC's Mountain Beer That's Brewed Right Here," a tag line that if used from the beginning would have forestalled all the nonsense in the first place. (The other option, shipping the stuff from the Creston, British Columbia, brewery, as it had done for the western provinces, was judged too expensive.)

Labatt's Hugo Powell, mindful of his masters in Belgium, did not wait long to respond to Molson's Kokanee attack. By the May long weekend, he'd launched a $2-per-case discount promotion on Blue, still Labatt's biggest seller. Molson responded with an even deeper discount the following long weekend, and throughout the summer beer drinkers were treated to price-off promotions offered by the duelling duo during peak buying times. The price discounts on the brewers' top brands during the biggest beer-selling weekends were previously unheard of in provinces such as Ontario. When it was all over, the two had damaged their key brands with discounts, encouraged drinkers to swap (thereby eroding brewery loyalty as well), and primed drinkers to expect the same thing the next summer. The result was another market share dip for Molson, down from 46.1% to 45.4% for the year ending March 1998. Labatt took much of that share, although now that it was a private company, it no longer had to divulge market-share figures. Discount pricing upped consumers' expectations and was in large part responsible for the follow-on blizzard of in-case promotions that would see the two give out key chains, mugs, hats, and T-shirts, the expensive "trinkets and trash" game that encouraged even more brand switching.

Hugo was not content with making Molson's life difficult in the marketplace. In the summer of 1998, as the breweries' marketing teams were grinding away at each other, Hugo presented his side of the beer wars to a group of Molson's big shareholders. The audience of pension and mutual fund managers was told how Labatt made about $160 million more operating profit than Molson, even though Labatt ran one more brewery and the two each employed about 4,000 people. Analysts might have quibbled about the numbers, but few doubted that there was a profit gap between the two. Some said at the time that Hugo was laying the groundwork for taking the company public and performing trial runs. That is exactly what Hugo himself says, years after the series of meetings with Canada's investment community. "I do remember early on people saying, 'Why are you doing this? Are you going public?'" Hugo recalls. "No, but we are getting the experience to understand how you think. To give you some feel about us." Hugo's uncomplimentary comparisons with Molson, which Molson never disputed, were just a logical by-product of these "get-to-know-you sessions," the Labatt chief claimed.

Hugo's descriptions of Labatt's operations had their compelling elements. Blue may have been in unstoppable decline, but the company had Interbrew brands to bring to market, it had the Budweiser juggernaut, and it had an interesting regional brand beyond Kokanee. Labatt had learned its lessons from the Kokanee fiasco. The brewer's other regional "stealth beer," Alexander Keith's India Pale Ale, was introduced in a far different fashion. Brought to Ontario about the same time as Kokanee with less fanfare and lower expectations, Labatt originally introduced it as an import and never strayed from that strategy as it grew, mindful of the "BC or BS?" attacks on Kokanee. Keith's was priced and positioned as a "domestic import," meaning it had come all the way from an overworked brewery in Halifax, Nova Scotia, inspiring people to pony up more for the beer. In fact, a large percentage of Ontario beer drinkers believed an independent brewer produced Keith's: surely it could not come from Labatt or Molson. Keith's was also introduced without any Kokanee-style ad campaign because the brand started small, popping up as a niche draft beer. Molson itself was hardly in a position to go after the Keith's cash-cow as it had its own stealth brand, Rickard's Red. Named after a brewmaster at Molson's Vancouver brewery, Rickard's descriptions featured the same "cloaked in the mists of time" imagery as Keith's and Kokanee. Rickard's Red is described as "Canada's top-selling red beer for over 10 years." The brand also has a bit of the microbrewery mystique, said to be "first brewed in Vancouver at the original site of the Capilano brewery in the early 1980s." CBC's consumer show *Marketplace* went after Molson for this description, noting that the quaint-sounding Capilano Brewing Co. identified on Rickard's labels does not in fact exist. Molson brewmaster Rob McCaig, interviewed for the show, tackled *Marketplace*'s assertion that Rickard's Red is made "at Molson's big brewery in Vancouver" and that there really was no Capilano Brewery. "Not anymore," said McCaig, "but that is the heritage of the brewery. The brewery was called the Capilano Brewing Company." Thorns in the sides of true microbrewers, the stealth brands are proof that Labatt and Molson will still do a lot for an extra couple tenths of market share.

The *Marketplace* piece went on to make several startling observations: Molson and Labatt's mainstream beers are designed to appeal to mainstream tastes. To be fair to Labatt and Molson, they have a much harder marketing job than do the microbrewers or quasi-big brewers such as Sleeman Brewing Ltd. Day in and day out, the country's two megabrewers trying to get today's just-of-age drinkers to make the switch from sweet, sugary soft drinks to beer. The core consumers, those legal drinking age to 24, are not going to be drinking anyone's Oatmeal Stout in great numbers.

Not surprisingly, Hugo's presentations to Molson's shareholders annoyed John Barnett and the other Molson brass. They would privately admit, however, whose company was less profitable. To narrow the gap between the two, Molson was taking steps to close the Barrie brewery. By this time, it was going to be two or three times more expensive to shut the Toronto brewery even though management wanted to keep Barrie because of its more agreeable union. John Barnett and his management group had drawn up a strategic plan outlining how Molson should deal with its profitability gap with Labatt, and that included closing the Barrie beer factory. "We tried for months to get the board to read it," said a former member of Barnett's management group. Barnett himself did not suffer for long. By October of 1998, frustrated with the delays and other factors, Barnett simply took his leave from the beer business for the top job at cigarette maker Rothmans Inc. "The job just walked in the door," said a colleague. "Philip Morris [Rothman's owner] called John on a Wednesday, he flew to New York on a Friday," and accepted the job.

Barnett, who lustily swung the management axe while inspiring devotion among his employees, may have bailed out too soon. Just a few months earlier Molson had finally bought out Foster's after nine years of partnership in Canada. Molson owned Molson again, and all the other distracting stuff, with the exception of the Habs, was gone. The road appeared clear for Barnett to trim Molson to profit parity with Labatt. But now the president was gone.

Of course, the way was also clearly marked for anyone else who wanted to sign on.

14
Molson Gets Focused

James Arnett was stunned and angry about Barnett's defection. Still relatively fresh in his first stint as chief executive officer of Molson Companies, the corporate lawyer had done what Norm Seagram had balked at: he'd sold off the old bits and pieces of Molson's now-abandoned diversification scheme. Most importantly, he'd repurchased the 50% of Molson Breweries held by the Australians since the Carling merger in 1989. Now with Molson finally a brewer once again, there was no one to run it.

With no obvious replacement waiting in the wings, it was February 1999 before Molson finally had its man: Daniel O'Neill, 47, an Ottawa-raised executive who'd worked as president of Campbell Soup Canada, and more recently in the United States and South America for H. J. Heinz Co. The "ketchup man," as he was known originally in beer circles, definitely had no "beer man" in him, though he had a solid-looking resumé. (He soon became known simply as "Dan" to friend and foe alike, given the honour of a first-name moniker, just like Mickey, and Hugo, over at Labatt.) It is not widely known that O'Neill began his career in Toronto as a corporate recruiter, gaining skills that served him well with Molson. Dan's start date with Molson was April Fool's Day 1999, but it was also notable because it fell one day after the end of Molson Cos.' fiscal 1999 year-end. That meant his employment arrangements with the company, guaranteed to be the most interesting reading in Molson's circular to shareholders, would not be revealed until the following year's version. By the time the compensation arrangements of the awkwardly titled "executive vice-president, and chief operating officer, North American brewing operations" were finally made public – 15 months into the job – few people cared, beyond some nosy journalists. More than a year into the job, Bay Street was in love, and Dan was the brewing industry's pin-up boy.

Investment analysts and institutional shareholders are typically less interested in pay than they are in performance. As a group, they were impressed that the new brewery chief talked frankly about Molson's problems and appeared to be tackling them energetically. He talked a great deal about Molson's share price, which was trading at about the same level near the end of the decade as it had in 1992, missing one of the great bull markets in history. The 1999 annual report, entitled "Reinvent," was full of the buzzwords and statements that analysts wanted to hear. Management pay would be linked to improvements in shareholder value. Molson would win the market-share war profitably (although no details were given as to how the company would accomplish these two conflicting aims). The cost base would also be reduced and an international strategy would be formulated.

Dan certainly attracted attention. Barely two months into the job, with the release of the company's annual results that May, Molson's new beer man acknowledged that a $100-million "cost-gap" existed between the company and Labatt, the first such admission by Molson that such a profit shortfall existed. "We are going to go clear after that number and it is going to be a major focus of our organization," Dan said in a conference call with analysts and investors. You could practically hear them weeping with joy on the other end of the telephone line. "We had a little cheering section over here," Scotia Capital Markets analyst Steve Holt said following the call. "You hear $100-million over three years and double-digit EBIT growth in brewing this year and you definitely sit up and take notice." Molson's class A non-voting shares, the ones everybody but the Molsons owned, ended that day at $21.55, still pretty close to where they'd been at the start of the decade. In 1999, the stock market was still focused on the Internet "revolution" and the unlimited wonder and potential of e-companies and their stocks, but Molson's time would come.

Just in case the analysts and investors were not paying attention, the full story was repeated a few weeks later at an invitation-only presentation to analysts at the Air Canada Centre, the new home of the Toronto Maple Leafs and the Raptors. While Molson was determined to locate its top executives in Montreal, Dan, as the mere brewing chief, was where the action was. The 1999 annual report was distributed along with a presentation of just how Molson would close the publicly acknowledged profit gap. Dan's presentation, after about two months on the job, was instructive of what the new brewing czar hoped to accomplish. Earnings before interest, taxes, and depreciation, known as gross profit to most, would increase by $100 million over five years, erasing any profit gap between Molson and Labatt. "Project 100" it was dubbed. Dan, who was into easy-to-remember names for absent-minded analysts and investors, would attack marketing and sales expenditures and capacity utilization, shrink the number of brands and package sizes, reduce supplier costs, and benchmark the company against "world class" competitors such as Anheuser-Busch. Molson also pledged to boost its return on capital to 11.5% from a lethargic 7%, and drop the amount of capital it had invested in the business by $400 million over the next five years. Looking at the three years from 1997 to 1999, Dan showed production costs had risen moderately (4%) to $104 million per year while distribution had fallen 4% to $92 million annually. The real savings potential looked to be in the marketing and sales expenditures, which had risen nearly a third in a brewing-industry competition equivalent to an arms race: up to $265 million annually from $200 million in 1997.

Two weeks after his coming out with the analysts, Dan gave his first one-on-one interview with a Toronto business journalist. Dan sipped Diet Coke rather than coffee at breakfast, a sign he'd become more than a little Americanized in his career working for US multinationals. The reporter kept bringing up job cuts and asked, "When will Barrie be closed?" Dan kept responding with a variation of "I don't want to talk about Barrie." The next day, a version of the interview appeared in the *National Post* with the headline, "Molson mulls closing an Ontario brewery: Worst case scenario." The 400-word article, buried as usual in the dot-com madness on page 4 of the business section, quoted Dan saying innocuously: "We will have a study completed between the end of the calendar year and the end of the fiscal year." The morning the article appeared, Dan's public relations department phoned the reporter and said the new president was never going to speak to him again.

Molson, however, had no choice but to continue talking with the media. Dan had set out an ambitious agenda for change and was giving every indication he intended to follow up on it. Boosting Molson's worth, or building "shareholder value," became a mantra. The most visible sign of that effort, Molson's share price, became something of an obsession with Dan. Updated Molson ticker prices were on near-constant display at the brewer's downtown Toronto offices, and the brewing chief admitted to checking the price "umpteen times a day" in an interview five months into the job. Molson's stock was responding to all that attention: up 21% to $26.25 over that span.

Dan was busy. The brewery fired MacLaren McCann in May. Its ad agency of four decades, initially hired to launch Molson Canadian, MacLaren had steered the brand to the number-one position in the country, introduced rock video–style TV commercials, and created the "I Am Canadian" tag line. Dan, who had made his intentions known after refusing to take the calls of MacLaren's president since joining Molson, used the brewer's promotions agency to produce two low-budget TV commercials for the spring-summer selling season. It didn't really matter. The summer would be Labatt's after its first Stanley Cup promotion and the collectible craze those plastic miniature cups emblazoned with team logos created.

Molson would continue to be in the news for the rest of the year. In September, Molson said it would fire 287 white-collar employees, or about 18% of its salaried workforce, to save $30 million a year in operating profit. Some of the terminations were caused by the company's transition from a conglomerate to a brewer. With the cuts, the decentralized structure set up by Barnett was junked in favour, once again, of a centralized, top-down marketing-and-sales system. A week later, the brewery signed an unprecedented six-year labour deal with the troublesome union representing its Toronto brewery workers. Dan continued to talk about contract brewing opportunities to sop up excess capacity, but the new contract with Toronto was a clear sign that the Barrie brewery's days were numbered. Less than a month later, Molson announced the planned closure of the Barrie plant, which meant a one-time charge of more than $200 million and the elimination of more than 400 jobs. Investors, clearly primed and less sympathetic than news media who played up the "tragedy" angle, sent Molson stock up $1.20 a share.

The business of sports also proved to be a distraction. That summer rumours cropped up that the brewer might go so far as to put the storied Canadiens hockey team up for sale. It was in the company's interest to keep the story smouldering as it was in the midst of appealing the $10-million tax bill on its new Molson Centre, "a state-of-the-art sports and entertainment facility" located a puck's throw from the storied Forum in downtown Montreal. That September, after more than a year spent considering the future of the Habs, Molson claimed the team was not for sale at any price. During a conference call the following week, Dan said it was the horror of Labatt winding up with the team that swung the decision. "It was a fear of our competitor getting a hold of that unbelievable brand, the brand being the Montreal Canadiens, and using it against us." Molson, of course, could simply have signed a long-term marketing deal with any buyer of the franchise. Interbrew-owned Labatt may have gone into hockey with its NHL-sponsorship arrangement, but it was no more interested in buying professional sports teams than Molson was. Ever since Labatt ownership had shifted to Belgium, the brewer had been attempting to unload the Blue Jays, an on-again, off-again process that had been going on for five years.

It's possible that Molson was having trouble finding a buyer at a decent price. In the recently completed 1999 fiscal year, the club and the building lost $3.8 million after excluding a $4.4-million expansion fee for the Nashville NHL franchise. That franchise fee windfall was nice: Molson expected fees of US$3.1 million and US$6.1 million over the next two years as teams were added in Atlanta, Minnesota, and Columbus. But all that expansion watered down the league and diluted the value of existing teams, including the Montreal franchise. Sports fans in Montreal would support the Habs if they were winning, but empty seats would be visible at Canadiens games if the team was playing poorly (unlike Toronto, where long-suffering Leafs supporters packed the rink regardless of the standings). Montreal's other major league franchise, the Expos, were a continual candidate for relocation, and the prospect of landing an NBA franchise to help fill the new stadium the way the Raptors did in Toronto was not worth mentioning. Few doubted Molson's commitment to the Habs, which had been sold away once before and repurchased a few years later from the Bronfmans. The Molson clan retained its prize seats just behind the team's bench and Eric Molson continued to refer to the club as a "legacy" asset.

Dan's star was rising, as was that of his opposite number at Labatt, Hugo Powell. That fall, as Molson was energetically firing salaried and unionized employees to narrow the gap with Labatt, Hugo was named to the newly created post of president of Interbrew. The appointment ended an unworkable structure of having co-chief operating officers in Europe and the Americas. Hugo was the logical choice for the job, as Labatt's North American operations were providing the lion's share of Interbrew's profit and the 55-year-old executive had the experience of working for a public company, a claim few Interbrew officials could make. Hugo steered Interbrew through its first big acquisition since it had swallowed Labatt in 1995, a US$1.5-billion investment in South Korea's Doosan, and in the spring of 2000 he announced that Interbrew would go public. It was just the beginning of a four-year buying binge that would transform the centuries-old company from a little-known European brewer to the world's second-largest beer-making company behind only Anheuser-Busch.

Hugo's spending spree saw Interbrew spread across Europe and into Russia. The Belgian company also moved into the United Kingdom with the purchase of Whitbread and later the US$3.3-billion purchase of Bass (raising the ire of the country's competition regulators), and on into Asia. The effort culminated with the acquisition of Germany's Beck's in 2001 for US$1.1-billion. Analysts immediately objected to the hefty price, but Interbrew had determined it needed another "global brand" in markets such as the United States where Stella Artois had been slow to gain acceptance. The purchase illustrated the brewing industry truism that companies will pay for brand equity, not profits or sales. A puny seller in its home market of Germany, Beck's is an import powerhouse. It is the top-selling international premium lager, compared to Interbrew's top brand Stella Artois, the international number six in sales.

Beck's is now the key brand in Interbrew's assault on the US market, which remains the world's richest, but the acquisition of Beck's and its promotion under Labatt USA sparked a lawsuit from its Mexican partner, FEMSA Cerveza. The Mexican company, which receives a 30% share of the US division's profit, objected to the inclusion of the Beck's brand, which it claims will hurt US sales of its FEMSA-made beers such as Dos Equis Lager and Tecate. "For a variety of reasons, they almost regretted from day one that they gave us control of the US market, which in the end is 90% of the dollars" of the Labatt-FEMSA partnership, Hugo said in an interview. FEMSA's court action "represents perhaps the only or best chance that they think they have to create a problem for us that requires a negotiation." Interbrew subsequently lost its legal fight with its Mexican partner, and was forced to continue selling its Beck's brand separately in the United States.

By the beginning of 2003, Hugo had worn out his welcome in Europe. Not for the FEMSA dispute, or any problems in the highly profitable North American operations, but for the hectic and expensive international shopping spree. Analysts complained that Interbrew was paying too much for beer companies (such as Beck's), that some acquisitions were botched (such as the Whitbread and Bass deals in the United Kingdom, which caused government regulators to step in), and that key operations such as those in Russia were not running smoothly. Hugo was handed a three-year deal to work as a "consultant" to Interbrew, and has since been replaced by John Brock, an American who, like Hugo, is a long-time packaged-goods executive with no brewing experience.

Interbrew investors may doubt the wisdom of some of Hugo's acquisitions, but none can criticize the wisdom of the Belgian company's takeover of Labatt, since the Canadian and US businesses remain the profitable core of the ever-expanding brewer. Although the two countries account for just 16 million of the 100 million hectolitres produced worldwide every year by Interbrew, the Canada-US operations earned a total of 340 million euros ($530 million) – more than Interbrew's Western European businesses (326 million euros) or its so-called emerging markets in Asia and Eastern Europe (140 million euros). Operating in a duopoly as Labatt does in Canada has provided Belgium with a steady stream of profits.

While Hugo was off trying to conquer the world, Dan was busily remaking Molson according to his plan. In many respects, that blueprint was not much different from what Hugo had done earlier in the decade and what Barnett had unsuccessfully proposed. Costs were being cut, suppliers were brought in line, a new ad agency was hired, and Dan brought in his own management team. Dan soon became synonymous with Molson's "Rant" ad for Molson Canadian, the national sensation of 2000. The widely popular TV spot was held up as proof that Molson's turnaround was on track. Even if it didn't sell much more Molson Canadian (market share for the brand was flat from 1999 to the end of 2000), the "Rant" cemented Dan's reputation. So when Molson announced in June that James Arnett, now 61, was stepping down as chief executive officer of Molson Companies, no one questioned Dan's appointment to the top job.

Shortly after the announcement of Dan's elevation, the curtain was finally raised on the beer boss's salary. The 2000 circular accompanying the annual report proved interesting reading. Dan had been granted a princely 1 million share options at the time of his hiring. By comparison, his boss, James Arnett, had been granted 304,000 options over a three-year period following his hiring. For fiscal 2000, Dan was paid a base salary of $750,000, or 25% more than Arnett earned, and he was granted a bonus of more than $1.1 million. Dan was also paid a signing bonus of $2 million, the after-tax proceeds of which were invested in Molson shares. Dan was earning nearly four times in salary and bonuses what John Barnett had pulled down before him.

Fiscal 2000 was an ugly year when viewed from the bottom line. The cost of closing Barrie and firing all those white-collar workers resulted in a net loss of $44 million, compared with a profit of $170 million a year earlier. For those looking on the bright side, analysts for example, Molson presented plenty of good news: brewing profit was up 15.1%, beer sales for the industry were up, and even the company's seemingly unstoppable market-share slide was halted, as market share had risen minutely to 45.1%, from 45.0%.

Dan's major accomplishment at Molson was, in fact, the end of the pursuit of market share at all cost. Success and failure would now be measured by the Boston Consulting magic of EVA (economic value added), attacking costs, and putting marketing and promotional spending behind fewer and fewer beer brands. A complicated-sounding measure, it essentially called for weighing the added value of a certain action against what it cost. And the flurry of activity continued, rather than abated, to the seemingly constant approval of analysts as well as investors, who viewed Molson as a safe haven after the dot-com bubble burst so spectacularly in the spring of 2000. Beer was one of the ultimate defensive stocks, and here was a company that was boosting profit at rates unheard of for the industry.

Molson has continued to hack away at costs under Dan. In addition to Barrie, the company closed the Regina plant, giving it a total of just five breweries across the country. Molson could now point to lower fixed costs compared to Labatt, which was running eight plants across Canada. Beverage analyst Michael Palmer calculates that Molson's costs are about $50 million lower than Labatt's annually, a function of running fewer, bigger plants and from having a flatter management system.

It was similar thinking that earlier moved Molson to buy out its US partner Miller Brewing, which still handled the marketing and distribution of its US brands (Molson Golden, Molson Ice, and Canadian). Molson paid US$133 million to reacquire the rights to its brands in the United States and the next month turned around and sold 49.9% of Molson USA to its oldest US partner, Coors Brewing Co., for US$65 million. Clearly, the wounds of the arbitration battle of just a few years earlier had healed. Business was business after all.

Like Labatt before it, Molson was not satisfied operating a geographically limited — if extremely profitable — brewing company serving half the Canadian market, with only a small US import presence. In the fall of 2000, a month before it repurchased its US brands, Molson dipped its toe into the huge Brazilian market, spending $150 million to buy the Bavaria beer brand from AmBev. The giant Brazilian company, formed by the merger of the country's two largest brewers, controls 70% of what is the world's fifth-largest beer market, but was forced to sell off the Bavaria label to satisfy antitrust regulators. Bavaria gave Molson a 4.5% share of the country's beer market and five breweries. For Dan, who spoke "smooth, Brazilian-accented Portuguese" thanks to his time running SC Johnson in Brazil in the early 1980s before his Campbell and Heinz days, Bavaria would be just a first step.

In March 2001, the company announced one of the largest acquisitions in its history, the $1.1-billion purchase of Cervejarias Kaiser, Brazil's second-largest brewer. The deal was said to give Molson roughly 18% of the South American country's beer sales when combined with Bavaria. Outbidding Heineken, Dan softened the sting by selling 20% of the Kaiser-Bavaria combination to the Dutch brewer for US$218-million. (In just a few months, Molson had made equity sales to Adolph Coors and Heineken, signalling who its friends were in the rapidly consolidating beer business.)

An ecstatic Dan said at the time of the purchase that the company had been working on the deal for 14 months and that the purchase would transform Molson. It likely will. Brazil represents an enormous gamble for the company, given its history of economic instability. In the early 1990s, inflation ran at 45% a month. Leftist candidate Luiz Inacio Lula da Silva was running for president and scaring foreign investors, and the Brazilian real was tanking against foreign currencies. Lula, who won the election, has toned down his left-wing rhetoric and moved to reassure financial markets, but the Brazilian real has yet to recover. Molson says the risks of entering the Brazilian market are justified by the growth potential of a market where so much of the population is just entering its prime beer-drinking years.

Then, in the winter of 2001, the company did what was unthinkable even just a few years earlier. It sold the Canadiens, a painful call for the Montreal-based organization. Under Arnett, it had explored selling the team, suddenly unprofitable under the changing NHL, but it always pulled back. Arnett had put the new Molson Forum, called the Molson Centre and later the Bell Centre, up for sale to little interest. The hockey arena, unprofitable virtually from the day it opened, was not saleable without including the hockey club. So on a dark day in January, Molson sold the most successful franchise in hockey (and the stadium) to Colorado-based businessman George Gillette, Jr., for $190 million in cash and preferred shares worth $86.5 million at the end of 2008. Molson, retaining 19.9% of the club but none of the building, agreed to take over Gillette's debt from the purchase in the event the American businessman defaults. Molson's sale provoked the expected teeth grinding and national soul-searching from fans, social commentators, and the media, but the company toughed it out.

Dan has made a lot of money for investors, including the Molson family. The company's stock has more than tripled from the time he joined the company to mid-2003, from a stock trading in the low 20s, to a share-split-adjusted $75. The soaring share price has also made the Molson chief executive a rich man. Depending on the share price, Dan could be one of the best compensated CEOs or he could move into the Frank Stronach–Gerry Schwartz stratosphere where compensation is measured in the tens of millions. In fiscal 2003, Dan recorded his first huge payday, which is likely not going to be his last. In addition to his salary of $900,000 and bonus of nearly $4 million (up two-thirds from $2.4 million granted the year before), he realized $13.9 million from the execution of stock options for the year ending March 31, 2003. According to Molson's shareholder circular, Dan has another $19.2 million worth of stock options he can exercise at any time, plus another 1 million options worth $16.6 million he cannot yet exercise. On paper, Dan's the $50-million man.

Investors and the vast majority of analysts certainly think Dan is worth the money they are paying him. At the time the circular was distributed, just 3 of the 13 analysts who follow Molson had neutral "hold" or "peer perform" ratings on the shares, according to the Bloomberg newswire service. The rest rated it either "out perform" or "buy." Molson stock has also roughly tripled during the Dan O'Neill era. But Michael Palmer, one analyst who no longer rates Molson for shareholders, has a far less rosy view of Dan's era at Molson. His analysis of Molson's costs per hectolitre of beer brewed suggests the company's vaunted savings of $150 million over Dan's reign are an illusion. Profit has been driven largely by cost increases, not savings from employee reductions and the two brewery closures, he says. For the last four fiscal years, Molson has generated $300 million from price hikes, or an average of $75 million per year, accounting for much of the gross profit gains in three of four years, the analyst contends.

In Ontario, the largest market for sales, the price of a mainstream two-four case of Molson Canadian or Labatt Blue before deposit has risen from $25.80 to $31.35 or 21.5%. Those savings from closing breweries and concentrating on fewer, larger beer plants, in Molson's example, are not being passed on to the beer drinker. Molson and Labatt, however, are now paying the penalty for all those price increases. In Ontario, the price for mainstream, so-called premium brands (Blue and Canadian) are set at $33.75 a case including bottle deposit, a full $10 above the province's minimum floor price of $23.70.

While the market and the Molson family are no doubt still in love with Dan and his management team, a number of troubling developments have arisen for the brewer. Share of its most important brand, Molson Canadian, peaked around the time of the "Rant." Since then it has gone down about 1 share point nationally to approximately 11 market share points. That means the Budweiser brand, Labatt's under-licence brew from Anheuser-Busch that began the modern-day beer wars in 1980, is the top-selling bottled beer in Canada. If you'd told someone back then that "American piss" would be the country's top-selling beer, he would have laughed you out of the bar, but Molson Canadian has peaked for a number of reasons. As former Labatt marketing vice-president David Kincaid predicted at the time, the "Rant" spot painted Molson into a corner. The commercial was too successful in a way because it summed up in one neat little package all the underlying truths about the brand and what it meant to be Canadian. If you tell the whole story in one 60-second ad, however, what's left to be said? The ad also resonated most deeply with the wrong people, those one or two decades too old for the big brewers. Molson might like to think differently, but wrap-yourself-in-the-flag patriotism can be downright "Dad-ish" for the legal-drinking-age-to-24 target. Especially if the hockey glory shown in the "Rant" is taken from a series that happened in 1972, about a decade before they were born.

Besides Canadian, Molson has few beer brands to call its own. Molson Export has all but disappeared as a national brand. An attempt to resurrect the once-mighty beer with the "Had Ex Today?" campaign failed to resurrect the ale and Export has since been abandoned. Of the top five brands in the country, the only other company-owned brand is Molson Dry, which has about a 5 share nationally. Molson Dry is a great brand for the company in Quebec, where it is premium-priced, but it's far less profitable in Ontario where Dry, like Ice, is now a discount category contender.

Molson is in danger of becoming a brewer and seller of other people's brands. Over the last five years Molson's market share has held relatively steady, sliding about 1 share point from 45% of the market in 1999 to 44% in 2003. But the market share of the company's own brands, which make it the most money, have been sliding, almost unnoticed, and those sales have been replaced by more cases of Coors Light, Miller Genuine Draft, Heineken, and Corona. The share of those "rented" brands has gone from 9.3% of the market in 1999 to 14.6% in 2003, an increase of 50%.

The profits are even slimmer for Molson's sales agent brands, Corona and Heineken, which the company doesn't even brew. Molson represents the Mexican and Dutch brews in beer and liquor stores, and bars and restaurants, receiving a sales commission for its efforts but no long-term control of the brand. That is the main reason for the Canadian launch of Brazilian-made A Marca Bavaria by Molson in the spring of 2003. The "super-premium" brew, priced at the same level as Corona and Heineken, is certain to take sales away from those two brands, which are Molson clients. A Marca Bavaria is packaged in clear glass bottles, the same as Corona. (Industry sources have said the makers of Corona are less than happy with their Canadian salesmen for their introduction of A Marca Bavaria.)

Dan is touting Brazil as the rosy future for Molson, but its own financial statements tell a different story. The South American business earned $56.5 million in gross profit in 2003, barely a tenth of what the boring old Canadian brewery made. When negative factors such as depreciation and amortization are taken into account, the numbers appear even worse. Brazil contributed an operating profit of $36.5 million, while Molson Canada earned $485.4 million. Under Molson's direction, the Brazilian unit raised beer prices, and Brazilians reacted by switching brands. The market share of the Brazilian venture fell from 17% in fiscal 2002 to 14.3% in 2003, Molson disclosed in its annual report.

The story is currently no rosier in the United States where Molson sells its beer in a 50-50 joint venture with Coors. Molson USA had an operating loss of $6.3 million in 2003, worse than the $5.7-million loss the year before. Molson finally stabilized its market share in the United States after a number of years of decline, and it has made the decision to emphasize its Molson Canadian brand at the expense of Molson Ice and Molson Golden. This in the wake of Canada's refusal to back the war in Iraq and a generally more patriotic, post-September-11 US population. Not a great time to be selling a beer named Canadian.

So what does it all mean? Following the Mickey Cohen era, Molson has become a tightly focused beer company. The conglomerate is dead. Even the "legacy asset" Montreal Canadiens have been sold off. Molson and Labatt have raised beer prices over the past five years about as much as the consumer can take, or perhaps more than he will take judging by the success of discounters. Dan, with $50 million in stock options, is getting a payout worthy of a dot-com entrepreneur. Molson has bet its future on Brazil, a vast country, geographically distant, linguistically and culturally alien, and, from an economic standpoint, downright frightening. The Brazilian upside may be huge as Molson executives claim, but so is the downside. On the homefront, Molson is weaker than at any time since before the merger with Carling O'Keefe. Sales of its own brands have been on a long-term slide, and all the growth in the market is taking place in the discount end and the imported super-premium category, where it is a salesman, rather than a player. Molson also faces a far stronger rival than it ever has in an Interbrew-owned Labatt, which is flooding the market with its company-owned green and brown foot soldiers: Stella Artois, Beck's, Hoegaarden, and Leffe.

"It is obvious to any knowledgeable observer of the industry that Molson's brand equity has been considerably damaged for the last few years," said Michael Palmer. "That has been offset through very aggressive pricing and the stock has responded. Longer-term beer companies are dependent on brand equity and Molson's has deteriorated. Even as its earnings go up, its equity goes down. [Rival beer companies] pay for equity, not earnings."

Meanwhile, the beer world is shrinking and Molson is not growing fast enough. When it bought Kaiser in 2001, the company said it was the 12th-largest brewer in the world. Two years later it is number 15. Not so much from lost sales as because everyone else grew bigger faster. That does not mean Molson will be acquired anytime soon. The family still controls the company's fate and, given the run up in value over the Dan years, why would they sell now? Potential acquirers similarly will be in no rush to buy. Given the slow growth in the Canadian business and the volatility of the Brazilian venture, why pay premium prices for something that looks to be headed into the discount aisle?

15

Postscript:
Last Call

Molson investors, and beer industry watchers generally, received their first real glimpse of the health of the brewer's Brazilian venture – its first major investment in more than a decade – when the company reported its first year-over-year financial comparison in mid-2003 on the $1-billion investment. The results were anything but pretty.

After just a year operating what was solidly the number-two beermaker in Brazil, Molson reported its market share plunged nearly a third, to 12.7% of the country's beer sales from 17.8% the prior year. Molson also ended a deal with a third-party distributor that handled 16% of its sales in the country and closed a brewery there, taking a $43.3-million charge.

"At a certain point in time, you have to bite the bullet and make the tough decisions, and we made them," Dan O'Neill said on a conference call. Investors, who sent Molson shares down about 5%, or $1.80, on the day the financial results were released, thought differently. "The end conclusion is Molson has got their hands full," said David Hartley, an analyst with First Associates Investments. Hartley, who'd travelled to Brazil with Molson executives the year before, concluded then that the company's arrangements with soft drink bottlers, who act as third-party distributors, posed a bigger risk to Molson than Brazil's economy or falling currency.

The steady profit machine of Canadian beer sales continued to chug along, as sales rose 2.8% thanks to relentless beer price increases. Molson's all-important market share, however, fell to 44.1% from 44.7% as the brewer lost ground in Ontario and western Canada. "I'm not at all happy," said Dan. "Tactically we are being beaten and I don't like being beaten."

Two weeks later the company showed what the price of failure would be. It announced that Michael Downey, Molson's president for Ontario and Western Canada, had "decided to leave" rather than accept a lesser position with the company. Downey's departure came after a 1.5 market-share drop in the region, which accounts for 65% of Molson's volume. Around the same time Mr. Downey was headed out the door, Molson saw the departure of its vice-president of marketing for the Canadian brand, Sean Moffitt, after six months on the job.

Downey, who had worked as a marketer for Labatt prior to joining Molson as its top marketer and later divisional president, was replaced a week later by Les Hine, a 21-year marketing veteran with consumer products giant Procter & Gamble.

At Labatt, meanwhile, which remained out of the glare of scrutiny for the most part despite its status as the most profitable division in the Interbrew empire, changes were being made at the top. About the time Dan shuffled executives, the Belgian parent company announced that long-serving Labatt officer Bruce Elliot was leaving the post of president of Labatt Canada (and the company). He would be replaced by Stewart Gilliland, most recently Interbrew's UK president and the executive credited with making the Stella Artois brand one of the country's top-selling beers. It's too early to tell whether Gilliland will be a cost-cutter in the Dan O'Neill mould or will look to raise market share through marketing and promotions to end the Molson-Labatt deadlock.

Still controlling nearly 90% of the country's beer sales thanks to their hold over the fast-growing import brands such as Heineken, Corona, and Stella Artois, it's certain that Molson and Labatt will continue to put pressure on smaller brewers such as Sleeman Breweries Ltd. and Brick Brewing Co. Based in Guelph, Ontario, Sleeman has worked to stay away from the Molson Canadian–Labatt Blue middle of the market, focusing on premium-priced beers sold in clear bottles and discount-priced beers under the Stroh's and Old Milwaukee brands. New Brunswick–based Moosehead, long the country's number-three brewer until it was eclipsed by Sleeman, continues to be an East Coast power, a major beer exporter, and a niche seller in the rest of the country.

Brick Brewing of Waterloo, Ontario, which lays claim to being the country's first microbrewery, began in 1984 and has until recently contented itself selling premium-priced brews and niche brands such as Red Baron and Red Cap. Brick, which like most small brewers has far more capacity than sales, caused a stir in the spring of 2002 when it reintroduced the long-dead stubby brown beer bottle. Bringing back the squat bottle, now with a twist top, has provoked a furious reaction from the brewing establishment. Ontario's Beer Store distribution monopoly (owned by Molson, Labatt, and Sleeman) reacted by cutting off Brick's supply of tall standard bottles, arguing that the little brewer violated a standard bottle agreement which has been signed by most of the country's beer makers. Brick founder Jim Brickman, who says his company never agreed to such a pact, won an interim court judgment forcing the Ontario beer distributor to keep sending him used bottles. The stubby bottle dispute appears headed to court for an ultimate resolution.

While Molson, and to a lesser extent Labatt, erode the sales of their Canadian and Blue profit engines by pushing imports, they still hope to reverse the growth of microbrewery offerings like those coming from Brick or Calgary's Big Rock, which Dan O'Neill famously referred to as "mosquitoes or black flies buzzing around your head."

Interbrew has continued the aggressive expansion that began with the acquisition of Labatt in 1995 and picked up pace with the appointment of Hugo Powell as chief executive four years later. Powell pursued a dual-track strategy of buying huge but less profitable breweries in emerging markets such as Russia and South

Korea, as well as buying well-established companies such as Bass Brewers and Whitbread Beer Co. and Germany's Beck's. Not to be outdone, Hugo's replacement, John Brock, made a $736-million play for German brewer Lowenbrau. Although Lowenbrau is not the international sales powerhouse that Beck's is, the brewer is a force in Germany, making Interbrew the number-one player in what is the world's third-largest beer market. "This is the right deal, at the right price, in a key market," said Brock after the acquisition.

Although still fragmented when compared to consumer product sectors such as soft drinks, the beer industry is fast consolidating, led by the likes of Interbrew, Heineken, and the new giant SAB-Miller, which was formed by the combination of South Africa's largest brewer and Miller Brewing, the US number-two beer company.

Interbrew can be expected to continue to look for the "right deal, at the right price" as its Labatt holdings are all but guaranteed to churn out steady profits. It's far less clear whether Molson, now suffering indigestion from its Brazilian acquisitions, will be predator or prey as the brewing world shrinks.

At a now-infamous analyst briefing in the fall of 2003, Dan O'Neill predicted the world brewing industry will go through another round of consolidation, one Molson has decided to sit out. Instead, Molson will focus on its Canadian business and fixing what it has purchased in Brazil. "The beer market continues to consolidate much faster than we expected," Dan told analysts and investors at the meeting. "The gap between us and the four big guys [Anheuser-Busch, SAB-Miller, Interbrew, and Heineken] has actually widened." The beer industry has seen US$25 billion worth of acquisitions since 1999, but Dan said the big acquirers have generally overpaid. He contended that some of those high-priced brands would become available at a discount in a few years' time, when Molson will once again be on the acquisition trail.

Dan's comments were overshadowed by his suggestion during the briefing that the Molson family might stand aside should the consolidation wave wash over it. "This is going to shock a lot of people. If [a bid for the company] was right, I don't think the family would stand in the way of it. I don't think so," Mr. O'Neill was quoted as saying in *The Globe and Mail*, which made his comments the banner business story of the day.

Within hours, Molson had put out a statement refuting their CEO's words, which a public relations executive at the company said came in response to a "hypothetical" query about a sale, and that he answered hypothetically. Dan, in a company-wide e-mail to staff, was more blunt: "Clearly, I was misquoted, misinterpreted, and under no circumstances is Molson considering or entertaining selling the company nor are we open to bids."

The controversy was the first hint of disagreement between Dan and the retiring Molson family, who for the most part prefer to stay out of the headlines. Given the speed with which the international beer industry is consolidating – and Molson's refusal or inability to participate – it is doubtful that Molson can stand an island apart over the long term. Molson's Brazilian venture does not appear to make it stronger than it would be on its own, and its major competitors in the United States and Canada only grow larger and more powerful.

Going it alone as a geographically isolated, family-owned business is a luxury the Molson family is not likely to be able to afford for much longer.

Bibliography

Baum, Dan. Citizen Coors: An American Dynasty. New York: William
    Morrow, 2000.
Hernon, Peter, and Terry Ganey. Under the Influence: The Unauthorized
    Story of the Anheuser-Busch Dynasty. New York: Simon & Schuster,
    1991.
Molson, Karen. The Molsons: Their Lives & Times 1780–2000. Toronto:
    Firefly Books, 2001.
Van Munching, Philip. Beer Blast. Toronto: Random House Canada,
    1997.
Winn Sneath, Allen. Brewed in Canada: The Untold Story of Canada's 350-
    Year-Old Brewing Industry. Toronto: Dundurn Press, 2001.
Woods, Shirley E. The Molson Saga: 1763–1983. Toronto: Doubleday
    Canada, 1983.

Index